Library of Congress Cataloging-in-Publication Data
Peter Hartshorn, We All Have Fathers: A Red Sox Memoir, baseball, Red Sox, memoir
Summary: A memoir of a father and a son and the love for the Red Sox that sustains and connects them.

ISBN: 978-1939282392

Published by Miniver Press, LLC, McLean Virginia
First edition July 2017

We All Have Fathers:
A Red Sox Memoir

Peter Hartshorn

Miniver Press

To the memory of my father,
in peace

"You know, this baseball game of ours comes up from the youth. [But] you got to start from way down, at the bottom, when the boys are six or seven years of age. You can't wait until they're fourteen or fifteen. You got to let it grow up with you, if you're the boy. And if you try hard enough, you're bound to come out on top."

- Babe Ruth

Table of Contents

Introduction

With the youthful intensity of a slugger barely out of high school, Tony Conigliaro turns on a fastball and hits a towering shot to left field, the ball, a mere speck travelling in the illuminated night sky, settling softly in the vast net above The Wall at Fenway Park. This image, once so vivid in my mind, now recedes slowly with each passing year. Instinctively, I cling to it as a treasured marker of a time filled with the boundless hope and the absolute loyalty that perhaps only a child can summon for a major league team—in my case, the often inept but always captivating Boston Red Sox of the 1960s.

Sitting in a closet in my home, up on a shelf, are several aging boxes that must have once held new shirts or sweaters, probably to be opened on Christmas morning. But those boxes retain little connection to clothing or to Christmas. For decades, they have been stuffed with yellowed newspaper clippings, torn magazine articles, weathered scrapbooks, well-thumbed photo albums, and a dizzying variety of other fragments of sports history, most covering the baseball decade of the 1960s.

The boxes have sat largely undisturbed for years. As I sift through them now, I recognize that much of the meaning of my childhood lies in the contents of those tattered cartons. Relics all, each brings me back to the striking freshness and excitement of youth, which in my case involved the daily pursuit of baseball. Many cover the spectrum of Major League

Baseball, a nostalgic reminder of my keen interest in teams in both the American and National Leagues.

The assortment of items still fascinates, five decades later. A 1964 *Sport* magazine cover featuring a photo of a smiling Sandy Koufax gripping a ball alongside headlines of "Yogi Berra's Burden" and "The Fight to Remodel Wilt Chamberlain." A 1965 *Sports Illustrated* cover of Juan Marichal, with his left leg extended up past his cap in his trademark windup, and a headline of "Latin Conquest of the Major Leagues." From the *Boston Globe*, a black and white photo of a pensive Eddie Mathews, at a ten-year commemoration of the 1957 World Series championship for the Braves, with a somewhat bittersweet headline to many locals, "Boston Remembers, Too." Another *Globe* clipping, "Shadow of a Rose," showing a dashing, hatless, crew-cut Pete Rose frantically racing toward first base trying to beat out a grounder as the Pirates' Donn Clendenon stretches for the throw (and, on the back, Sam McCracken's "Rockingham Handicaps" next to a photo of smiling Sam himself). A *Globe* drawing of a very young Jerry Koosman, done by a very young Larry Johnson, entitled, "Shea Hey, Jerry!" And two of my favorites as a baseball fan living in the past as often as in the present: a photo of Willie Mays crossing the plate, being congratulated by Willie McCovey, after hitting his 500th home run, under the head-scratching headline of "Giants' Players Hold Mays Almost in Awe" (almost?), and black and white, side-by-side newspaper photos of Stan Musial taking a swing in 1942 and in a similar shot taken twenty years later, headlined "One of the Greatest Says 'So Long.'"

Above all in importance, though, is the Red Sox archive covering teams that I thought of in nearly reverential terms, although not often deservedly so. Again, the items take me back. A large, color photo of manager Johnny Pesky sitting on the dugout steps with a deeply concerned look on his face, as if he could see the futility that lay ahead. A peel-off sticker of Red Sox pitching coach Sal Maglie, with an even more pronounced facial expression of misery that made him appear as if he hadn't seen a twenty-game winner since 1951, when The Barber himself won 23 games in that immortal year for the New York Giants. A scrapbook dedicated to the Impossible Dream team, featuring a rather jaw-dropping photo of a totally clean-shaven, clean-cut Red Sox rookie, identified as "Albert W. Lyle," better known to history as Sparky. A Red Sox photo of ex-Indians Jose Azcue, Vicente Romo, and Sonny Siebert with the not quite politically correct headline of "Meanwhile, On the New Reservation ..."

While many of these items were not cut out with the greatest care—I apparently wasn't exactly a surgeon with a pair of scissors—they were looked at studiously and preserved with affection. And much of my warmth was extended to the first Red Sox teams of my memory, those sorrowful squads of the mid-1960s. As underwhelming as they were on the field—and frequently off it as well—they were the home team and the daily focus of my considerable attention. I supported them with heart and soul.

Those consistently poor teams of the 1960s lost because of dropped fly balls, missed cutoff men, fielders colliding, slow runners being sent home, careless runners bounding through stop signs, too many runners who couldn't steal second base, too many batters who couldn't get to first base, pitchers who couldn't remember to cover first base, pitchers who couldn't bunt, pitchers who couldn't *pitch*—basically, they lost because while they understood that the main concept was to keep the other team from scoring more runs than they did, they had great difficulty in doing so. While my memories of those very mortal players of fifty years ago have faded a bit with time, I remember enough to know that if they had understood how hard I was rooting for them, they couldn't possibly have lost so many games.

The better teams of later years, starting in 1967, lost because they were *the Red Sox*, meaning a talented team that sometimes did not have quite enough talent, sometimes did not have quite enough managerial/front office wisdom (has any other team ever lost a Hall of Fame catcher because they forgot to mail him a contract?), and always had very little luck. There was no talk of a "curse" or anyone blaming the ghost of Babe Ruth during my earliest days of following the teams of the 1960s. The heyday of "The Curse" came much later. From the mid-60s to the mid-70s, in fact, the Yankees were no better, and were often *worse*, than the Red Sox. How Mel Stottlemyre, who helped the Yankees win a pennant by one game with a brilliant, stretch run (9–3) as a rookie in 1964, must have wished he had put on the pinstripes about five years sooner.

No, those teams could have and probably *should* have done much better. After all, the Red Sox did have some very skilled teams that won divisions and pennants, teams that had hitting, pitching, hitting, fielding, and hitting. Speed blessed few Red Sox players, with Tommy Harper and Jerry Remy heading a regrettably short list—on three occasions, Carl Yastrzemski himself led the team in steals. Clearly, most Red Sox players were not born to run.

Talent and management issues aside, it did seem that those Red Sox teams lost at least partly because they had unbelievably bad luck. Even the Mets, after years of setting the standard for failure and undoubtedly making manager Casey Stengel wonder if Mickey Mantle and Whitey Ford had been playing the same sport back in the golden Yankee days, eventually managed to win a championship—*twice*. For teams that good to lose the way the Red Sox did demanded the patience of Job from their fans, who understandably may have felt that only divine intervention could bring a World Series victory to Boston. Good or bad, though, the Red Sox were never boring.

My most intense days as a Red Sox fan came when I was a young boy, in the 1960s, playing baseball on a daily basis with friends who also loved the sport. Baseball pretty much held the meaning of life in those long summers of elementary school vacation and steamy days spent on countless playgrounds and ballfields, and the Red Sox provided much of that meaning for me. Even with baseball being the sport of choice for so many baby-boomer kids, though, the abysmal Red Sox could not attract them—or, more importantly, their parents—to come out to see the team play. A trip to Fenway was an afterthought for most families, something they did maybe once a year, if at all.

In my case, fortunately, going to Fenway in those days was not only not an afterthought but was a major piece of my life. My late father, Lewis Hartshorn, who seemed to know more about baseball history than anyone else I knew at that young age, brought me to Fenway on a regular basis, each game, in my innocent mind, being at least as momentous as my race down the stairs every Christmas morning. Actually, Yaz and Tony C and Dick Radatz may have even been higher than Santa Claus on my list of heroes at the time—it was pretty close. And whether I was about to see Roger Maris and the New York Yankees or Mike Hershberger and the Kansas City Athletics was of little concern to me—major league ballplayers of any caliber were a thrill to watch, and I never tired of the experience.

Change, however, was coming, both for the Red Sox and for my father and me. In genuine amazement, I saw the Red Sox go from an annual doormat in the American League in performance and attendance to a legitimate contender playing regularly in front of large crowds both at Fenway Park and in nearly every other city they visited. Suddenly, not only boys and fathers who loved baseball but other boys, girls, their parents—*everyone* seemed to be eager to get tickets to Fenway. This remarkable transformation of the team and its fans was the true birth of Red Sox Nation, a coast-to-coast BoSox mania still going strong fifty years on. The story of baseball and the Red Sox in my own life, I suspect, will recall a past warmly familiar to many others who were also present at the creation of Red Sox Nation, while informing younger fans that from many years of pain may come unimagined beauty, a perfectly fitting truth for the Boston Red Sox.

Sadly, for my father and me, the beauty of our own early baseball days of enjoyment together gradually was eclipsed by the pain of experience in the real world beyond the white lines. A debilitating mental illness progressively sapped my father's interest in both baseball and nearly life itself, while creating a chasm between us that became increasingly challenging for either of us to bridge. Decades of strained relations seemed destined to last into the grave until his final days, when long-forgotten memories of baseball, much of it documented in those decaying boxes in the closet, brought us final redemption and peace.

1. The Creation

No one asks to be born. But once you are here, you must find something, or something must find you, to occupy your time. I'm not sure which way it worked in my case, but baseball entered my life, I am told, at the age of four in 1960. In a journal that my mother, Vera, kept on my life at that time, she wrote "[Peter] loved playing ball with Daddy. First bat and ball on 4th birthday." Two years later, she simply noted, "Crazy about baseball."

I don't doubt that this commentary on my youthful passion is true, as I still have some once-treasured 1961 baseball cards, roughly cut out from the backs of Post cereal cartons, buried in the boxes. The following year I was lucky enough to get a rookie card of Carl Yastrzemski, but being a mere child and not having an inkling of the future of Yaz or the yet-to-exist value of old baseball cards, I practiced writing the alphabet, in blue pen and in nice, carefully written letters, on the front of the card, leaving it a sentimental but totally profitless memory.

The age of four was important for both me and my father. When I turned four, it was a time of great hope and pride for America. John Kennedy was elected president, the country was thriving in the midst of "the American Century," and, from what I remember of my childhood in the Boston suburb of Norwood, my impression was that all things seemed possible—at least in sports dreams—for a young boy growing up in those days.

My father turned four, however, in 1929, a year that, along with 1861, 1941, and 2001, has only the darkest connotations in the American psyche. Who knows what parents thought as jobs disappeared, food became harder and harder to put on the dinner table, and poverty stretched as far into the future as they could see while President Hoover, from the comfort of the White House, worried that helping the poor too much might damage the moral fiber of the country, undoing much of his well-deserved reputation as "The Great Humanitarian."

For a young boy in the 1930s, one imagines that the grinding poverty gave the dreamful, heroic world of baseball a special allure. I'm sure that my father, who also grew up in Norwood and was a Boston Braves fan, did not get to many games at Braves Field, but he had his baseball cards and a radio, and that must have given him many hours of pleasurable distraction from the daily worries of his parents. (To be completely accurate, the team was briefly known as the Boston Bees, and the field as National League Park, or "the Beehive," from 1936 to 1940, undoubtedly a time of intense interest on the part of my father, who turned eleven in 1936.)

In any event, at an early age I began the happy ritual of bringing glove and ball into the backyard, throwing myself some practice popups, hitting the ball a mile—or at least ten feet or so—and chasing it down before hitting it another mile. I didn't ponder it much then, and I can't explain it now, but in some way, I fell very hard for the game of baseball.

Like riding a bicycle, there were lumps to be taken in the learning process. It could be quite frustrating trying to hit a ball "where they ain't," rather than where they were, or catching an in-between hop with my glove and not my groin. While I never mastered the various skills required of a baseball player myself, I was "good enough," as they say, to always enjoy the effort, and no baseball game or practice, from the time I started playing, could last too long.

In those days, a new baseball itself, with its smooth surface and its perfectly sewn, rough laces, so important for grip, made it seem somehow indecent to hit the ball and give it its first grass or dirt stain. On the rare days that my friends and I actually had a new ball, we tended to admire it more than use it,

17

generally going with our baseballs already darkened an admittedly unappealing shade of greenish-brown from hours of play, some so abused that the cover had ripped off, to be replaced by a thick, rather mushy layer of black masking tape. And to think that major leaguers got to wear full uniforms, play with new gloves, bats, and balls, and were paid large sums of money for doing it—that had to be the best job in the world, and of course was the job I wanted more than anything else.

These warm memories, as with most boys, may exist as much in my dreams as in any reality, but they remain a treasure of childhood nonetheless. And in those very early days, many of the memories came courtesy of my father's efforts to teach me the game that he himself had loved so much as a child. When he got home from work on warm, summer evenings, he would spend hours playing catch with me behind our house, and later, after I had learned how to catch a ball more easily, he would hit what seemed to me to be very sharp ground balls and towering fly balls in the backyard until I was comfortable catching those as well.

And on Sunday mornings, while most of the education occurring across America involved the Bible and Christian worshipers packed into church pews to hear priests and ministers pass along the word of God from on high, mine went blessedly further. A believer himself, my father would faithfully attend the ten o'clock service while I was in Sunday school class, but after we went home and changed, he often brought me to a nearby park where I could go on the swings and, of course, play baseball. There was a large screen behind home plate, and he would pitch to me as I batted in front of the screen, with each of us taking turns chasing down the one or two baseballs we had. Sunday may have been a day of rest for some, but the same was not true for my father, at least during baseball season, and I was the fortunate beneficiary.

On one of these mornings, however, the baseball universe went awry. As a pitcher, my father had very good control, and I was used to swinging at nearly every pitch he threw. Even pitches that were not strikes were usually hittable. But one at-bat produced a very much unanticipated result. As my father released the ball, he immediately shouted, "Watch out!" But my instincts betrayed me. So accustomed to swinging, and so *eager* to swing, I remained locked in on the job of hitting the pitch even as it bore in on me until I realized, too late, that my bat was not going to connect with this pitch. At the last second I jerked my head away, but the ball struck me on the side of my head.

I did not want to show that I was hurt, and I did not want my father to feel bad about hitting me, but I was unsuccessful on both counts. He came running in to check the damage, and I leaned over, holding the side of my head while being unable to hold back the tears that came streaming down my face. I could see that he was upset about hitting me, and I felt bad about not being a slightly braver baseball player. In fact, the pitches my father threw were not fast, and I was injured a bit but not mortally so—I should have been stronger.

But one thing that I could never tell my father, and barely could admit to myself, was that I always had a fear, as long as I played, of being beaned. A baseball is not a soft object, and while it had mostly positive qualities to me, at the same time it also put a sense of dread in me that I constantly struggled to stifle. In that moment, when I came unglued, I felt that my secret was out. But my father, who undoubtedly could see that I wasn't seriously hurt, offered minimal reassurance but not more, allowing me my dignity. Who knows—maybe he had harbored the same fear himself, decades earlier. The bottom line was that my father took my development as a baseball player seriously, and part of that development meant learning to get back up when I had been knocked down in some way. It was a lesson that was useful then, and remains so.

One evening around the same time in our lives, my father went up to the attic and came back with something that was a guarantee to catch my attention. He showed it to me with the comment, "I bet you've never seen one of these before," a bet he would have easily won. It was an old, faded brown glove from his own youth that, unlike the stiff gloves of my earliest memories, was quite broken in—actually, it was falling apart—but the fascinating thing about that glove was that it did not have five fingers. I don't remember if it had four fingers or three fingers, but it did not have five.

Although the glove was for a lefty and I was right-handed, I was fairly obsessed by it, so my father readily agreed that I could use it to play with. I often practiced catching balls with that very odd glove, awkward as it was for me, as I was using the wrong hand, just so I could try to figure out exactly where all of my fingers were supposed to go. Making the task of catching the ball more challenging was the fact that there was no lacing attaching the fingers together, and the webbing itself was pretty flimsy. The only safe place to catch the ball was right in the pocket, as any ball hitting the fingers of the glove was likely to keep right on going. I thought that was why old-timers—that would be anyone out of high school—always told you to use two hands in catching the ball. It was not possible to catch a ball one-handed with such a glove, and that pearl of wisdom must have been handed down through the generations. If there is a phrase I remember from my father while I was shagging fly balls, it is "Both hands!!"

Seeing my enthusiasm for his weathered glove, which took its proud place with my own glove in a paper bag near the back door, he ventured once more up to the attic and produced an equally aged bat, worn but still in pretty good shape, with some pre-World War II masking tape barely protecting the bat handle. It was much too long and heavy for me to use at that time. But whenever my father gave me his well-worn line of "Probably Mel Ott and Ducky Medwick used bats like that," I would take a few more practice swings with it, imagining all of the baseball gods that might have swung a bat such as the one in my own hands. These moments, and there were many of them, were the essence of my early baseball education.

My father's own baseball beginnings, also in Norwood, were somewhat different. I knew from an uncle, my father's brother, that he had played a lot of baseball as a boy, and had played very well. But growing up during the Depression, he learned mainly what he could from the unfortunate but timeless school of hard knocks, never finishing high school and paying the same lifelong, economic price that too many others have paid for the lack of a formal education.

And I don't think his family life at home was particularly easy. I never heard him talk about his father hitting him fly balls in the backyard. In fact, my few memories of my grandfather, generally from occasions when he visited us on Sundays for lunch, were that he always had a very stern look on his face. If I complained to my father about some punishment he was about to inflict on me for what I felt was a harmless transgression, his standard response was, "Just be glad you're not dealing with *my* old man!" Nevertheless, I used to imagine that my father had the same baseball dreams I had as a child, although I don't truly know if children in the Depression had dreams or not. Perhaps dreams were *all* they had.

To support himself, my father took a job working at a local book bindery as a young man. When I was a boy, he had moved on to an equally dead-end job in a clothing factory, which he never escaped until retirement, going in every day at 7:30, getting his half-hour respite for lunch, and coming home tired at 5:00, always for barely more than minimum wage. Naturally, such wages required my family—my parents, my older sister, my younger brother, and I—to live accordingly. For my father, buying third-hand cars that were constantly breaking down and tended to rot in front of our eyes (he measured the value of any car he bought by the extent of the rust on it, and by how many turns of the key it took to start the engine), having no savings (benevolent aunts and uncles quietly and generously provided cash when necessary, particularly regarding rent and cars), never owning a home—all were daily reality.

What he really wanted to be was an artist, a passion he pursued most of his life. He told me of art classes he had taken at the Museum of Fine Arts in Boston, when he must have been in his twenties. Wistfully recalling his commuting days on Huntington Avenue (where the Boston Americans/Red Sox played at the Huntington Avenue Grounds from 1901 to 1911 before moving to Fenway), he usually ended by saying, "Well, the whole damn thing's probably all changed now." Largely self-taught, he painted landscapes and seascapes, using oil paints that he often mixed on his own to get the desired color. There was a small room in our attic that functioned as an art studio of sorts and that doubled as my bedroom. It was an unheated room, which made the long New England winters seem even longer to both of us, but it was what it was, and we got used to it.

On summer weekends, he would display a dozen or so of his paintings along the side of a well-travelled road near our house and sit there in the heat for hours, as car after car shot past, hoping, Willy Loman-like, to "make it" in some way that would have been nothing short of miraculous. One day I joined him, thinking rather blankly that it might be a worthwhile excursion, or at least something different on a hot afternoon. Mainly what I saw was the pathos of a man imprisoned by his dreams, determined to keep hope alive when there was no plausible reason to do so. He passed the day alternately pacing back and forth on the sidewalk, arranging and rearranging the paintings, staring into space, and sitting in the car for some shade to escape the heat, as cars beat past us, all on their way to somewhere more important.

After a couple of hours of futile waiting, with me sitting on the ground awkwardly trying not to feel bad about a situation that had no silver lining whatsoever, my father summoned up whatever optimism he had left by saying a version of, "Well, nothing's happening. Must be vacation season or something. I'll try it again in a couple of weeks – people should be around then, damn it." So we packed the paintings with care in the back seat of the car, although, sadly, the care wasn't really necessary, as many of the paintings would never leave his possession. He certainly had some artistic skill and did sell a fair number of his paintings to passers-by and at church sales, just enough to sustain the illusion of future success for years. What should have remained an enjoyable hobby became, instead, a "somewhere over the rainbow" fantasy that he never quite shed.

In addition to painting, my father had an equal fascination with U.S. naval warships, his focus being on those of World War II, although he never served in the military. Just as I would spend hours immersed in studying my favorite baseball cards, he used to pore over his copies of *Jane's Fighting Ships*, filled with black and white photos of ships that all looked the same to me but were statistical goldmines to him, with a dizzying array of numbers that, disappointingly to my father, did not strike me with the same sparkle as those on the back of a 1965 Yaz baseball card.

When he wasn't painting, much of his free time was spent building ship models. In his improvised workshop in our cellar, he would use rectangular blocks of wood, two to three feet long, to meticulously make what would eventually amount to dozens of warships, his focus being on cruisers, destroyers, battleships, and carriers of World War II. His main "tools" were a handsaw, a hand drill, a vise, a chisel, and some sandpaper and paint that he used on his ramshackle bench. The ships' guns and decks he fashioned out of wood, while the railings and flags he made from various pieces of string and cloth. To hawk his ships, he visited local VFW and American Legion halls and Navy recruiting stations. As with the paintings, he actually sold a number of his ship models over the years, sometimes to sailors who had been on the ships, or to relatives of sailors, but never enough to rescue the family finances.

Two memories concerning his interest in ships remain vivid in my mind, both occurring when I was a young adult. They also reflect my father's somewhat quirky personality. At times mild-mannered and genial, he also could be uncomfortably gruff and pointedly honest, though he never meant to hurt anyone with his comments, and in my mind it is this forthright side of him that endures, however unfair that may be to him.

The first story regarding ships involved a visit we made to the Naval War College in Newport, Rhode Island, where an officer had kindly agreed to meet my father to discuss his ship models. When we entered the room, the officer got up from his desk to greet us, but my father, having spied a warship model across the room, strode right past the officer and gave the model one brief look before turning back and asking, "Is that the best you have? Christ, it's made of *plastic*!" From there, the meeting could only improve, and largely through the graciousness of the officer, it did, with all of us sharing a few laughs at the end over Rhode Island politics and New England weather.

On another occasion, we went to see the USS Massachusetts at Battleship Cove in Fall River. As one of the sailors on board was giving some information about the ship's World War II service in the Pacific to a couple of tourists, my father listened rather impatiently before brusquely gesturing for us to move along. I understood what this meant: the guide was not on the top of his game that day, to put it politely. As we walked away, my father muttered, "Christ, if he had been running the ship, the Japs would have sunk it in ten minutes." Pity the person who made a mistake on World War II naval history in the presence of my father, and I sometimes pitied myself for being stuck in the middle of such uncomfortable moments. To be fair to all sides, my father also had several enthusiastic exchanges over the years with ship guides and other naval personnel, never tiring of finding someone willing to revisit epic sea battles such as Guadalcanal or Leyte Gulf.

When he wasn't using his spare time to paint or make ship models, he was often reading, and he read a lot when I was young. In the evening he would sit in his favorite chair in the living room and go through the *Boston Globe*, growling his conservative disagreement ("a bunch of god damn kooks!") with almost every editorial in it. He would then seek out the antidote on the comics page, starting with "Mutt and Jeff," a strip that usually gave him a good laugh every night.

Across the room was a small bookcase full of books, mostly on presidential and military history and poetry. As he grew older, his reading narrowed almost entirely to material on the U.S. Navy. Two books in particular that I remember were *The Two Ocean War* by Samuel Eliot Morison, and a huge volume on the history of the U.S. Navy in World War II. "Damn good book" was a common utterance from my father while he was immersed in such reading. For a period of years, he also faithfully read the U.S. Naval Institute's monthly publication, *Proceedings,* up until the family budget had no more cap space for such luxuries. Occasionally I poked through his books and magazines, knowing little about the content but catching names and faces and phrases—"tin can sailors" and "seabees" were two that remain stuck in my memory—that would interest me much more as an adult.

My father did not watch a lot of television, and he knew what he liked. Mainly he enjoyed baseball games and the *Red Skelton Show*. And any World War II movie starring John Wayne, Henry Fonda, Robert Ryan, Robert Mitchum, Cliff Robertson, Sean Connery, James Coburn, Eddie Albert, or Lee Marvin was one that he had probably seen several times, never enjoying it less than he had the first time. Of course, if I happened to be watching *Combat!* or *Twelve O' Clock High*, he usually had the time to sit down with me.

When he had read enough or finished watching television for an evening, he would often put on a record from his small collection, maybe Mitch Miller or something Western. "Red River Valley" and "Home on the Range" were played enough so that I still remember some of the lyrics. Above all, he enjoyed classical music, especially Beethoven symphonies, which is generally when I would leave the room, being rather more interested in the Beatles and Herman's Hermits at the time. Even "Georgy Girl" or "Born Free" was better than Beethoven, I thought. At some point during the music, he would ultimately doze off, most often repeating the performance the following night.

My father spoke to me pretty frequently in those days, but not much about school, possibly out of a subconscious sense of his own educational shortcomings. We certainly talked about baseball, as much about the 1930s as the 1960s, and the Navy as well, although that was mostly a case of him telling me about the history of this ship or that ship and me thinking that it was all not quite capturing my attention. But we did talk—I simply found his animated retelling of the history of Dizzy Dean, Pepper Martin, and the Gashouse Gang, for example, more interesting than that of the U.S.S. Bainbridge.

For baseball conversations, he often started with a kind of Socratic approach, asking a question along the lines of "Did you ever hear of Johnny Logan?" to lure me in to the baseball line of thinking, not a challenging task. On one occasion, he got started on Dizzy Trout, who wasn't even a National Leaguer. When I told him that I didn't know of Trout, that was all he needed to hear, and such conversations always led down the same path of astonishment followed by a blast from his own archive of hardball history. "Never heard of Trout?" he asked in amazement. "Christ, you probably think the only 'Dizzy' was Dean. You gotta do more reading. Trout was a right-hander for the Tigers. Talk about 20-game winners—Trout was up there every year [not exactly, but he did hit the mark twice, including 27 wins in 1944]. Him and Newhouser were great together— and don't tell me you never heard of Newhouser, for Christ's sake! Newhouser was like god-damn Koufax back then. But old Dizzy Trout—I can't believe you never heard of him."

And to finish the story of Trout, after his long career with the Tigers, he was traded to the Red Sox in 1952 for, among others, Johnny Pesky. But Trout's mediocre record (9–

8) in his one season in Boston only confirmed why the Tigers had shipped him out.

Such was the method by which I initially learned a lot of the diamond history that had transpired before my birth. And World War II was never far from any discussion, including baseball. Even as a young boy, I knew the difference between knuckleballer Eddie Rommel and Hitler favorite (for a while) Erwin Rommel, as taught to me—in detail—by my father. When I watched episodes of *The Rat Patrol* on television, I always remembered the Desert Fox.

So, to me, my father was a reliable and entertaining baseball confidant and instructor. One longstanding myth that can be dispelled, however, is that of all fathers playing catch with sons back in the day. Many fathers did, in fact, play catch with sons in the backyard, and some even took the next step and generously coached various Little League teams, particularly if their son was on the club. So there certainly was a good amount of father-son baseball going on.

But fathers had other lives as well. Some liked watching an occasional baseball game on television, but did not have much interest in going to Fenway or playing baseball with their sons or with anyone else. Others preferred tinkering with their cars in the driveway, doing some kind of woodwork or home improvement project, often in the cellar or in the garage, or sitting in the yard or on the porch and reading the newspaper or just relaxing for an hour or two on a weekend. So fatherhood had many forms, and not all involved the national pastime.

The one constant about *every* father in my neighborhood is that each day, Monday through Friday, they got up in the morning and went to work for the whole day. I don't remember anyone being unemployed, or working part-time. It was the father's job to bring home the bacon, and they did. And in that pre-internet age, no one "worked from home," and flex schedules were non-existent. (Even three-day weekends were yet to be established—holidays fell on holidays, regardless of the day.) My friends' fathers were firemen, policemen, mailmen, bus drivers, truck drivers, mechanics, plumbers, janitors, town workers, and so on, and they had alarm clocks and punch clocks and overtime to deal with in their daily lives. All of this came before any thoughts of baseball.

Beyond the invigorating world of baseball, though, lay the discomforting realization, dawning on me slowly but unmistakably, that my father was not normal. At least, through my inexperienced eyes as a child, I could see that his behavior did not match that of other fathers. In my initial wave of baseball mania, encouraged and facilitated by my father, I think I just blocked out such thoughts and lived by the mantra, "Play Ball!" And as my parents never openly discussed the matter of my father's erratic behavior, my task of willful ignorance was made easier. But as I passed through elementary school, I found it harder to ignore the obvious.

While my father's symptoms were physical, the cause was mental. Whether he was sitting or standing, his body would twitch in a seemingly uncontrollable manner, often while he was loudly swearing about one thing or another, although sometimes about nothing at all. He just seemed to be in another dimension. And the episodes could last for moments or minutes or longer, depending on reasons that I could not begin to comprehend. When I was sprawled on the couch, reading a baseball book or poring through my cards, the relentlessly rustling noise of the newspaper in the unsteady hands of my father, sitting across the room, became a kind of background music to which I became oddly accustomed. Yet when he was painting or building ship models or, most importantly to me, playing baseball, he was quite relaxed, giving him the appearance of having alternate lives.

Later, I would learn that he had Tourette's syndrome, and had suffered from it since he was a boy. As an adult, I tried to imagine the frustration and discouragement that my father undoubtedly felt as a young baseball player, playing a game he loved but trying to do what his muscles could not always agree to do. But as a child, I was left to observe, largely in bewilderment, the troublesome behavior of my own father that would eventually grow to depression and, ultimately, a diminishing interest in life itself.

2. Fenway Up Close

Although I wish it were otherwise, my father's struggles with his health are some of the strongest memories of my childhood. Memory, though, is a strange and often peculiarly selective guide. In 1963, for instance, when I was seven and in second grade, President Kennedy was shot, but despite the great stir that must have been occurring all around me for days, I have only the vaguest recollection of that tragedy. Yet, at the same time, I was quite familiar with the career of utility infielder John Kennedy of the Washington Senators, who later had several decent seasons off the bench for the Red Sox and, oddly enough, shared the same birthday—May 29—as President Kennedy.

I also still clearly recall my second grade teacher, our classroom (which, for some reason, was actually split between second grade and third grade students), my friends, the elementary school itself, and, of course, some early baseball experiences. Included among my most precious memories of those years of innocence was my introduction to Little League baseball, to pick-up baseball games, to the Red Sox on their infrequently televised games, and to Fenway Park, courtesy of my father's patience at bringing me to what would be five games a season over the next few years.

We started attending Red Sox games regularly in 1963. The first Red Sox game of which I have even a vague memory of attending was against the Los Angeles Angels that year. The only game details that I recall are that the Red Sox won, slugger Dick Stuart hit a homer, and Dean Chance, one of the best starters in the league and also one of my favorite pitchers, with his sidearm, whiplash-type delivery, came in as a reliever. (In his

Cy Young year in 1964, Chance had the rather yeoman-like stat line of 20 wins, 15 complete games, 11 shutouts, and 4 saves.)

The aftermath of the game, however, has a more distinct mark in my memory. My father brought me to a souvenir stand, where I marveled at each item, almost salivating at some of the choices (badges with faces of Red Sox players and an impressive red, white, and blue flag-like cloth attached below were always a favorite, not that I could often buy one), before deciding to purchase an Angels pennant. I already had a selection of pennants at home, including one of the Red Sox, but none for the Angels, so I bought it to add to the collection. The pennant was rather large, made of dark green cloth and attached to a wooden stick, and I waved it out the car window all the way home. How out of place this must have looked in the Boston area did not occur to me at the time.

When I got home and pulled the flag inside the car, though, I was distraught to see that about half the pennant had been shredded by the wind. "How the hell did that happen?" was my father's unsurprising response, seeing that my souvenir had been destroyed less than an hour after we had spent his hard-earned money on it. Feeling both guilty and more than a little annoyed that such ridiculous things happened in life— how was a seven-year-old boy supposed to know the effect of wind dynamics on a cloth baseball pennant?—I took the remains of the pennant and stubbornly put it up on the wall in my room, where it remained in its ragged grandeur, along with about a dozen undamaged major league pennants, for the rest of my childhood.

Those first Red Sox games I attended have left impressions of moments or scenes more than distinct memories of entire games. But many of those images have stayed with me, decades after the fact. Of course, Fenway Park itself, which over half a century had played host to baseball moments ranging from historical to hysterical, was at the heart of my experience. I came to know the park pretty well, and much of what I observed was certainly memorable, if not always encouraging.

Present-day Red Sox fans may regard Fenway as a shrine of sorts, and any suggestions of tearing it down and replacing it with a modern stadium featuring comfortable seats and aisles that someone with a moderately protruding gut might be able to fit through are seen as heresy. In the 1960s, though, Fenway Park was no shrine, and getting the Red Sox mercifully out of there was a Hot Stove topic year after year. A group known as the Greater Boston Stadium Authority was created specifically to that end, having been granted "Authority to Construct, Operate and Maintain Multi-Purpose Stadium and Appurtenant Facilities in or in The Vicinity of Greater Boston."

Suggestions were not lacking. Various reports had the Red Sox playing in a new stadium at the nearby Fens, somewhere around South Station, along a suburban highway, or, it seemed, wherever else an open piece of land existed within thirty miles of Jersey Street. There was even a proposal for a *domed* stadium. The new park would be paid for by the team, by the city, by the state, or by some combination of any or all of the above.

The only certainty was that it was going to happen because if people talked about something as much as people debated how to replace Fenway Park, it was destined to happen, and because the park, everyone agreed, was too small and antiquated. In fact, Fenway Park was the best possible advertisement for watching a game on television or even listening on the radio—it was the Riker's Island of baseball parks, which was one reason why the Red Sox barely got 10,000 fans a night to show up. Tom Yawkey himself, the Red Sox "plantation" owner, as he was known, threatened to move the team if a new stadium did not appear on the horizon. "The House That Ruth Left" might have been an appropriately negative moniker for Fenway in those days. There were no "Save Fenway" campaigns that I can recall, and for good reason.

As far as fans are concerned, any discussion of 1960s Fenway Park must begin with the restrooms. Before or since, I have never truly appreciated—*feared* would be a more appropriate word—the strength of the human sense of smell. The odor of those men's rooms, not to mention the sights and sounds, left an indelible impression on my young and unfortunately inquisitive mind.

The physical setup of the restrooms was simple. When I ventured in, what I found were dimly lit, open space areas featuring long troughs running around the perimeter of the room, with drains here and there. Everyone, men and boys together, did their business communally, usually as fast as possible, preferably without inhaling, as the fumes coming up from the constant flow and mixing of bodily fluids below were well beyond the design limits of the human nose. And you had to look straight across at the wall or, heaven forbid, down, as the thought of turning your head sideways to avoid some of the odorous onslaught was totally out of the question, at least for a young boy. Occasionally, patrons seemed to enjoy a noisy and elongated spit into the trough, as if that somehow added to the ambience of the moment. Mainly it only added to the horror, as far as I could tell. Other unwelcome bodily utterances were frequently heard as well.

The sinks, with leaky faucet handles and drains that enjoyed backing up to contribute to the overall discomfort level, were not used often and only in a hurry. There was no reason to linger in a Fenway Park restroom. If there were any mirrors at all, they have left my memory. Maybe I just wasn't tall enough to see into them. Of course, anyone worried about taking the time to check their physical appearance at that particular moment had personal issues that one does not want to contemplate.

The restrooms were the major but not the only drawback at Fenway. If you sat under an overhang—and many of the seats were under an overhang—the chances of having water or other fluids dripping on your head at some point during the game were high. In the case of a rain delay, there was hardly any reason to move from an open seat to the overhang area, as the amount of precipitation may have been equal all the way around. As a result, some fans chose to sit under their umbrellas or self-made tarps, apparently content to know that what was hitting them from above was only rain. More than once my father and I sat under the rain with *no* umbrella, only our baseball hats protecting us from the elements.

The possibility of having a pole situated somewhere between you and the field was also not out of the question. But, from a young fan's point of view, the beauty of the early and mid-1960s Red Sox was that almost no one went to the games—more than 10,000 was an excellent but rare turnout, which gave fans welcome seating options. Once the sixth or seventh inning rolled around, if not earlier, my father and I would join the migration downward, moving from our accustomed right field seats to the empty seats closer to the actual field, sometimes nearly in the first row, and no one ever said a word about it. Obstructed view seats were not an issue in those days.

The seats themselves could only have encouraged fans to stay home or, once seated, to wish they had gone to see John Wayne in *El Dorado* or Jimmy Stewart in *Shenandoah* or Omar Sharif in *Doctor Zhivago* in the comfort of an air-conditioned movie theater or in their car at a drive-in. I personally didn't know exactly what "hardwood" was, but I always assumed that those Fenway seats were made of something called hardwood. They certainly were not meant as a friend to anyone's posterior. People who got up to get food were just as likely trying to give their rear end some well-deserved relief. The backs of the seats were also made of the same hardwood, so I got into the habit of leaning forward to watch the game and saving my back at the same time. Nearby spectators may have thought I was just a particularly avid fan—which, in fact, I was—but I was also concerned about being able to stand up and walk normally at the end of the game.

Another memory of the ballpark was the growing fog of slowly drifting smoke that collected around the light standards, being quite visible in the late innings. Many fans did smoke (always legal products, I should add), not that I minded, as it was such a common occurrence in any setting in those years. Even my father smoked his pipe occasionally. But with so few fans at each game, it seems a little hard to believe that such a group could produce a burgeoning cloud of smoke overhead. Still, I saw what I saw.

Perhaps because of all of this, not to mention the product on the field, ticket prices were very reasonable. My father paid $1.50 for each of our seats, and we could have sat in the bleachers, where there were no dripping overhangs, for a dollar each. We never sat in the pricier seats behind home plate, but sometimes when we entered the park, we would walk up one of the ramps near the infield to get the rich folks' view for a moment, especially during batting practice.

To my young mind, it was somewhat incredible that you could get that close to a real major league player. Even my father couldn't restrain himself from saying, "Look, there's Colavito!" or "Hey, isn't that Norm Cash?" The players themselves seemed to take it all very casually, a few patiently signing autographs or joking with one another, sometimes talking to players on the opposing teams while hanging around the batting cage or playing catch in foul territory. When the pitchers and the backup catcher walked across the outfield on their way to the bullpen, they moved like any normal person just strolling down the street. Didn't they realize that they were walking on *major league grass* that most of us would never get to touch? They didn't seem too impressed by that fact. Being a major leaguer was truly a different life, I imagined.

The streets and sidewalks around Fenway at that time were not a cross between a shopping mall and a food emporium, as they are now, but there was still plenty of major league atmosphere to savor or fear, as the case may be. The area certainly had its own sights and smells, the smells being mainly the floating plumes of cigarette and cigar smoke that competed, for the most part quite successfully, with the greasy odor of hamburgers and hot dogs being grilled by vendors of dubious culinary skill. I saw one of them once drop a hot dog on the ground and then pick it up and put it in a bun, having lined up a few for immediate sale. In the fine backyard tradition of youth (male youth, at least) at that time, my friends and I often shared cans of soda, candy bars, ice cream cones, and other assorted products destined for your stomach, all embellished with various amounts of someone else's saliva, but there was something about the sight of that hot dog on the ground that challenged even *my* sense of acceptable hygiene.

With my father, generally around the fourth or fifth inning, I had some popcorn or an ice cream bar, along with a coke that I would say was a mix of approximately eighty percent mud-like syrup and twenty percent water, depending on how fast the ice cubes melted. Overall, I guess I failed the Fenway food test, possibly to the unintended benefit of my health. One related food memory was the accuracy with which the Fenway vendors—mostly young urban guys, I figured, judging from their swagger—could lob those ice cream bars and Cracker Jack boxes to customers. Until 1967, there usually was no need to throw them at all, as most nights the vendors could walk right up to fans and handed them over. But once people started showing up for games and the seats were filled with bodies, the vendors, heeding the evolutionary call, developed quite capable skills at standing in the large aisles between sections and tossing the bars and boxes the full distance to fans, often with pinpoint accuracy. The fact that some fans could not actually catch the items in no way reflected poorly on the throwing ability of the vendors. I was duly impressed.

The souvenir stands, however, were a different matter from the food. I never tired of looking over all of the pennants, player photos, yearbooks, hats, helmets, T-shirts, badges, bumper stickers, and other assorted objects that, I imagined, would significantly improve the quality of my baseball life. Occasionally I could buy one of the items, which always made the ride home extra special, often even taking the sting out of yet another Red Sox defeat. Yes, I definitely preferred souvenirs to food at Fenway.

As a boy, though, I didn't go to Fenway to focus on the restrooms or food or overhangs or poles or seats or cheap prices—the park itself did have its own charms, which certainly cast their spells on me. But first came the actual game-day excitement of just *knowing* that I would be at Fenway soon to witness a major league game. I don't know if facebooking, video-gaming, youtubing, texting youngsters of today, knowing that they will shortly be making their way to Fenway to see the Red Sox, experience the same sense of heightened anticipation that I certainly felt in the hours before a Red Sox game back in the Luddite 1960s. The end of such innocence would be a mark not of progress but of deprivation, based on my own memories.

Given the woeful teams that the Sox put on the field in those days, it may be hard for younger fans now to wonder what all the fuss was about. It may seem that people who spent their time and money at those Red Sox games just had no life. I don't remember it that way at all. The whole process to me was special, from finding out that I would be going to a particular game to the day of the game itself.

We always went to weeknight games—I'm not sure why—so I would often be in school during the day, and those days absolutely seemed to drag by, even though I would get a bit of envy from friends when I told them that I would be going to Fenway that night. Then the two hours after school from 3:00 to 5:00 seemed to be even slower.

Finally, when the time came to get in the car and go, I was in full game-day mode. I would look at the pitching match-up to see who had the advantage, and go over the line-up of the opposing team to see who might give Red Sox pitching the most trouble (some nights, that could have been almost any hitter), pondering all of this, and maybe what souvenir to get at the game, during the trip in.

Our travel to Fenway relied on the family car and the public transportation system of the Massachusetts Transit

Authority (MTA), replaced by the more ambitious Massachusetts Bay Transportation Authority (MBTA) in 1964 and now widely referred to as simply "the T." From our home in Norwood, we drove along the VFW Parkway before turning left on Baker Street in West Roxbury and parking the car at a station in Newton, where we got on a Green Line trolley to the park. What I recall about the Green Line was that we had to stand and wait a long time for a train (some things never change), and that was the first time that I had ever been among any black people, not that many blacks took that line. Later, I would understand why black people felt such discomfort at Fenway Park and largely stayed away.

Night games were like a spectacle at Fenway, even if not many people were there. The light standards surrounding the park resembled something from another planet, lighting the field so well that it seemed better than daylight itself. I remember thinking of my own frustration at having to stop playing baseball each night with my friends when it got dark out, and how lucky these players were to be able to play at night. It struck me as almost exotic. And, again, they got *paid* to do it—unbelievable. And the grass was so green and so well mowed, fitting seamlessly around the dirt areas of the field. The smooth infield dirt itself was such a perfect light brown color that it looked almost clean in a strange sort of way. I heard people say that the Fenway grass could be tough on infielders, but compared to the fields that the rest of us were playing on, it looked like heaven.

Many people over the years obviously have commented on the unique shape of Fenway, but I had never personally been to another big league park, so it became a normal sight for me, although no less magical. At the time, there were no signs around the outfield advertising W.B. Mason or McDonald's or Foxwoods or some other sponsor of the team—just the large Jimmy Fund billboard in right that reminded us of the charitable connection between the Red Sox and children with cancer. (To be accurate, the Braves started the charity, and it was taken up by Yawkey and the Red Sox when the Braves left the city in 1953.) And the jumbotron was still to be imagined. The right field foul pole, not yet widely referred to as Pesky's Pole, was inviting to left-handed batters who liked to pull the ball, and I came close on several occasions to getting a foul ball or a short home run as a souvenir.

My memory of the two bullpens in right field was that the relief pitchers, slouching on their bench or leaning forward against the outfield wall or the wall between the pens, often chewed a lot of gum or tobacco, spit a lot, and generally looked bored. I couldn't believe that a major leaguer could be bored, though, so I just assumed that they had their own way of concentrating on the game, and it merely appeared to be boredom. Between innings, however, the right fielder would often play long toss with someone in the bullpen, and it was possible that that action would be the *only* action a reliever might see all night, so the boredom theory likely has some support.

When the time came for one of the relievers to enter the game, which did not happen as early or as frequently as it does in the present age, even for those woebegone Red Sox teams, someone—presumably a licensed Massachusetts driver—would drive the bullpen cart from the runway out to the bullpen and collect the new pitcher, who almost always was wearing a windbreaker no matter the temperature, and the two would ride back to the mound, with the pitcher taking off his jacket and putting it in the cart before getting the ball and then briefly, or not so briefly, kicking at the dirt in front of the rubber to customize the mound as the cart was driven away. The entrance of a reliever in 1960s Fenway Park was a ritual now gone but not forgotten.

The triangle in center field was no man's land for the center fielder, and more than a few of them got twisted and turned badly enough while racing back on fly balls to either turn outs into extra base hits or, in the worst cases, slam their bodies into the wall and crumple to the ground, forcing the

39

right fielder to race over and get the ball back to the infield. For the more graceful centerfielders, all that space presented opportunities to make spectacular catches, and some did, although not usually while playing for the Red Sox. From my fan's point of view in right field, when a fly ball disappeared in the triangle, I had to wait for the reaction of the crowd to know if there had been a superlative catch or an extra base hit.

The left field wall, however, was the soul of the park. Now commonly referred to as "The Green Monster," the 37-foot high wall was better known as "The Wall" when I was growing up, and that is how I still think of it. Of course, in the 1960s, there were no Monster seats where you could get a bird's eye view of the game. Instead, there was The Wall and a huge net above it, which gently snared most home runs to left. A ball that was crushed, though, might sail over both The Wall and the net and eventually hit somewhere between Landsdowne Street and the Massachusetts Turnpike, possibly reminding an unsuspecting driver or two that baseballs can travel a great distance when launched from the bat of someone like Dick Stuart or the Twins' slugging outfielder, Bob Allison. From our right field seats, my father and I had a pretty good angle on such blasts, and watching the ball rise into the night sky, clearing The Wall and the net, and sailing majestically beyond, was impressive every time it happened, and at Fenway, as always, it happened frequently, often for both sides.

With its sheer size, The Wall was the first thing fans noticed as they walked into the park, and it undoubtedly was on the mind of every pitcher and batter during the game, helping and hurting both on many occasions. Any reasonably deep fly ball to left field was an adventure for the spectators, not to mention most left fielders, and even more so on nights when the wind was blowing out. Who knows how many home runs The Wall added or subtracted from players' totals, how many pitchers were intimidated by it and threw accordingly, how many hitters got big eyes at the plate and put themselves into slumps by doing so, or how many left fielders played an out into a double by giving up on a ball too soon?

As I sat perched in my seat and imagined each at-bat playing itself out, as if I were on the mound or at the plate, The Wall was always there, ever present, looming over the entire game. Players have said it doesn't affect them, but based on how well or poorly many players have performed over the years at Fenway, that seems like brave talk more than honesty. The Wall was a daunting but compelling presence at the same time. Yawkey, in the team's dark days of the mid-1960s, lamented, "Damn it, that wall hurts: it has an effect on the organization from top to bottom. We have to go after players who have that Fenway stroke, but then they get in the habit of pulling the ball and they try it on the road—in Yankee Stadium or Comiskey—and it's no good. Hitters' habits are hard to break."

Unfortunately for the Red Sox, not many people were there to observe all of this. Commenting on the team's popularity, *Globe* writer Clif Keane once quipped, "A lot of people will come dressed as empty seats tonight." Even a half century later, Yaz still vividly recalled the solitude of playing at Fenway in those years. "The stands were empty," he said in an interview. "You could throw raw meat up there. You could hear every little thing they were saying. We had no real hope."

The numbers back him up, as the Red Sox never reached a million fans in any season between 1963 and 1966, hitting rock bottom in 1965, attracting barely 8000 fans a game. On five occasions that year, my father and I were among them, sitting in a ballpark that was three-quarters empty. Interestingly, though, the Red Sox were hardly bringing up the rear in the American League in terms of attendance. During that same four-year span, a period in which the Red Sox never finished higher than seventh place, their attendance, almost respectably, ranked fourth, fifth, seventh, and eighth. So while Boston fans may not have been clamoring to see Yaz, Mantle, and other stars, neither were fans in many other cities.

Of course, helping to limit the attendance were the higher number of day games and the fact that nearly all potential spectators—males—were at work or in school during that time. Females were not usually among the hardy souls who made it to Fenway in those days. Girls my age were not often seen, nor were women with other women unless you happened to be at Fenway on Nuns' Day, which was never the case with me. Mothers with husbands and children were also not among the mainstream.

With minimal attendance at most Red Sox games, and this being long before the appearance of cell phones and Sweet Caroline and even the Wave, games at Fenway Park were often fairly sedate affairs. Of course, there was a roar, which included my own screams, whenever a ball soared up toward The Wall in left, the triangle in center, or the bullpen in right, but for the most part the games were played before a politely quiet crowd. This suited me fine, as I really wanted to concentrate on the game, pitch by pitch, in true baseball-fan fashion, as much as possible. From my invaluable cards, I knew the names of nearly every player on every team, and at least for the starters I knew what they could and couldn't do, so I would try to "manage" both teams, in my mind, from my seat. I anticipated what each batter might do, and how they should be played. For example, if the Angels' 5' 5"Albie Pearson (once a Red Sox signee) was at bat and any outfielder was not playing shallow, that was a cause for concern.

On the other hand, if 6'7" Frank Howard of the Senators was up, everyone could back up ten steps or so. If the ball didn't go over The Wall, lumbering Frank was not often going past first base, and if he tried to do so could be thrown out from nearly anywhere in the outfield. Howard was certainly menacing at the plate—the bat looked like a small stick in his hands as he flicked it back and forth waiting for the pitch—but it always struck me as slightly ludicrous seeing him hit a bullet off The Wall and then casually rounding first base and stopping, as if he had simply hit a ground ball through the hole out to Yaz in left. To make a baserunning contrast, Jim Rice hit the same number of home runs as Howard—382—but to that total Rice added 373 doubles and 79 triples, while Howard produced 245 doubles and 35 triples. Regardless, I loved watching both hit a baseball.

At the games, my father and I did not keep up a running conversation once the action started. The games moved along at a significantly quicker pace than most games of recent years, so I kept up a silent concentration on each pitch, lest I miss one. My father, for his part, was content to enjoy a night of baseball—he didn't need me to entertain him.

But when there was questionable baseball strategy/execution taking place in front of us, which was often the case, he would come to life with his unique brand of commentary, generally in the form of muttering some bird-dog wisdom about the ineptitude unfolding before him. Hitters taking third strikes ("For Christ's sake, what does he think the bat's for?") or failing to get down a bunt ("For Christ's sake, what do they do all that time in spring training?"), pitchers walking any batter with less than a .250 average ("For Christ's sake, let him hit it—it ain't going anywhere!"), outfielders missing the cutoff man ("For Christ's sake, didn't these guys play Little League?"), or starters being taken out of the game with the lead, especially if the incoming reliever for the Red Sox was not Dick Radatz ("For Christ's sake, let him stay in there—why just give it away?") were all bromides offered up by my father, most to be repeated verbatim at the next game.

And, naturally, to my father, all of the players we saw paled in comparison to the goliaths of the 1930s and 1940s. "How many balls would (Hack Wilson, Ralph Kiner, Ducky Medwick, Hank Sauer, Wally Berger, Gabby Hartnett—take your pick) have hit over that wall?" he repeatedly asked, leaving me with the boyhood impression that these National League players of yore had biceps bursting through their sleeves and used tree stumps for bats. Anyway, I doubted that they had bigger biceps than Willie Horton or Harmon Killebrew.

On the ride home, the highlight, brief as it may have been, was the huge drive-in movie screen we passed on the VFW Parkway in West Roxbury. I always looked forward to seeing whatever fleeting glimpse of the big screen I could catch as my father slowed down the car on that stretch of road, quite possibly so that he could catch his own glimpse of the action. The movie scenes generally fell into one of the following categories: a sheriff or a posse gunning down an outlaw in the canyons of the wild West, blue and grey uniformed Civil War soldiers shooting each other on a battlefield strewn with dead bodies, American soldiers fighting the Germans with tanks and howitzers, or a man and a woman kissing each other with their eyes closed. All except the last were of great interest to me in the few seconds of action that I could capture before our car, frustratingly, left the big screen behind.

3. Help Wanted

In my young baseball mind, the 1960s was like a Golden Age for dreaming. I started playing Little League baseball in 1963, on a real team with a real Little League T-shirt (white with a blue Little League emblem on the front), and was convinced that I was well on my way to a future at Fenway Park. I noticed that some of the boys on my team couldn't throw or hit as well as I could, which was a clear sign that I was headed in the right direction. The fact that there were other boys on the team who *could* do those things better than I could was an inconvenient truth that I put aside for the moment.

All I had to do, I figured, was make it to the lowest of the Red Sox minor league teams, and from there it would be an easy ride up. I saw on the backs of my baseball cards that some players never spent more than a few years on minor league teams before getting promoted, and some skipped whole leagues in the process of their upward mobility to the big club. I knew that there were players like Bob Feller, Al Kaline, and Ernie Banks who had spent *no* time in the minors, and others like Willie Mays and Roberto Clemente who had spent less than a full season there, but I was willing to acknowledge that I might not be quite that good yet.

Anyway, at least according to my baseball cards, there were not many players at that superlative level, so I wasn't too worried about them. Heck, Yaz himself had spent two years (.356) in the minors. And I had about ten years before I would even finish high school. Ten years was longer than I had yet lived—imagine how much you could improve in that much time, I thought. For sure, I was going to the majors. It was just a question of how fast it would happen. In the meantime, I kept playing baseball with anyone willing to get a game together, at

45

school or in my neighborhood, figuring that the better I got now, the less hard I would have to work when I got to the big leagues.

The Red Sox apparently could use someone like me as soon as possible. But in those tender years of youthful optimism, when I was drinking the Red Sox Kool-Aid by the gallon, I had no idea of the size of the problem. As all members of The Nation know, the transformation of the Red Sox from misfits to marvels was neither gradual nor anticipated.

That the Red Sox were bad in the first place seemed surprising to me, as a child, and was a condition that would absolutely improve, I believed, with each new spring training. After all, this was a team, as I heard and read, that had featured Ted Williams, Bobby Doerr, Joe Cronin, even a DiMaggio—how could they really be bad? (In the 1941 game against the Red Sox at The Stadium when Joe DiMaggio broke Wee Willie Keeler's major league hitting streak record of 45 with a home run against 31-year-old rookie—and ultimately 19-game winner—Dick Newsome, Dom DiMaggio had made a terrific catch on a fly ball off his brother's bat earlier in the game, leaving one writer in the press box groaning, "Joe ought to sue his old man on that one.") Surely the Red Sox were destined for better things.

The Red Sox themselves had a number of All-Stars even in the lean years, and in one of those lean years, 1961 (76–86), actually had two players in the top five in the Rookie of the Year voting: Don Schwall, the winner, and Chuck Schilling, both of whom also received MVP votes. So hope sprang eternal for young fans like me.

What I hadn't grasped yet was that the pre-1967 Red Sox teams of my youth were fun to watch if you simply wanted to be entertained by frequent gaffes and rather less frequent moments of fleeting glory, particularly moonshots over The Wall. The Red Sox were quite adept at hitting balls over The Wall, and at allowing the opposition to do even more of the same. And, if you were lucky—or wise—you might see a visiting team that had some genuine stars on it.

The one constant at the end of each year, however, was the Red Sox' poor record. Usually the better teams, like the Orioles and the Twins, positively thrashed them. In 1965, against almost impossible odds, the Red Sox managed to lose nearly every game against the pennant-winning Twins, going 1–17. The following year, the Red Sox, in a hollow achievement, finished in front of the Yankees for the first time in nearly twenty years, ending up in ninth place, a half-game ahead of the cellar-dweller Yankees.

All of it was disappointing but not discouraging, for every time that Dick Radatz struck out the side or Tony C hit another home run or Yaz lofted an opposite field double off The Wall, I knew that success was just around the corner. But I would be in sixth grade, almost in junior high school, before the corner was turned, and then only to experience the unique brand of BoSox heartbreak that would cruelly mark the team until 2004. "Wait Till Next Year" became a time-honored mantra with the Red Sox, but I didn't realize it was said by veteran fans not with honesty and hope but with an exhaustive and painful cynicism.

My innocence aside, the Red Sox in the early to mid-1960s were a perplexing and largely inglorious collection of players, and I knew them all, perhaps too well. Through my trips to Fenway, my dedication to each radio and television broadcast of a game, and my studious attention to my baseball cards, I had a very personal relationship with nearly every player on the Red Sox, not to mention most of the rest of the players in the American League. But while the Red Sox were always the great hope in my heart, they were also memorable for all the wrong reasons at too many spots on the field.

Going position by position through a major league lineup was something I often did in my dreamy baseball head, thinking up changes in the batting order, defensive improvements, or the like. And I did it with every team.

Sabermetrics was not even a gleam in anyone's eye at the time, as far as I knew, but such things as Dave Nicholson of the White Sox striking out at a rate of more than once a game and struggling mightily to keep his batting average within 100 points of the league leader had to relegate him to the bench, I thought, no matter how many home runs he hit or how anemic the White Sox lineup was. When Nicholson struck out 175 times in 1963, it was the third consecutive season that an American League hitter had set a major league record for strikeouts, but somewhat amazingly, the Red Sox' own strikeout machine, Dick Stuart, was not one of the offenders: Harmon Killebrew (142) and the Tigers' rookie Jake Wood (141) had preceded Nicholson. His dubious mark had far more staying power, though, as no one in the American League passed him for nearly a quarter of a century.

I did this position-by-position analysis most of all with the Red Sox lineup. At the time it was done with intensity and almost a sense of pride of ownership, as the Red Sox were "my" team, and I really wanted to see them improve. In the hindsight of adulthood, of course, it is clear that improvement was a bridge too far for those dysfunctional teams.

To indulge in the nostalgia that has always been a huge part of the appeal of the national pastime, I will momentarily resurrect that old pleasure of player analysis, going through the Red Sox lineup and looking at the good, the bad, and the ugly of those boys of summer.

First Base. Dick Stuart had come over from the National League in a trade with the Pirates (in exchange for Schwall and Jim Pagliaroni, two of the first Post cereal Red Sox baseball cards I collected, in 1962), so my father had a certain regard for him, and since it was true that something actually might happen when Stuart was up, we paid attention to him. Stuart was a genuine slugger, one of the best of his time, and he did hit 75 homers in his two seasons (1963–64) with the Sox, in the process becoming the first player to hit 30 home runs in each league. But Stuart was one of those flawed "instant offense" players who, in every sport, are so tantalizing to teams that don't have them but wish they had, and so easy to get rid of for the teams that do. He struck out easily and often, 274 times just with the Red Sox. What I probably remember most about Stuart was that his home runs to left could soar over the net entirely, bringing my father and me to our feet, and that, like many sluggers before and since, when the pitch to him did not leave the yard, if often landed in the catcher's mitt as the third strike. He also had the name of being a headache for any manager. Thus, Stuart was a well-traveled power hitter.

And he was an adventure in the field, a legitimate Dr. Strangeglove, as he was known, leading the league in errors for seven consecutive seasons. Whoever was writing the annual scouting reports for *Sports Illustrated* apparently had a certain fascination with watching Stuart trying to field his position. In its 1964 preview of the Red Sox (well-preserved in one of my boxes), the report notes that "a clubhouse boy claimed this spring that he was bitten by Stuart's first baseman's mitt. Stuart, however, needs more than teeth in his glove to improve his fielding." The next year's report only added to the legend: "With Dick Stuart's powerful bat and five-thumbed glove on hand last season, the Red Sox finished first in batting, second in homers and eighth in the American League." Stuart was on deck when Bill Mazeroski hit his home run to win the 1960 World Series for the Pirates—that fact alone made him worthy of being on those Red Sox teams.

Lee Thomas replaced Stuart in 1965 with a solid year (22, 75, .271 in 151 games) before being traded in the off-season to the Braves and replaced by The Boomer, George Scott, who played in all 162 games the following year, enthusiastically entertaining the press along the way and establishing himself as the ever-quotable and quite talented Red Sox first baseman of the future.

Second Base. Pete Runnels, winner of two batting titles (and just missing another, in 1958, by 6 points to Ted Williams) while playing at second base and first base, had been traded just before I started going to games, and there would be no more batting titles coming from either position anytime soon. At the plate, second basemen Chuck Schilling and Dalton Jones did not remind anyone of Pete Runnels, although both, like many Red Sox flameouts, had been hailed as "can't miss" prospects before they reached the big club. They did not start the trend, and they would not end it. Schilling certainly could field—my father used to say that he was "not a bad fielder," which was high praise from him—but Schilling's offense had faded to barely above anemic by the time I saw him. His averages of .234, .196, and .240 from 1963 to 1965 were, unfortunately, not deceiving. Jones's numbers were better than anemic, but still were much closer to Schilling than to Runnels.

More encouraging was the performance of Felix Mantilla, who played second base and nearly everywhere else, hitting 30 home runs in 1964 and 18 the following year. As a boy, I always loved the sound of Felix Mantilla's name, and he had played with Hank Aaron, Eddie Mathews, and Warren Spahn in Milwaukee—in fact, he had been signed by the *Boston* Braves—so that gave him a certain status as well in my baseball history evaluation. I cheered for him at every opportunity.

Shortstop. There was always hope at shortstop for the Red Sox. Eddie Bressoud, who had come up with the New York Giants in 1956, put up some impressive offensive numbers for several seasons with the Red Sox. I saw Bressoud, a good pull hitter, often hit the ball off The Wall—his 41 doubles in 1964 were second in the American League, just behind Tony Oliva— and send a fair number *over* The Wall. But he quickly learned that playing for the Red Sox was not like playing for the Giants. In 1962, his first year with the Red Sox, Bressoud observed, "On the Giants, I felt if I didn't come through, there were always such guys as Willie Mays and Orlando Cepeda to pick me up. We don't have that kind of guys here and you instinctively bear down harder." But by the end of the 1965 season, Bressoud himself was not able to bear down quite hard enough and had the unfortunate fate to be traded to the Mets for outfielder Joe

Christopher, going from a team of 100 losses to one that had lost 112 games. Reflecting the karma of the teams they played for, Bressoud went on to bat a lowly .225 for the Mets, which was 158 points higher than Christopher (.077) hit with the Red Sox.

Bressoud was replaced by Americo Peter Petrocelli, better known as Rico. He shared his rookie card with Jerry Stephenson, another can't-misser who totally missed (8-19, 5.54 in five Red Sox seasons), but Petrocelli avoided a similar fate. Once he got comfortable emotionally at the major league level, which seemed to be his biggest challenge, Petrocelli developed into an outstanding player, one of the best on the rejuvenated teams that followed. He had a short, compact stroke that many called a "perfect Fenway swing," and Rico did send a good number of balls sailing over The Wall in his career. Later, he was moved to third base, where he continued to perform at a high level. Deservedly, he went on to become one of the most popular of the Red Sox players.

Third Base. During those difficult years, third base was never a joke for the Red Sox. The Bronx's Frank Malzone was one of the best of his time. Signed by the team in 1947, he did not become a regular until a decade later, as injuries and military service slowed his progress. But he more than made up for lost time, going on to make 6 All–Star teams. Malzone could field better than any third baseman of the time until Brooks Robinson came along, and he was a steady, above average hitter who, unlike most Red Sox right-handed hitters, used most of the ballpark. And he was durable, playing in at least 150 games for 7 consecutive seasons.

Unfortunately for Malzone, he was good only when the Red Sox were bad, and was not around for the success of the later teams, having been let go following the 1965 season. Timing counts, and Malzone was rather unlucky in his, although, unlike most Red Sox players of the time, he could ease the pain with memories of playing in All-Star games with

Williams, Mantle, Kaline and other Hall of Famers. That was no small consolation.

Replacing Malzone in 1966 was Joe Foy, who was no Malzone but went on to have several decent seasons with the Red Sox, of course 1967 being the most memorable of all.

Left Field. Yaz deserves a chapter of his own in this book and will get one later. For the moment, it is enough to say that with Yaz, the Red Sox could be considered a major league team with a future, even with all the blemishes, but without him, cause for hope dwindled dramatically. There was so much to admire about Yaz, particularly his flawless one-handed grabs of balls caroming off The Wall before twirling and firing a strike to whatever base the soon-to-be-dispatched runner was heading. And how he hit those doubles off The Wall with regularity was a kind of magic I never tired of witnessing. Finding his baseball card in a pack was just about the best thing that could happen in a day. (Had Bob Costas been a Red Sox fan, he would have put Yaz's card in his wallet.)

In those early years, though, Yaz was still ascending, a bright star in the night sky, but all alone in the Red Sox universe. In time, more stars would come, and Yaz did shine for years in a Red Sox uniform, the only one he ever wore. But in his own way, he remained a lone star, a private, self-reliant individual who played hard and well, yet remained an acquired taste for many Red Sox fans. *Enigmatic* is the unfortunate word that describes much of Yaz's experience in Boston, but by the time of his retirement, he had become a beloved player, and rightly so.

Center Field. With the exception of the year (1964) that Yaz was out there, center field had the much more typical Red Sox flavor of the time. Jim Gosger fit the bill nicely. When the back of your first baseball card highlights your "hustle and desire," that's not a good sign. Gosger was a fine fielder and a great hustler who, if he could have hit consistently, might have become a fan favorite. But while he did add a left-handed bat to the roster, as I grew older I figured out that if the bat does not make contact with the ball, it doesn't matter which bat you bring to the roster. Never quite surpassing mediocrity at the plate, Gosger lasted a couple of nondescript years with the Red Sox before bouncing around the major leagues for a decade, ending with a .226 lifetime average. Why teams keep latching onto .226 hitters, year after year, as if they are going to adequately fill some niche, until they eventually do hit .226 yet again and then are sent to the minors or dumped in a trade has always been an unsolved baseball mystery. It continues to the present day, with no end in sight. Gosger does hold a place in trivia history by being the last major league batter to face ageless Satchel Paige, grounding out to shortstop against the 59-year-old Paige, who highlighted one of Charlie Finley's many creative promotions by throwing three scoreless innings for the Kansas City Athletics in a September 1965 start against the Red Sox.

Another Sox center fielder, Lenny Green could run down some balls in the outfield and had had two very good seasons with the Twins, but his best days were behind him by the time he reached Boston. Gary Geiger, who was a decent player in his prime, had seen health issues and, to a lesser extent, a fear of flying bring his prime to a close at the tender age of 27, in 1964. He played only sparingly for the next several years. Reggie Smith was the first centerfielder I remember clearly, and happily.

Right Field. Lou Clinton and Lee Thomas both played right field in my early years at Fenway, but my fondest memories are of Tony Conigliaro, whose name lives on in sadness and pride among Red Sox fans of a certain vintage. Who can forget the immortal, brash, but lovable Tony C from Swampscott, Massachusetts? Or the Conigliaro family, sending two brothers, Tony and Billy, to the Red Sox, the proud Conigliaro father, Sal, beaming over his boys, and the girls and women who swooned at the sight of the handsome right-fielder? Tony C was Bo Belinsky with talent, Joe Pepitone without sideburns. He made an immediate statement at Fenway Park by homering in his first at bat. In fact, he hit 100 homers so fast—he was only twenty-two—that he was already considered well on his way to Cooperstown.

As my father and I always sat in right field, Tony C was directly in front of us. When he ran over to the right field corner to dig out an extra base hit and fired the ball to second, the hitter had to run with abandon or there would likely be no "extra" in his base hit. And as much as many right-handed hitters have salivated at the sight of The Wall, all were in line behind Tony C. To say that he was a fan favorite is insufficient. I'll just note that vendors were not racking up sales when Tony C was up. All eyes were on the plate, absolutely including my own.

Then came the tragedy of August 1967, when Jack Hamilton hurled a fastball into the face of Tony C, the slugger crumpling to the ground, his left eye blackened, destroying what truly might have been a Hall of Fame career. But in the mid-1960s, Tony C. and Yaz were the youthful, rock-solid cornerstones of the outfield, one that looked like it would be set for the next decade, if not longer. Who could have foreseen the sadness that lay ahead? F. Scott Fitzgerald's old line, "Show me a hero and I'll write you a tragedy," could serve as the title for any biography of Tony C.

Catcher. Catchers are the backbone of some lineups, but such was not case at Fenway. The whole catching trio of Bob Tillman, Russ Nixon, and Mike Ryan was not greater than the sum of its parts, unfortunately for the Red Sox. Tillman could hit for power, if the pitcher were foolish enough to throw him a fastball. Even Tillman himself admitted, "I could not hit a curve ball with a paddle." A newspaper article at the time summed up what was obvious to all who saw Tillman at the plate: "He might hit a ball into downtown Boston or he might not hit it at all." (To be technically accurate about this, Tillman's home runs rarely were hit toward downtown Boston, which would have been roughly in the direction of the right field foul pole.) Still, power is relative. Tillman's best four-year period for home runs was 45. Orioles catcher Gus Triandos, a contemporary of Tillman's, once hit 95 home runs in a four-year period and, along with Yogi Berra, held the American League record for homers (30) by a catcher in a season, not broken until more than two decades later by Lance Parrish. Yet, who remembers Gus Triandos today? All in all, Tillman deserved to be a platoon player, and he was certainly not destined to be, as Johnny Pesky once said, "a right-handed Bill Dickey."

Nixon could hit respectably, but not for power and not enough to get a steady job, never getting into 100 games in a season for the Red Sox. Doing anything offensively was a challenge for Mike Ryan, who nevertheless, Houdini-like, lasted eleven seasons in the majors with a lifetime batting average of .193. In his four seasons with the Red Sox, it should be noted, he did keep his head above what would later be known as the Mendoza line—barely—at .201.

Pitching. The pitching staff, perhaps in a way that only the optimistic eyes of a young boy could see, seemed to me solid from the starters to the bullpen. The questions I pondered had answers that didn't match the reality of the standings. Hadn't Earl Wilson, Dave Morehead, and Bill Monbouquette all pitched no-hitters? (Not surprisingly in either case, Wilson contributed a home run in his gem, while Morehead's took place in front of barely 1000 fans.) Wasn't Jim Lonborg a rising star? Last but certainly not least, hadn't Dick Radatz established himself as the most feared relief pitcher in the major leagues?

But there certainly was no arms race on the Red Sox pitching staff. Radatz was exceptional. Wilson and Monbouquette were good to very good. Morehead probably should have been better than he was, and would have been better on a decent team. (Of course, that description could be placed next to the names of many big leaguers.) Lonborg had talent but was still learning. After that, a fan in the stands might have been as effective as many of the hurlers who took the mound for the Red Sox. The team had a penchant for scoring runs. It had a stronger penchant for giving them up. In a ten-team league, the Red Sox team ERA was 9th (1963), 9th (1964), 9th (1965), and 10th (1966). More need not be said.

The Red Sox of those days were a good example of why some people like to say that statistics are for losers. Pete Runnels (.320, .326) and Yaz (.321) won batting titles. Tony C (32) led the league in homers, Stuart once hit 42 home runs, and Felix Mantilla 30. Earl Wilson himself hit 17 home runs for the Red Sox before hitting another 17 for the Tigers. Monbouquette was a 20-game winner, and Dick Radatz won 31 games in two seasons—*in relief*. To put Radatz's dominance in perspective, in 1964, The Monster struck out 181 batters, placing him seventh in the *entire* American League—and ahead of Sudden Sam McDowell—and every one of those strikeouts had come in relief. In fact, the closest relief pitcher to Radatz was the Athletics' Wes Stock with 101 strikeouts, barely half of Radatz's total.

All of the promising numbers, however, could not produce enough runs or get enough batters out when needed. Perhaps the cards themselves were trying to help me understand why. When Red Sox cards, year after disappointing year, included veteran players such as Garry Roggenburk, Jack Lamabe, Darrell Brandon, and George Smith, maybe I should have understood the problem.

Even Roman Mejias, who was obtained from the Colt .45s for batting champion Runnels and who had shared a 1955 "Star Rookies" baseball card with Roberto Clemente ("Mejias is the best prospect in the Pirates' farm system"), staggered through two years with the Red Sox before his .229 batting average during that time sent him deservedly into retirement.

Nor were the younger players, fresh out of the farm system, immune to the affliction of mediocrity, or worse. How many of them—the names of Bill Spanswick, Pete Charton, and Jerry Moses spring quickly, if not pleasantly, to mind—had unlimited potential and were sure to be All-Stars as soon as they had a little seasoning. They did play, but not for long and not particularly well. But at the time, I thought they were destined for greatness.

Most misleading of all to my youthful and eager-to-believe mind were the "Rookie Stars" cards heralding the arrival of whiz kids who, sadly, would barely have the proverbial cup of coffee in the major leagues. The Red Sox had a bountiful supply of such prospects, whose main purpose seemingly was to make me, and many other fans, wonder how a "star" could actually be a baseball nobody.

There was Guido Grilli, who appeared in 22 games in the big leagues, just six with the Red Sox. Others played even less in the majors, and only with Boston. Dave Gray pitched in nine games, Pete Magrini in three. Bill Schlesinger, an outfielder, got into one game and produced a single hitless at bat. (Amazingly, despite his complete lack of success at the major league level, Schlesinger was acquired and dispatched on *three* occasions by the Red Sox, once bringing Ray Culp in return from the Cubs. Truly, the Cubs earned their misery.) Pitcher Gerry Vezendy's star was never to shine even a single day at the major league level. His Rookie Star cardmate, Brookline's own Bobby Guindon, made it into only five games himself, after having created great expectations in Boston by signing a $125,000 bonus and producing a monster minor league season of 37, 121, and .320.

Finally, there was the case of Ed Connolly and Ed Connolly, Jr. Like father, like son was not a winning recipe for the Connolly family. The son, a sometimes starter in the 1964 starting rotation, put up a 4–11 record with a 4.91 ERA while managing to walk the rather incredible number of 64 batters in a mere 80 innings. He never pitched another game for the Red Sox. His father, as a backup catcher in the 1930s, played sparingly, but in the 1932 season, he evidently did not play sparingly enough, earning the unwanted distinction of finishing 2nd in errors among catchers in the American League, having appeared in only 75 games. It was his fourth, and final, season in the big leagues, all spent with the Red Sox.

I remember the names of these BoSox lesser lights of the 1960s well, but have little or no recollection of actually seeing them on the field. Such was the reality of too many Red Sox up-and-comers. The Red Sox had a great farm system that was constantly pumping out prospects that other teams would love to have—that was my naive interpretation of my trusty baseball cards and the Red Sox PR efforts. But, in some way, our prospects too rarely turned into Yaz or Tony C and more often into Bob Heffner (11–20, 4.60 in three years), another in a long list of players about whom you could say that no one wished they had played longer.

4. Lovable Losers

Another unfortunate issue for those losing Red Sox teams, as I heard in passing or would read about in detail later, was the absurd, at times carnival-like atmosphere in which they seemed destined to operate. Examples over the years were legion to the point that many Sox fans must have looked upon the team the way a parent looks with both love and exasperation upon a wayward child.

Of course, as with much that concerns the Red Sox, the legacy of disbelief covers generations. Babe Ruth being sold to the Yankees in 1919, or local boy (Somerville High School) Pie Traynor slipping from the Red Sox' grasp the following year, or Denny Galehouse being picked over Mel Parnell to start—and, naturally, lose—a playoff game for the pennant in 1948, or prospects Jackie Robinson and Willie Mays being ignored because of their skin color, or Ted Williams giving the finger to fans—*at home*—are only a few of the memorable missteps.

In my lifetime, there was the 1962 head-scratcher of Gene Conley, a pitcher tall enough and talented enough that he played for the Celtics as well, jumping off a team bus in New York, apparently lubed-up, as Tom Brady might say, and deciding to hop a flight to Israel. Turned away at the airport because of passport problems, Conley decided it was best to take a few more days leave before returning to the team. To make this a true Red Sox story, it should be added that Pumpsie Green was to be Conley's traveling companion, until Green got cold feet a day later and made his way back to the team, and that the irrepressible Conley went on to win 15 games that year, tying Monbouquette for the lead on the Red Sox staff.

Then there was the truly sad case of Jimmy Piersall, who suffered from bipolar disorder but tried valiantly to play through it. In the 1950s, Piersall was an All-Star outfielder for the Red Sox who went on to have a lengthy and distinguished career with several teams in the major leagues. But to many fans, the name Piersall didn't mean just baseball—it meant bizarre. He fought with opposing players, fans, and even his own teammates. He once wore a Beatles wig to the plate, ran around the bases backwards after hitting a home run, sprayed a water pistol on home plate, and ran in circles between pitches while playing center field.

While some fans laughed at him, the Red Sox, according to Piersall, did show great patience and provided mental health counseling and treatment, to their credit. I had Piersall on several baseball cards and, not knowing much about his mental health problems, regretted only that his great years for the Red Sox had come so long ago.

Another scenario involved Red Sox players who, besides having limited talent, just seemed to find misfortune at every turn. One of them was pitcher Galen Cisco. During the 1962 season, Cisco's second with the Red Sox, the team suffered a prolonged shellacking in late July, dropping the last of a four-game set to the Yankees, 13–3, before losing the next three games in humiliation to the last-place Senators, 11–2, 14–1, and 9–1. In the 14–1 drubbing, Cisco, the starter, was left on the mound to endure 5⅓ merciless innings, being relieved only after giving up 16 hits and 13 runs. His numbers of 4–7, 6.72 got him waived before the end of the season, and in September Cisco was selected by the woeful Mets, where he spent most of the next four seasons, his record of 18–43 aptly summing up the experience. He then was signed again by the Red Sox and pitched sporadically in the 1967 season before being banished to the minors after the All-Star game, missing out on the best moments of the Impossible Dream. Perseverance, if not victories, was the hallmark of Cisco's unfortunate career.

That Marv Throneberry never played for the Red Sox of those lean years seems, even now, like an imperfection in the baseball universe. The Throneberry family had genetic consistency on its side, though: Marv's brother, Faye, *did* play for the 1950s Red Sox and had a lifetime batting average that was a mere .001 lower than Marv's. Unfortunately, the two averages, .237 and .236, only served to remind fans of what it meant to be a Throneberry in the major leagues.

One of Marv Throneberry's teammates on the 1962 Mets was five-time All-Star Richie Ashburn, who tried to put his finger on the mystique of that spectacularly flawed team:

> Any losing team I've been on had several things going on. One, the players gave up. Or they hated the manager. Or they had no team spirit. Or the fans turned into wolves. But there was none of this with the Mets. Nobody stopped trying. The manager was absolutely great, nobody grumbled about being with the club, and the fans we had, well, there hadn't been fans like this in baseball history. So we lose 120 games and there isn't a gripe on the club. It was remarkable.

The situation with the Red Sox was far less remarkable simply because the team not only *did* have a sizable number of players who gave up, who hated the manager, and who had no team spirit, but it also suffered from a terminal case of apathy. Most of the players apparently believed that silence is, indeed, golden. The Red Sox clubhouse, as described by Yaz himself in his 1968 autobiography, was a portrait of failure. Noting that Malzone and Conley were likable teammates, as was Schilling, his roommate, Yaz found little else to warrant much optimism during his first years at Fenway under manager Pinky Higgins:

> Win, lose, or draw, the locker room was like a morgue after every game. There was no exuberance, no cheering, no backslapping when

we won, no grumbling, no sulking, no anger when we lost. Schilling and I went for weeks at a time without talking to anyone except each other. We roomed together on the road, lockered side by side, warmed up together before ballgames, sought each other out for meals and movies, and ignored everyone else. I didn't know the guy who lockered on the other side of me—I can't remember now who it was—and Schilling didn't know the guy on the other side of him. As far as we could tell, we were about the only ones who talked to each other. Sometimes, as we looked around the room, we marveled at the utter lack of communication among the other ballplayers. Some of them must have been friends, I suppose, but you'd never know it by their actions. They all seemed to be loners.... It was as if someone had hung huge *SILENCE* signs all over the walls. You walked in expecting to see a dead body on a slab, and you acted and talked as if it were right behind you.

While not intending to criticize his players, Yawkey himself confirmed the disinterest of the team by commenting, "Players are the most helpless people in the world. If you told them to go to San Francisco by themselves, they might wind up in Mexico City."

Thus was born "twenty-five players, twenty-five cabs," years before Frank Duffy made it official. And when widespread jealousy and resentment set in toward Yaz from his own teammates, Bressoud took him aside and advised the rising star, "You're a great young ballplayer and you'll be greater. Some of these chowderheads would like to see you collapse. Don't let them get you down." No wonder Yaz became such a complex figure.

Where were the managers during all of this, one may ask. In the case of Johnny Pesky, he was certainly devoted to the Red Sox organization and expected his players to perform as he had, with effort and pride, which they did for the first half of Pesky's initial season in 1963. On July 15, the Red Sox, at 49–39, were in second place and just 5½ games behind the Yankees. But then it all went south. As the momentum changed and losses piled up, the team went 27–46 over the second half, finishing up at 76–85, in seventh place and 28 games out of first.

Dick Radatz's own season mirrored that of the Sox. He was an astonishing 12-1 on July 21, possibly on his way to becoming the first reliever to win 20 games in a season. But he struggled somewhat over the remainder of the season, going 3-5 to finish up at a still superlative 15-6. To this day, no reliever has ever been a 20-game winner.

For reasons apparently known only to himself, Higgins, having been promoted to general manager after being fired as manager in 1962, went the whole season without making a single trade, despite the team's precipitous fall. Sniping between players and Pesky intensified during that time, and it was clear that Pesky was not the man for such a toxic environment. He had numerous issues with Dick Stuart, who ribbed Pesky to the point of mocking his salary, about half that of Stuart's. At one point, Pesky went so far as to bench Stuart for his glaring lack of hustle (replacing him with, interestingly, Dick Williams). That was no shock—from my right field seat, even I could see that Stuart was averse to running anywhere.

Yaz, who also had his gripes over Pesky's penchant for commenting privately to reporters on players' performances, recalled that "the collapse of morale was total, with everyone bickering, criticizing, blaming others for his own shortcomings, falling back into those deadly cliques. Pesky ... practically lost control of the ball club." And that was a year in which Yaz *won* the batting title and came in 6th in the MVP voting. Perhaps worst of all for Pesky, Higgins resented having been replaced by

Pesky as manager, and Higgins was now his boss and had the ear of Yawkey.

The 1964 season was no better for Pesky. Although Tony C demonstrated the greatness that lay ahead of him by hitting 24 home runs as a 19-year-old rookie, the bad news far outweighed the good. Of the 13 Red Sox pitchers who had a decision that year, 12 finished under .500—only Radatz won more than he lost. Earl Wilson alone (5) hit one less home run than second basemen Dalton Jones and Chuck Schilling combined. The team was nearly helpless on the road, at 27-54, and dropped to eighth place at 72–90. Predictably, Pesky did not even make it to the finish line, being replaced with two games remaining by a former Boston Brave—and buddy of Higgins—William Jennings Bryan Herman.

Also among the departed that season would be Dick Stuart, traded in the off-season to the Phillies for Dennis Bennett. Stuart may have had stone fingers at first base, but his bat had done considerable damage and would clearly be missed. The numbers told the story. In 1963, Stuart had knocked in 118 runs, with Lou Clinton a distant second on the team with 77. In 1964, the RBI differential only grew, as Stuart drove in 114 runs and Yaz was next with 67. Bennett himself would be a model of mediocrity for the Sox, with a 12-13 record over three seasons, although in fairness to him, 4 of the wins came in 1967, a year in which every victory mattered.

A personal footnote to that 1964 team involves two-time All-Star outfielder Al Smith, who held a place of interest to me in baseball history. Nearly all washed-up by the time the Red Sox signed him in August of that year, Smith's career ended in Boston on a forgettable (.216) note. But in my private world of favorite baseball players at that time, Smith was in good standing. By chance, I seemed to get at least one baseball card of Smith every year from the time I started collecting, so I knew his career well, and his numbers were always impressive. Also, Smith was black, and I could see from his cards that his career stretched back to the days when black major leaguers were not exactly flooding the marketplace. In fact, Smith had been signed by the Cleveland Indians in 1948, one year after the club made Larry Doby the first black player in the league. And Smith had been the starting left fielder on two very memorable teams, the 1954 Indians and the 1959 White Sox, the only clubs in the American League to take the pennant away from the Yankees during their stretch of dominance between 1949 and 1964. Smith gained some unwanted notoriety in the 1959 World Series against the Dodgers when a fan accidentally but quite accurately dumped a beer on Smith's head as he ran back to the wall trying to chase down a home run by Charlie Neal, a moment that was captured in embarrassing detail by cameras. But I looked upon Smith as an accomplished player over many years, even if he unfortunately had nothing left in those final days spent in a Red Sox uniform.

What I knew too well at that time was that the Red Sox teams I watched with my own eyes had reliably lost more games than they had won every year, and few baseball experts ever mentioned them in a serious voice. Of course, *I* took them seriously—after all, the guys on the field were the same players I had on my treasured baseball cards—but I was just a kid, so hope I always had.

But the floundering Red Sox of those days did garner sympathy, if not much respect, from some legitimate—i.e., adult—baseball observers. I still have a 1965 "Baseball Facts" booklet ("from Gramps" it is noted on the cover, courtesy of my grandfather) that put the Red Sox in eighth place in its assessment of that upcoming 1965 season. At the time, I'm sure I was impressed, if not delirious, to read even the faint optimism expressed by booklet's handicapper: "Could move up if pitchers and youngsters come through for new manager Billy Herman. Got good mound performance only from Radatz in 1964. Monbouquette, Wilson & Co. can do better. Rookies Guindon and Horton will be tried at first. Outfield is strong sector."

Sports Illustrated, in its annual baseball prognostication, preferred to stick with reality, noting, "[Billy] Herman predicts the Red Sox will climb two notches, to sixth, and hopes for fourth. Fourth place is a possibility only if Yastrzemski returns to his batting-championship form, if Lonborg and Stephenson become reliable starters, if Monbouquette becomes a 20-game winner again, if Geiger stays relaxed and healthy, if Mantilla keeps hitting home runs, if Conigliaro avoids the sophomore jinx and, most important, if Bennett can come back from his ailments and be the first-rate left-hander the Red Sox need. That's too many ifs."

Herman himself, wearing the rose-colored glasses of a baseball manager during spring training, looked over his starting rotation of Bennett, Jerry Stephenson, Dave Morehead, Bill Monbouquette, and Earl Wilson and, echoing my own wishful sentiments as an eight-year-old Red Sox fanatic, observed, "You look at that list of pitchers and you have to agree there are five good arms there. I'm going to find out why they shouldn't give us a good solid staff."

Yes, that was something I myself could have said at the time. But no, people didn't have to agree, and Herman did indeed find out why. His team was blessed by the same abundance of hitting and the same absence of pitching that had afflicted so many previous teams. The "five good arms" that he invested so much of his hope in went on to finish 39-62 for the year. One game at Fenway painfully epitomized the problem. On May 14, in a Friday night game against the Tigers, Red Sox hitters teed off on Denny McLain, chasing him in the second inning after McLain had allowed five runs on five hits, including two home runs. The Red Sox went on to score three more runs in the game, and Yaz hit for the cycle, finishing the night with a single, a double, a triple, and two home runs, driving in five runs and amassing fourteen total bases. But Bennett couldn't get through the third inning, and the team came up empty in a 12–8 loss.

The curious case of reliever Bob Duliba illustrated the too often inexplicable strategy of the Red Sox front office. Duliba, 30 years old, had what might be considered a stellar season for that struggling staff, as he appeared in 39 games, going 4–2 with a 3.78 ERA. In fact, he was the only Red Sox pitcher with a winning record. His reward was to be traded the following year, in May, to the Athletics for three players, two of whom would never play a day in the major leagues and the third, infielder Syd O'Brien, who passed another three years in the minors before spending a single season, 1969, with the Red Sox, hitting .243. Duliba, a journeyman, was not headed for baseball immortality, but that he was judged not even good enough to remain on the roster is yet another mystery among many in the Red Sox annals.

With Felix Mantilla leading the team with 92 RBIs and Tony C driving in another 82, the 1965 Red Sox did manage to make up for some of the offensive production that was lost with Stuart's departure. But Murderer's Row itself might not have been enough. Under Herman in that long season of ineptitude, the club lost early and often, finishing in ninth place at 62–100, 40 games behind the Twins.

The oratorically and intellectually gifted Abba Eban, a key founder of Israel and long-time diplomat, once observed, "History teaches us that men and nations behave wisely once they have exhausted all other alternatives." The same can be said of many baseball owners and teams, particularly in the case of Tom Yawkey and the Red Sox in those years. Having patiently endured the stagnant oversight of the club by Pinky Higgins, his devoted cohort, Yawkey finally—and most appropriately—fired his GM with two weeks left in the 1965 season (and on the same day that Dave Morehead pitched his no-hitter). Higgins had been either the manager or the general manager of the club since June 1960, a stretch in which the Red Sox never finished less than 19 games out of first place. His replacement, Dick O'Connell, had his work cut out for him.

Displaying some benevolence toward the Red Sox by preventing them from falling even farther in the standings during those years was the unimposing lineup of the Kansas City Athletics, who were described by one handicapper with four words that would put fear in the heart of any manager: "Need help almost everywhere." A cynic might have said that was the reason behind owner Charlie Finley having shortstop Bert Campaneris play all nine positions in a September 1965 game: not to attract the ever-elusive Kansas City baseball fans to the stadium—fewer than 7000 a game bothered showing up that season—but to improve the team at every spot on the field.

SI itself was nothing if not consistent with the Red Sox competition, noting that in Kansas City, Finley's Athletics "have a good infield and a very impressive mule, but neither does much to change the conviction that this is a solid last-place club." And the Athletics did indeed bring up the rear in the American League standings by losing 103 games of their own, the two teams combining to finish 83 games in back of the Twins.

Curiously, the sorrowful pitching staffs on the 1964-65 Athletics teams (total losses: 208) included Diego Segui (13-32), John Wyatt (11-14), Jose Santiago (0-6), Lew Krausse (2-6), and Ken Sanders (0-2), all of whom went on to pitch for the Red Sox, and Ted Bowsfield (4-7), who had originally been signed by the Red Sox before being traded to Cleveland for the immortal-to-be Carroll Hardy. Even the A's manager, Haywood Sullivan, the youngest skipper in the major leagues, had been signed by the Red Sox as an amateur free agent in 1952 and would depart the Athletics after that forgettable 1965 season for his own memorable run in the Red Sox front office. The two clubs in the mid-60s were clearly peas of a very unfortunate pod, although I always thought of the Athletics as a bad team and the Red Sox as a rising team in my less than impartial assessment at the time.

In 1966, the Red Sox picked up right where they had left off, staggering through a 7-20 start, dropping 12 games off the pace by May 15. Tony C, at 21, continued his slugging ascent, going on to lead the team in homers (28) and RBIs (93), but the pitching staff remained abysmal. Even the Monster, Dick Radatz, had lost it after his yeoman's work over the previous four years and was shipped off to Cleveland in June for Don McMahon and Lee Stange in what would turn out to be a surprisingly good deal for the Red Sox. For the moment, though, the team continued to be as dysfunctional as ever. Herman contemplated his golf game as much as his lineup. Camaraderie was nil. It was a house divided, and it wouldn't stand much longer. Like Pesky, Herman didn't make it through his second season, getting the axe on September 8, with Pete Runnels chosen to complete a year that would end at 72–90 and a second consecutive ninth place finish.

As each neared the end of the line, Pesky and Herman must have felt like saying a Hail Mary nearly every time their team took the field. Having both been exceptionally good players back in the day, they probably wished they could have been on the field themselves on many an occasion. Even at their advanced age, they might still have been able to run as fast as most of their players. The team stole a grand total of 127 bases in the four years that Pesky and Herman managed, with a lowlight of 18 in 1965. The Dodgers' Maury Wills alone stole 225 bases during that span (and that does *not* include the year—1962—he swiped 104, and his own teammate, Willie Davis, came in second with 32). But the Red Sox were not in the habit of obtaining players with a skill-set like Wills. Appropriately, Russ Nixon maintains the dubious distinction of holding the major league record for most career at bats (2,504) without a stolen base, while Bob Tillman is not far behind, having stolen a grand total of one base (in his only attempt) in 2,329 at bats.

And there was always the matter of why other teams seemed to be able to evaluate talent—and acquire it—better than the Red Sox could. Having seen most of the players in the American League, I enjoyed doing my own general manager-ing of the team with an eye on improvement. Bill Freehan, for example, was a catcher who could both catch *and* hit the ball well. Why couldn't we get a player like him behind the plate? Juan Pizarro of the White Sox (and formerly of the Braves' championship team of 1957) was an outstanding left-hander who had little trouble beating the Red Sox or most other teams. In 1963, the Red Sox had three left-handed pitchers—Wilbur (pre-knuckleball) Wood, Arnold Earley, and Chet Nichols—who went a combined 4–15. That same year, Pizarro went 16-8, and 3-0, 0.67 against the Red Sox. Chicago did not deserve Juan Pizarro more than we did. Then, five years later, the Red Sox *did* obtain Pizarro, who proceeded to go 6–9 before being sent away in a trade to Cleveland after getting stopped by police in a car driven by Joe Foy, both men drunk, Foy having collided with a taxi. Even as I type this, I remember the frustration of wondering how these things could happen so easily to the Red Sox.

I turned ten during the 1966 season, the team's last year of ignominy before graduating to a nearly four-decade run of winning the minds but breaking the hearts of Red Sox Nation. From his own childhood experiences with the Boston Braves, my father felt my pain and commented accordingly, although always with affection for those old Braves teams. He certainly could remember, and talked about, Red Sox players Ted Williams, Joe Cronin, Joe Vosmik, Tex Hughson, Doc Cramer, and other blasts from the past, but he was much more a lifelong, still-in-mourning Boston Braves fan. The names that glowed in his memory were Warren Spahn, Johnny Sain, Tommy Holmes, Wally Berger, Buck Jordan, Tony Cuccinello, Connie Ryan, and Alvin Dark, among many others, with Spahn and Holmes being his favorites. But the reasons for his mourning were all too real, as I would hear from my father and learn from my own reading.

Historically-speaking, *I* should have been the one sympathizing with my father, for when he was ten in 1935, the Braves had a spectacularly unsuccessful season of their own.

They finished a staggering 61½ games out of first place by going 38–115, with a winning percentage of .248, the worst National League record in modern baseball history. Not surprisingly, the team featured a starter, the unfortunate Ben Cantwell, who finished up at 4–25—this, from a pitcher who had won 20 games just two years earlier. Slugger Wally Berger, rather amazingly, not only led the National League in home runs (34) and RBIs (130), but his RBI total eclipsed that of the team's next two RBI leaders combined. Saddest of all, the Sultan of Swat joined the team for his final season and showed only that he had outlived his nickname. While hitting 6 home runs in a total of 28 games—the final three coming in the same game, against the Pirates—Babe Ruth finished with a pitiful batting average of .181, just over half that of his remarkable career average of .342. At forty, Ruth was done.

But as dismal a record as that 1935 Braves team had, it could not have come as a shock to the team's dedicated, but unfortunately sparse, fan base. For the Braves/Bees of my father's youth were not the frequent pennant-winning teams of the prior century (known then as the Beaneaters, the Red Caps, and, in the National Association, the Red Stockings) but were consistent mainly in their annual effort to reach mediocrity, a feat not often attained. In this case, the numbers don't lie. In the first twenty years of my father's life, from 1925 to 1944, the Braves average win-loss record stood at 66–88, and that does not include the three previous seasons in which they lost exactly 100 games *each year*. The team never finished higher than fourth place during the entire stretch, and on ten occasions came in last or next to last. Not surprisingly, one of Johnny Vander Meer's two consecutive no-hitters in 1938 came against the lowly Bees.

Les Bell, a solid hitting third baseman for the Braves for a couple of seasons in the late 1920s, observed that the baseball acumen of Owner/Manager Judge Emil Fuchs was memorable if not admirable. While acknowledging that in 1929, "John McGraw, Joe McCarthy, and Connie Mack couldn't have done

71

anything with that team," Bell noted that it was also true the judge "didn't know a thing about baseball." For illustrative purposes, he recalled the time that a Braves hitter had a count of three and one, and coach Johnny Evers asked Fuchs what he wanted the batter to do. "Hit a home run" was the judge's reply.

Understandably, my father could not often brag about those teams of misfortune, but perhaps that made the Braves of his youth all the more endearing to him, and fascinating to me. And, Les Bell's assessment aside, Judge Fuchs did have great affection for his team—too bad that his affection did not result in pennants.

Casey Stengel became the manager in 1938. His star was not to shine in Boston, however, as the Braves/Bees continued to finish much closer to last than first during Stengel's painful years at the helm, which ended in 1943. Literally painful was a severely broken leg that Stengel suffered after being hit by a taxi in Kenmore Square in Boston just before the start of the 1943 season, and in a true Stengel moment, the Braves manager found himself placed in traction in a maternity ward at St. Elizabeth's Hospital due to overcrowding. Two fans mailed him Mother's Day cards, and in a biting summary of the dismal year, the *Boston Record*'s Dave Egan wrote, "The man who did the most for baseball in Boston in 1943 was the motorist who ran Stengel down two days before the opening game and kept him away from the Braves for two months." Perhaps fittingly, Stengel did not survive the season as manager. That Stengel finished with a 373–491 record as skipper of the Braves, didn't manage in the major leagues for the next five seasons, and then came back and won five consecutive World Series titles with the Yankees is one of those baseball stories that makes you scratch your head.

So I became pretty well-educated on the Boston Braves and paid attention whenever I came across the name. One of my own favorite Braves stories that I dug up long ago from my well-used version of the first *Baseball Encyclopedia*, published in 1969, was that when the Braves were known as the Beaneaters at the turn of the century, they had a pitcher with the historically impressive name of Kaiser Wilhelm who was an underwhelming 17–44 in his only two seasons (1904–1905) with the team. And for good measure, Wilhelm then missed two entire major league seasons before returning with the Brooklyn (pre-Dodgers) Superbas and losing another 21 games, but with a 1.87 ERA. It is fair to say that such a stat line will not likely be seen again.

Another story involves a pitcher with the Boston-appropriate name of King Brady, who, alas, was no threat to be the GOAT. Brady pitched for a total of four teams, including both the Red Sox (1908) and the Boston Braves (1912), while appearing in only eight games in his entire career. Evidently first impressions of him were quite consistent.

Out of respect for my father, and for the baseball education of any readers whose hair has yet to start turning grey, I must also note the astonishing career of Spahn who, as my father loved to say, was better at forty than most guys are at thirty. The fact that he won twenty games thirteen times (only Cy Young had more 20-win seasons) is well-known but certainly worth repeating, as most of us won't be alive the next time a pitcher matches that feat. But what always stood out to me most was that seven of those seasons came *after* he was thirty-five years old, the last, at 23–7, accomplished when he was forty-two. Had he done that in the age of steroids, he would have made Roger Clemens look like a choir boy, in the skeptical eyes of modern fans. And just to put an exclamation point on his career, he hit a total of 35 home runs, a National League record for pitchers that has stood for more than a half-century.

Spahn also had a sense of humor. After pitching under Stengel at the start of his career with the hapless 1942 Braves (59–89) and at the end with the more hapless 1965 Mets (50–112), he quipped, "I played for Casey before and after he was a genius." And following a prodigious home run given up at the Polo Grounds to Willie Mays in what was Mays's first career *hit* in 1951, Spahn was asked what kind of pitch he had thrown. "For the first sixty feet, it was a hell of a pitch," he replied. Undoubtedly to no one's surprise, Giants manager Leo Durocher described the blast somewhat differently: "I never saw a fucking ball get out of a fucking ballpark so fucking fast in my fucking life," The Lip observed. Mays would end that regular season in the on-deck circle, watching Bobby Thomson's immortal home run sail over Andy Pafko's head to clinch the pennant.

In one of my boxes, I have a lengthy, yellowing newspaper article celebrating the occasion of Spahn's 300th victory in 1961, when Spahn was forty and I was five. One of my first baseball card players ever, Braves' outfielder Gino Cimoli, hit a home run in the eighth inning to send Spahn into the history books. So, my Spahn/Braves indoctrination at the hands of my father began practically right out of the cradle and gave me a propitious start in my pursuit of a baseball education.

And not to forget Tommy Holmes—he was in rarefied air when he hit in 37 consecutive games in 1945, breaking Rogers Hornsby's National League mark of 33, set in 1922, and holding the record himself for thirty-three years until Pete Rose surpassed him with a 44-game hitting streak in 1978 with the Reds. Holmes was nearly a one-man wrecking crew that year, leading the league in hits (224), home runs (28), doubles (47), total bases (367), and slugging percentage (577), with a .352 average. While 1945 was a war year, for Holmes it was still a dominating performance. Maybe more impressively, as my father often said, "Christ, you couldn't strike that guy out!" It was true: Holmes knew how to put the bat on the ball. In 4992 career at bats, he struck out a total of 122 times. To put that in perspective, the only players since 1900 who have a better career at bat/strikeout ratio are Joe Sewell, Lloyd Waner, and Nellie Fox, all Hall-of-Famers.

A final point of interest on the Boston Braves also concerns Norwood, as there was a pitcher named Ray Martin who was from Norwood and, in fact, played for the Braves.

Born just five months before my father, in 1925, Martin led Norwood High School to the state championship in 1943 before being signed right after graduation by the Braves. Martin pitched in five games for the Braves over three seasons, including 1948, but none in the World Series that year against the Indians. Coincidentally, one of Martin's teammates on the Norwood High championship team was a player named Charlie Parker, later my own high school guidance counselor and whose son played on Little League baseball teams with me. Curiously, my father never mentioned Martin—I learned of him only upon his death in 2013. It is an omission that puzzles me still.

Even so, I did not equate my Red Sox teams with most of those Braves teams, although the comparison often would have been apt. But with the Red Sox, I always kept the faith. When I was lucky enough to be at Fenway, I got a scorecard for each game and studied it diligently, even though not much actually changed with each scorecard over the course of the year. I still have some of them. One is from 1964, priced at 15 cents and featuring a cover photo of a packed Fenway Park that must have been taken well before I started attending games.

The scorecard had photos of Pesky, Malzone, Bressoud, Yaz, Radatz, Monbouquette, Lamabe, Stuart, and Morehead. It also included a more disturbing front office photo of Pinky Higgins that, in retrospect, eerily resembles Jack Nicholson (think "Hoffa"). The opponent was the more talented Tigers, and in my best elementary school handwriting I recorded their starting lineup as

Don Wert
George Thomas
Al Kaline
Gates Brown
Norm Cash
Jerry Lumpe
Dick McAuliffe

Bill Freehan
Ed Rakow

Looking at the scorecard now, what catches the eye more than any baseball items are the advertisements that certainly reflect the "Mad Men" of the time. I'm not trying to cast any aspersions on the recreational tastes of the adult males who were in attendance at Fenway (although practically the only others in attendance were the male children of those adult males), but the advertisements lean most heavily toward just two products: booze and butts.

To start with the booze, I counted 16 ads for alcohol, including 3 full-pagers—this, in a scorecard of 24 pages. A sampling of the spirits would include beer (Knickerbocker, Narragansett, Ballantine, and Black Label, which, for the times, featured the fittingly sexist slogan, "Make your next call, 'Mabel, Black Label'"), whiskey (Four Roses, Seagram's, Schenley, and Melrose Place, the last highlighted by an attractive woman with windswept hair and a facial expression that suggested activities other than drinking whiskey), gin (Booth's and Seagram's), and even champagne (Great Western).

Cigarettes were also well-represented by Winston, Pall Mall, Lucky Strike, Tareyton, Carlton, Viceroy, Kool, Belair, Raleigh, Montclair, Kent, Lark, Chesterfield, L&M, and Marlboro ("Come to where the flavor is. Come to Marlboro Country"). Best copywriting would have to go to the makers of an unidentified beverage—a beer, apparently—whose ad suggested, "Give your cigarette-tortured taste a treat with BEGINNERS by BLACKSTONE—Ask the boy with the basket for a five-pack."

For any boys perusing the scorecard, there were tempting advertisements for Coca Cola ("Things go better with Coke"), Hood ice cream, Beech Nut gum, and Armour franks (which would take second prize in copywriting with "At Fenway Park you enjoy the hot dogs that are as nourishing as steak"). If the 1970s was the "me" decade, the 1960s had to be the "toxic" decade, at least for what the human body of a baseball fan was expected to endure. And let's not forget—more doctors smoked Camels than any other cigarette. Maybe even Yaz himself smoked Camels.

Speaking of Camels, one of the most memorable cigarette ads I've seen involves Jackie Jensen, a couple of years before he joined the Red Sox. A baseball and football sensation at UC-Berkeley, Jensen also made headlines with his romantic life. At twenty-two, he married Olympic swimming medalist Zoe Ann Olsen, eighteen, in an October 1949 ceremony attended by 1500 people. Three years later, Jensen, then with the Washington Senators, appeared in a comic strip illustration relaxing poolside with his bathing beauty wife, blue skies and palm trees in the background, with Jackie warmly encouraging her, "Here, honey, have a **Camel.**" Olsen, gratefully taking the cigarette, replies, "Thanks to you, I'll always have a **Camel!**"

Apparently even Camels couldn't relax Jensen enough for him to fly comfortably on airplanes, unfortunately for the Red Sox. Not many players retire after racking up 28 home runs and 112 RBI's, and just one year removed from winning the MVP, but such things happened to the Red Sox. Jensen did come back a year later to Boston, but a final, mediocre season in 1961, along with the new stress of cross-country flights on West Coast road trips, convinced him that the end had come.

Truly, though, the final word on the subject of cigarettes and baseball belongs to the Brooklyn Dodgers teams of the 1940s. Scrounging through every nook and cranny he could find for talent during the war years of depleted rosters, general manager Branch Rickey contacted thousands of high school baseball coaches in 1943 to hear about their local diamond prodigies, and set up tryout camps across the land. The Dodgers eventually signed about four hundred of the prospects. Two of the signees, Gil Hodges and Duke Snider, would prove eminently worthy of Rickey's nationwide search.

Achieving far more modest fame was one Tommy Brown, a candidate, among many, to replace the Navy-bound Pee Wee Reese at shortstop. Brown, to put it mildly, was not quite up to the task, going on to have a journeyman's career as a utility player for several National League teams. However, he made the big club in 1944 at the barely ripe age of sixteen, and the following year managed to hit two homers for the Dodgers, becoming the youngest player in major league history to hit one out.

And therein lies the tale of the cigarettes, for when a Dodger hit a homer in those days, Red Barber would call the shot "An Old Goldie!" in recognition of the team's radio sponsor, Old Gold cigarettes. A celebratory carton of the cigarettes would be tossed down the screen from the radio booth, where a batboy was waiting to catch them for the deserving player. But the unfortunate (or perhaps fortunate, from a modern health outlook) Brown was hardly considered old enough to be lighting up, so volatile manager Leo Durocher interceded by grabbing the batboy and demanding, "Give me the cigarettes, he's too young to smoke!" Presumably Brown decided that discretion was the better part of valor and, probably wisely, did not try to stand between Durocher and the precious cigarettes.

Cigarettes aside, the sorry truth was that one of the best reasons for going to a Red Sox game was to watch the opponents. As a baseball fan, I enjoyed watching visiting teams, although naturally I rooted only for the Red Sox. Still, it was always of interest to see Brooks Robinson, Boog Powell, and Paul Blair with the Orioles, Harmon Killebrew, Zoilo Versalles, and Tony Oliva (I almost felt sorry for the ball when he took his slashing swing, and he swung at nearly everything) with the Twins, Rocky Colavito, Leon Wagner, and Max Alvis with the Indians, along with many others. Talent-wise, there was no comparison to seeing the Yankees during my first couple of years at Fenway, with Mickey Mantle, Roger Maris, Bobby

Richardson, Tony Kubek, and the rest of their annoyingly fabled lineup.

With memories ranging from hazy to hallowed, I still recall some of the great ones of the time. Mickey Mantle almost always batted left at Fenway, as the Red Sox had few left-handers, especially in the starting rotation. He couldn't run much anymore in the years when I saw him, so I just had to imagine the speed he had shown a decade earlier. But Mantle was still a baseball god, and when he stepped into the batter box, there was usually at least a murmur of recognition from the sparse crowd, careful not to show too much appreciation for a Yankee. And Mantle was a classy player. Like Yaz, when he hit one out, he went around the bases in good order and back into the dugout. I couldn't bring myself to dislike Mantle, even if he was a Yankee. (Of course, like most fans, I knew nothing of Mantle's juvenile, and now legendary, off-field antics.)

An odd story concerning Mantle and the Red Sox was his connection or, in truth, lack of a connection with Walt Masterson, a Red Sox right-hander in the early 1950s. In his autobiography, which I first read nearly fifty years ago, Mantle went on at some length about how Masterson fanned him five times in a game at Fenway in Mantle's rookie year of 1951. "Each time I faced him I seemed to get worse," Mantle recalled. "I was always going for the distance anyway, unless I was bunting, so I really stirred that Boston air, until it must have ruffled the feathers of the harbor gulls." According to Mantle, his futility against Masterson led Casey Stengel, in a rather stunning move, to demote Mantle to the team's Triple-A club, the Kansas City Blues, to cure him of his propensity for striking out.

This scenario has been repeated in several books and even in obituaries for both Masterson and Mantle. One website has Mantle striking out *eight* consecutive times against him. Masterson, a two-time All-Star who had the misfortune of spending most of his career with the Senators (his record during the All-Star years was 20–31, which is clearly more of a commentary on the team than on the pitcher), did have some fine moments as a major leaguer, including 16 innings of shutout ball against the White Sox in a game in 1947. But he never struck out Mantle five times in a game for the Red Sox. In fact, in a Red Sox uniform, Masterson never faced Mantle.

The actual story was that Mantle did strike out five times in a doubleheader at Fenway in late May, but none of the strikeouts came against Masterson, and the games were played about six weeks prior to Mantle's demotion, obviously well before any decision on Mantle's status had been determined. Mantle's faulty memory may have stemmed from the fact that he did indeed struggle against Masterson, going 5 for 22, with no homers, in his career, and once striking out four times in a game against Masterson in 1952, when the pitcher was with the Senators. But Masterson was not the reason for Mantle's failures at Fenway Park as a rookie or for his banishment to Kansas City.

As with Mantle, Al Kaline was an easy player for me to like. What I most admired about him was his classic form, both at the plate and in the field. He had a smooth, seemingly effortless swing, and although he was generally a pull hitter, he could hit the ball anywhere, and did. There wasn't really a defensive strategy against him that worked other than to play him straight away, and hope. In right field, many times I saw him, like Yaz, charge a sharply hit ball at full speed, scoop it up absolutely in stride, and fire a strike to whatever base or cutoff man was necessary. He was so fundamentally sound and so sure in his movements that you could only admire his skill. And he let his play do the talking—he was one of the humblest players of his day.

Frank Robinson was a treat to watch in person, having come over to the American League in a surprising trade from Cincinnati, who apparently thought the 30-year-old Robinson was in the twilight of his career. He went to the Orioles for Milt Pappas in a swap that left Pappas, a fine starting pitcher for years, as the butt end of many unfortunate jokes about lopsided deals. The trade *was* lopsided, but in normal conditions, most teams would be very happy to have a pitcher the caliber of Pappas (209–164) in their rotation. Robinson's offensive numbers tell why he is in the Hall of Fame, and, like Kaline, he had a great arm from right field.

But his competitive nature is what stays in my mind. He had a habit of repeatedly glaring out at the pitcher and severely crowding the plate, essentially daring the pitcher to challenge him. And no matter what happened—even if the pitch hit him, which was the case 198 times—Robinson would be sure to repeat the scene in his next at bat. He had a Larry Bird-like intensity that was kind of chilling. There was no way that pitchers could be unaffected by his always menacing presence at the plate. Interestingly, although they were referred to as "the Robinson boys," Brooks had a very different approach from Frank, much more like Kaline's. It never seemed personal with Brooks, while it was *always* personal with Frank.

Other players stood out for other reasons. One of them was Eddie Brinkman, the sparkling shortstop for the Washington Senators. While a terrific fielder, certainly one of the best I ever saw, Brinkman was in foreign territory in the batter's box. It is a testament to his fielding prowess that he lasted fifteen years in the big leagues, playing over 140 games in nine of them, as he finished with a .224 career average, a number that would have plunged even closer to Mendoza territory if not for his two productive years (.266, .262) with Ted Williams in Washington.

At Fenway, however, he was a hitting machine, including one memorable ball off The Wall that sparked my father to say, in disbelief, "Was that Brinkman?" What it was about Fenway that appealed to Brinkman, I don't know. But during the years that my father and I attended games (1963–1967), Brinkman hit a robust .309 at Fenway. If he had played for the Red Sox and gotten half of his at bats at Fenway, he might have added a few more All-Star games to his meager one appearance, even with the stiff competition he faced annually from Luis Aparicio, Jim Fregosi (a Red Sox signee), Bert Campaneris, and Zoilo Versalles. After all, not many players can bat .203 and still finish ninth in the MVP voting, as was the case with Brinkman in 1972.

Additional favorites of mine included Chuck Hinton (the last Senators' player to hit .300), Vic Davalillo of the Indians (even at 5'7", he could cover center field exceptionally well), Don Buford of the White Sox (whose combination of speed and hustle was just what the Red Sox lacked), and Jimmie Hall of the Twins (he started his career off like Tony C but finished up like Willie Mo Pena).

So there was plenty to watch at any Red Sox game, exasperating as some of the games may have been for a Red Sox fan, particularly concerning the Yankees. In my early years of following the Red Sox, the Yankees still fielded a fearsome lineup, teaching me at the start to dislike the Bombers. A.J. Liebling, who very much preferred boxing to baseball in his years at *The New Yorker*, nevertheless raised the only relevant point regarding the Yankees by writing, "The Yankees are the least popular of all baseball clubs because they win, which leaves nothing to 'if' about." Possibly with the Red Sox in mind, he also wrote, "If you just try long enough and hard enough, you can always manage to boot yourself in the posterior."

More upsetting to me, though, was the increasingly erratic behavior of my father. His mood swings had always been wide-ranging and often without apparent reason, although one almost automatic trigger of a temper tantrum was a form of torture in our house known as party-line phone service. Ever in search of budget-cutting measures, my family shared our phone line with an unknown number of other cost-cutters, meaning that being able to make (or receive) a call was never a sure bet. As you could hear the people speaking if they were on the line, my father had little patience when he picked up the phone to make a call only to hear others enjoying their own conversation. After he slammed down the receiver and picked it up to try again a few minutes later, our phone comrades would get an earful of what was not exactly the Queen's English from my father if they were still rambling on. The maddening minutes—sometimes many of them—that I also spent waiting to be able to call friends in those days is not a treasured memory.

Of course, when my father's outbursts occurred in any situations involving baseball, I could be as unreasonable and impatient as any young child. There was one evening when my father had said he would hit me some fly balls, but he inexplicably changed his mind and planted himself in his living room chair, with the opened newspaper giving him cover from my increasingly shrill entreaties to get him out of the chair and into the backyard. As he brushed me aside with what I took as unacceptable indifference, I went up to my room and sat on my bed, where I went from brooding to boiling over at the unexpected turn of events. Whether my father was tired, annoyed, not feeling well—I didn't know or care. I felt that a kind of moral compact had been broken, and I grew only more upset dwelling on it. As unfair as that may have been to my father, that scenario played out on a growing number of occasions.

One of the reasons driving my petulance was that the creeping realization that my father was not sincerely invested in my life or that of the family. He kind of drifted in and out of being an involved father, spending time on his paintings and ships and music and what seemed to be a growing number of personal interests that, more and more blatantly, did not include his own family. And he was not happy to be distracted from his focus on himself. When he was required to attend to a family matter, his response, muttered barely under his breath, too often was, "It's always some damn thing!" Adding to my frustration was that my father, sticking to his conservative, time-honored principles, would sometimes punish me even for small infractions, the only justification for the punishment generally being a brusque "Because I said so!"

One beautiful sunny day, a perfect day for baseball, I had been confined to my room for "talking back" to my father, outbursts that occurred more regularly with my impatience over my father's part-time and indifferent approach to being a father. Looking out the window at the streaming sunshine, knowing that I should have been playing baseball and that my friends were undoubtedly on a ball field somewhere themselves, I was angry at—everything.

Sitting next to me on the bed were a number of baseball cards. One of them, a prized 1964 RBI leader card with a photo of Hank Aaron in the top half and Ken Boyer and Bill White below, caught my attention. I picked up the card, stared at it for a while, and nearly with tears in my eyes, in a pathetic, almost embarrassing form of protest, started to rip the card. My father probably could have imagined many things before the thought of me destroying a baseball card on purpose. But I wanted him to feel my pain, so, in growing anger, I tore that card, slowly, one small rip at a time, until I approached Aaron's face.

Then, a single motion away from mutilating Aaron's right cheek, in total frustration, I stopped. If I had disfigured the face of Hank Aaron, a Mount Rushmore face in my own version of baseball history, I think I would have hated myself for the rest of my life. And I knew that "punishing" my father was a delusion. Life had already punished him enough, anyway. I briefly left the card on the bed, half-hoping he might see it and understand the anguish he had caused me. Despondently, though, I soon put the card in the shoebox with the others. My father never saw it.

Some days later, in a useless attempt to undo the damage and ease my conscience, I taped the card back together, but that merely made the tear more glaring. I looked at the card many times in the following weeks, always dumbfounded to think that I had actually torn it and exasperated to know that something could bring me to such foolishness. Even now, when I hear or see Hank Aaron's name, I often remember that card and what it represented: the gathering distance between my father and me.

5. Blacks Unwelcome

The losing efforts on the field were not the only obvious flaw for the Red Sox. Another serious problem was the whiteness of its players, a racial imbalance that was not accidental and that reflected a managerial mindset no longer shared by other teams. Herman Franks, manager of the Giants, once saw Willie Mays sitting with the rest of the players in the coach section of the plane, and he demanded an explanation from the team's traveling secretary. When told that Mays had agreed to the arrangement and was equal to everyone else on the club, Franks exploded, "God damn, he's *more* equal than anyone else. From now on put him in first class!" It is safe to say that most black players on the Red Sox of my youth, talented or otherwise, had few illusions of being treated as "more equal" than anyone else. They may have considered themselves lucky to have been noticed at all.

As a boy, I didn't have quite the grasp of this issue as I would later, but even *I* could see that the team was whiter than most of the visiting clubs. I soon learned some of the uglier points regarding the Red Sox and the color of its players. Tom Yawkey was described by some who knew him as a benevolent, likable man who truly loved baseball and was dedicated to pouring large sums of his own vast wealth into producing a World Series victory in Boston.

But Yawkey also owned a 20,000 acre estate in South Carolina that was a former plantation, perhaps an appropriate circumstance for a man who oversaw a team that for years was segregated from the rest of the major leagues in terms of signing black players. The team's excuses were many, ranging from the Red Sox were looking for good ballplayers, not simply good *black* ballplayers, to black players, for some reason, were not

85

interested in signing with the Red Sox, despite the team's efforts to obtain them. The result was a very white team, and its track record with blacks does little to put Yawkey in a good light.

It should be noted that Yawkey's stance toward players of color reflected in some ways that of Major League Baseball's own complex view of players who were not white. Decades before Jackie Robinson broke the color line in 1946, Latinos, particularly Cubans, *were* playing in the big leagues. An important point, evidently, was the extent to which these players were non-white. "Latinos who made it into the major leagues are not welcomed as fellow whites," baseball historian Adrian Burgos, Jr., has written of that period. "They are welcomed as not black."

But some Latinos did get to the majors, including in Boston. In July of 1933, just a few months after Yawkey had purchased the team, the Red Sox acquired Baldomero "Mel" Almada from the Seattle Indians in the Pacific Coast League, making Almada the first Mexican-born player to reach the big leagues. He went on to hit .272 over parts of five seasons with the Red Sox on his way to a seven-year career. The first Latino ever to play for the team was Frank Arellanes, U.S.-born of Mexican descent, who joined the Red Sox in 1908, winning 24 games over three seasons. The immortal Boston Braves team of 1914 included rookie Dolf Luque, a Cuban, who went on to win 197 games in his distinguished career, although none in his limited action with the Braves.

Clearly, major league teams, including Yawkey's Red Sox, were not against signing non-white players. But signing black players was another matter. In 1945, before any blacks were in the big leagues, the Red Sox invited Negro League stars Jackie Robinson (Kansas City Monarchs), Sam Jethroe (Cleveland Buckeyes, where he would be teammates with Al Smith over the next three years), and Marvin Williams (Philadelphia Stars) to Fenway for a spring tryout, partly as reaction to pressure from a local politician for the team to give serious consideration to black players or risk losing the privilege of having games on Sundays. The players themselves, of course, expected little to come of the effort, figuring that it was just an excuse for the team to put a few blacks momentarily on the field and then say that they weren't ready yet for the majors. After they were done, Red Sox coach Hugh Duffy gave the players application cards to be filled out and said that the Red Sox would be in touch. Jethroe probably summed up the feelings of all three when he quipped, with unfortunate accuracy, "We'll hear from the Red Sox like we'll hear from Adolf Hitler."

Several years later, in 1949, the Red Sox scouted Willie Mays when he played for the Birmingham Black Barons of the Negro Leagues and could have signed him for $4500, but passed up the opportunity. The following year, the team purchased the contract of infielder and player/manager Piper Davis from Birmingham, with General Manager Joe Cronin, another favorite of Yawkey's, declaring, "If he makes good, I'm going to waste no time in moving him on to Boston." Davis did make good by leading his Scranton team in batting and home runs a few weeks into the season before the Red Sox, owned by one of the wealthiest men in Major League Baseball, released Davis for "economical reasons" in May 1950.

Three more years passed before the team signed its next black prospect, catcher Earl Wilson, to a minor league contract, later developing him as a pitcher. The scouting report on Wilson read, bizarrely, "He is a well-mannered colored boy, not too black." What the evaluator meant, considering that Wilson was certainly black, is very uncomfortably open to interpretation. (Years later, during spring training, Wilson was refused service in a Lakeland, Florida bar with the bartender's admonition, "We don't serve niggers here.") In the mid-1950s, the Red Sox showed some fleeting interest in Billy Williams but, as with Mays, again backed off.

A larger connection between Yawkey and racism in baseball came in a report issued by a Major League steering committee in 1946. Members of the committee included Yawkey, American League President Will Harridge, National League President Ford Frick, Yankees' co-owner and president Larry MacPhail, Cardinals' owner Sam Breadon, and Cubs' owner Phil Wrigley. The report dealt with a number of aspects of Major League Baseball, including the "Race Question."

While parts of the report sounded somewhat respectful and open-minded toward black players, others decidedly did not. The powers-that-be in baseball signed off on the following passages:

> Certain groups in this country including political and social-minded drum-beaters, are conducting pressure campaigns in an attempt to force major league clubs to sign Negro players. Members of these groups are not primarily interested in Professional Baseball. They are not campaigning to provide a better opportunity for thousands of Negro boys who want to play baseball.... They single out Professional Baseball for attack because it offers a good publicity medium.

> These people who charge that baseball is flying a Jim Crow flag at its masthead—or that racial discrimination is the basic reason for failure of the major leagues to give employment to Negros—are simply talking through their individual or collective hats.

> A major league baseball player must have something besides great natural ability. He must possess the technique, the co-ordination, the competitive aptitude, and the discipline, which is usually acquired only after years of training in the minor leagues.... The young

Negro player never has had a good chance in baseball.... This is the reason there are not more players who meet major leagues standards in the big Negro leagues.

The report went on to say that the Negro Leagues would suffer financially if the major league clubs "raided" the teams for talent, and that major league clubs who rent their stadiums to Negro League teams would suffer financially as well. In the summary, the report noted in a sentence emphasizing a very thinly-veiled but potent message, "The individual action of any one Club may exert tremendous pressures upon the whole structure of Professional Baseball, and could conceivably result in lessening the value of several Major League franchises."

Written after Jackie Robinson had signed a professional contract but before he had been brought up to the big leagues, the report clearly reflected the deep unease of top baseball executives with the imminent prospect of black players appearing on major league rosters. Most likely Tom Yawkey felt this unease as strongly as anyone.

The first Red Sox manager I remember was Johnny Pesky, who by all accounts was a true gentleman and no racist, but his predecessor, Pinky Higgins, apparently shared Yawkey's distaste for black co-workers and players, as well as a frequent fondness for elbow-tipping with Yawkey himself. Perhaps they should not be singled out for their drinking habits, as there were certainly other similar tandems (the Giants' Horace Stoneham and Herman Franks himself come to mind) who also enjoyed combining business with the pleasure of a bottle.

The most damning proof that a racial problem existed for the Red Sox had come in 1959, when the team became the last of the sixteen major league clubs to have a black player on its major league roster, and more than a year after any other team, as well as the last of the professional teams in Boston. By contrast, the Boston Braves had acquired Sam Jethroe nine years earlier from the Brooklyn Dodgers (and five years after Jethroe had gone through his "tryout" with the Red Sox). The Celtics had three *Hall of Fame* black players—Bill Russell, Sam Jones, and K.C. Jones—by the time the Red Sox got their first black player, and the Bruins had the first black player in NHL history, Willie O'Ree, who debuted in 1958. The Red Sox pioneer, well-known for the wrong reasons, was Pumpsie Green.

Before Green even got on the field for the Red Sox, the Massachusetts Commission Against Discrimination had already held a hearing on whether the Red Sox were a racist organization in light of Green's demotion to Triple-A Minneapolis in early April of 1959. Green ultimately returned to the big club in July and had a triple in his first Red Sox at-bat at Fenway on August 4 against Kansas City. Hopefully he enjoyed the thrill, as he would not experience many more at the big league level.

I never saw Green play for the Red Sox, but, thanks to my baseball cards, I did know something about him nonetheless, and it wasn't encouraging. I had him on a 1964 card for the Casey Stengel-led Mets, a ridiculously inept team that had lost 111 games the previous year, which was a nine-game *improvement* over the Mets' initial season of calamity. That was a definite strike one.

Strike two was the numbers on the back of his card—they were terrible. When your high water mark for hits in a season is 63, you'd better have a good classroom education you can fall back on. With other teams signing black players such as Willie Mays, Frank Robinson, Larry Doby, Ernie Banks—the Dodgers alone had picked up Jackie Robinson, Don Newcombe, Roy Campanella, Jim Gilliam, and Joe Black (the first black pitcher to win a World Series game) all long *before* 1959—how did the Red Sox come up with Pumpsie Green?

And strike three—again, so often it comes back to the Red Sox—Green had been traded from the Red Sox to the Mets with the luckless Tracy Stallard, who as a Red Sox rookie had surrendered Roger Maris's 61ˢᵗ home run and went on to lose 37 games in two years with the Mets. Some things, like injuries, may be bad luck, but clearly the poor talent level on the Red Sox was not due only to bad luck.

Somewhat surprisingly, Green harbored no ill-will toward the Red Sox, apparently happy to have been promoted to the big club at all. "People keep asking me time and again whether I think the Red Sox are prejudiced," Green said. "I can only judge by the way I was treated and at the moment, I have no complaints." Given both the experience of the previous black players with the Red Sox and the team's glaring ignominy of being the *last* team to integrate—and well over a decade after Jackie Robinson broke the color line—it is hard to know what to make of Green's comment. That he was personally treated well by the Red Sox is commendable to an extent but does nothing to erase the team's past, a history so clearly tainted by racial discrimination that the history itself may help explain why Green received such deferential treatment. All eyes were on him.

One of my personal memories on the topic of race and the Red Sox involved the less than exceptional talents of Willie Tasby. In 1960, a year after Green broke the color barrier in Boston, Tasby became the first black player the Red Sox acquired by trade. He hit a respectable .281 in limited action, but Tasby stayed in Boston for only that single season before he was on the move again, having been selected by the Washington Senators in the December 1960 expansion draft.

My first acquaintance with Tasby came when I got him on a very impressive 1962 Post cereal card, where his decent numbers for the Senators (17 homers, 63 RBI's), a batting stance in the photo that did make him look like a threat at the plate, and the fact that he had gone to the same high school as Frank Robinson and Vada Pinson (both of whom I also had on Post cereal cards that year and who both had ridiculously good years statistically) had me convinced that he was a future star. In fact, he would be washed up and out of baseball within two years, at the age of thirty, finishing with a grand total of 46 home runs and a .250 average, showing that the Red Sox (and the Senators), even when they tried to compete for black players, had great trouble finding the ones with actual ability. A final, and appropriate, point regarding Tasby occurred in 1959 when Tasby took his place in the Orioles outfield in his bare feet, having doffed his shoes out of fear of getting struck by lightning. Such diamond strategy destined Tasby for a stint with the Red Sox.

In terms of race, the Red Sox had nowhere to go up but up, and in fairness to them, they did improve. While in the standings they never lost fewer than 85 games while always finishing at least 26 games out of first place in the years 1963–1966, they did get better at having a team that reflected more the available talent pool than Tom Yawkey's, or general manager Pinky Higgins's, personal prejudices. By 1966, the Red Sox did have ten players of color on the roster, which brought them up to racial respectability while doing little to erase their shameful past.

My own connection to Pinky Higgins initially occurred not because of the racist mindset of the Red Sox management but through my father, who remembered Higgins as a very good third baseman for the Athletics, the Red Sox, and the Tigers in the 1930s. As most modern day players were not as good, in my father's mind, as the players of yesteryear, Frank Malzone was naturally not quite up to the level of Higgins in his view, a point that I obviously could not dispute from personal experience but did have rather strong doubts about, being a Malzone partisan.

Two other points of interest concern Higgins and my father. One involves a Red Sox trade that, too typically, did not go in their favor. When the subject of unusual pitching deliveries would come up in conversations between my father and me, he would mention the name of Elden Auker, a submariner who had a pretty successful career in the American League, mainly with the Tigers, including a 15-win season for the pennant winners of 1934. So I was quite familiar with the name of Auker.

At the end of 1938, the Red Sox decided to part with Higgins, despite the fact that he had had two very productive seasons in Boston. He was sent to Detroit for pitching help in the person of Elden Auker. The trade made some sense for both clubs, as the Tigers needed a third baseman and the Red Sox (as always) needed pitching. Higgins had knocked in 212 runs in his two years with the Red Sox, while Auker had won 74 games in the previous five seasons with the Tigers, so it was not an uneven swap—until it actually happened. Higgins, predictably, went on to have six very productive years with the Tigers, earning MVP votes in three of them, while Auker, in his one miserable season with the Red Sox, went 9–10 with a 5.36 ERA before being sold to the St. Louis Browns, for whom he naturally proceeded to win 44 games over the next three seasons. I don't mean to imply that the Red Sox were incapable of ever making a wise trade, but it does seem like too many of theirs did not come up roses.

The topic of Higgins's racism was not one that my father and I discussed, but if I have to be perfectly honest about it, my father may not have felt too differently from Higgins about the black players. My father was conservative in race matters—I never heard him express any sympathy toward the views of Martin Luther King Jr., who was in the news seemingly every day of my childhood.

Of lesser relevance, but simply in point of fact, my father, like most fans of the time, was very unlikely to have had black baseball heroes as a child because there had been no black major leaguers during those years when he followed the sport intensely as a youngster. And while there were various black ball clubs—no prominent Negro League teams, though—that played in the Boston area, I never heard my father mention them, making it very unlikely that he ever saw them or knew much about the players.

Still, for both Higgins and my father, feelings of racism are hard to ignore. Higgins was a lifelong southerner, having grown up amid segregation in Texas, which helps explain how he came by his feelings toward race. My father, as far as I know, never travelled any farther south than Newport, Rhode Island, so he did not have that excuse (not that Boston was a racial paradise), but it was true that his baseball world had been entirely white until he was in his twenties. That was the world he knew and was most comfortable with. I don't think he could have equated Bob Gibson with Carl Hubbell.

At the same time, while he may not have rooted for black players, I can't imagine that he would have tried to deny them a place in the sport, as Higgins reputedly did for years. Was this racism? Yes, but I try to cut my father some slack on it, hopefully for understandable, if not justifiable, reasons. The alternative—of thinking of him in the same terms as Pinky Higgins regarding race—is too disturbing, but not surprisingly so. When John Kennedy learned that Martin Luther King Jr.'s father had told reporters that he thought he would never vote for a Catholic before deciding to cast his ballot for Kennedy, the president observed, "Imagine Martin Luther King having a bigot for a father. Well, we all have fathers, don't we?"

In my own childhood, away from baseball, race was a kind of muddled issue, later made better over time by my daily newspaper delivery route, which gave me an education not just from front page news but from life itself. There were hundreds of kids in my elementary school, but none of them were black, so I didn't actually have any black friends. And while on baseball cards I had plenty of black baseball players that I rooted for, I didn't personally know any black people.

On my newspaper route, customers paid at the end of the week, and a number of them simply left the money "out"— in the mailbox, on a porch window sill, in an envelope taped to the door, or whatever. If they forgot to put the money out or just weren't home, I would go back another time to collect it. I don't recall exactly, but I think this is how I met the only black customers, a husband and wife, on my route. As far as I knew, they were the only black people in the whole town.

They lived in one of the last houses on my route, a small, neat home on a very residential street. As I rang the bell and waited on the front step, I felt very uncomfortable, half-hoping they wouldn't answer. But they did, and to add to my personal challenge, they didn't simply give me the money but invited me inside. This should not have been surprising to me, as many of my other customers often did the same thing in that circumstance, sometimes keeping me inside for a cookie or brownie and a conversation about the weather or how pretty the flowers looked this year. But I hesitated slightly as I entered, having never been in a black person's home. I went into the living room, where they smiled at me and made some brief small talk as they paid me. I tried to be as polite as I could, having little idea of what I was saying and just hoping I could get out as soon as possible.

Whether they could tell how nervous I was (probably), and how that may have made them feel (I don't like to think about that topic), I'm not sure, but I remember how I myself felt immediately afterward. Most of me was deeply ashamed over the whole episode. In hindsight, I knew that my discomfort was based on ignorance, and in that moment when they had smiled at me, their friendliness gave me a burning shot of guilt that mixed with the unwanted nervousness I felt, leaving me totally confused and upset as I went out the door.

One result of this experience was that when I read baseball history books as an adolescent, I remembered my day at the house, for I learned of black players, from Hall-of-Famers to utility infielders, being unable to stay in the same hotels as their teammates, being chased out of restaurants, being continuously taunted at ballparks by fans, opposing players, and sometimes even their own teammates and managers, and being expected to turn the other cheek and play as well or better than others while getting harassed at every turn for years.

And I learned that the media itself brought no less bias to the issue. Just after Jackie Robinson signed his first professional contract with the Montreal Royals, the *Sporting News* observed, "Robinson, at twenty-six, is reported to possess baseball abilities which, were he white, would make him eligible for a trial with, let us say, the Brooklyn Dodgers' Class B farm at Newport News...."

Sportswriters engaged in the ugliness as well. In the 1951 World Series, among the Giants' all-black outfield, Monte Irvin came up big but Mays and Hank Thompson did not in the Giants' six-game loss to the Yankees, leading a Chicago scribe to circulate among the press box his telling ode to the proceedings:

> Willie Mays is in a daze
> And Thompson's lost his vigor
> But Irvin whacks for all the blacks—
> It's great to be a nigger.

My history lessons through baseball, I imagine, made me a liberal, possibly before I knew what a liberal even was.

Regarding racism and Major League Baseball, skin color was not the only issue facing minority players. Speaking their own language evidently was an affront to the powers-that-be as well. Alvin Dark, managing a Giants team that included Orlando Cepeda, Felipe Alou, Marichal, and other Latino players, prohibited them from speaking Spanish while in uniform or listening to Latin music in the clubhouse. Alou, in fact, was once fined $10 by National League President Warren Giles for speaking Spanish on the field with Reds pitcher Orlando Pena before a game. (Alou, no one's fool, never paid.) "Seen but not heard" may well have been the appropriate motto in describing baseball's strained connection to that peculiar institution of the time—integration.

Years later, as a college student during the dark days of court-ordered busing in Boston schools, I often played basketball on weekends at the Fenway courts with a Norwood friend named Gary, and we were at times the only white players in the game. No one cared. It was a nice feeling.

6. Baseball 24/7

While waiting for the Red Sox to reach respectability, I was playing a lot of baseball myself, in preparation for my upcoming career with the team. A baseball field in my youth—and undoubtedly in the childhoods of millions of other American boys over decades—was my version of Mark Twain's Mississippi River. While a 19th century mid-western mother might have shooed her children out the door on a steamy summer day to go down to the local pond, river, or whatever body of water was big enough for a child to jump into and cool off, exasperated mothers in my neighborhood, with laundry and housecleaning and food shopping chores up to their necks each day (and with no air conditioning!), would wave their hands and half-scold us to go out and "play ball with the kids" whenever the heat reached a point where 90 degree temperatures and children in the house were no longer compatible. That particular ritual, as I recall, happened most days by noon at the latest.

I didn't think about this too much at the time, but for a boy who loved baseball, my hometown of Norwood was a great place to grow up. There was certainly no shortage of kids to play with and friends to be made through the sport. Also plentiful were fields to play on (although finding an empty one was a challenge at times), leagues to play in, and adults who supported all of this.

There was also the ultimate incentive of knowing that kids from Norwood could actually grow up and make it to the major leagues. Richie Hebner, part-time grave digger, was the best of a group that also included Skip Lockwood (a lifetime winning percentage of .370 and an ERA of 3.55—is that even possible anymore?) and Bill Travers (65 wins and an All-Star selection). And there were rumors that Reggie Smith, when he played for the Red Sox, lived at least briefly in Norwood as well. So even though Smith was a ringer of sorts, his presence counted for something in the baseball world of Norwood.

Hebner's, though, was the name most often mentioned regarding baseball. As a boy, I heard the townies speak of Hebner's prodigious baseball and hockey feats while playing for Norwood High School in the mid-1960s, surely (these voices said) putting him on the path to the big leagues in either sport. How Hebner could actually hit the ball with his hands positioned down by his waist remains a mystery, but it worked well enough to produce nearly 1700 hits, including 203 homers, in a lengthy and productive career, mainly with the Pirates.

Given the focus of this book, I would be remiss not to expand on the story of Hebner and his place, unknown to him, in my life. It had several phases, starting with the childhood chatter I heard about town and leading up to an afternoon that, rather ignominiously, remains etched in my mind.

On October 5, 1971, the Pirates were hosting the Giants in a critical playoff game, the Giants having only split the first two games at Candlestick and now facing elimination in the next two games at Three Rivers Stadium. Starting the third game for the Giants was my favorite player not named Yaz, Juan Marichal, in his first postseason appearance since a single start in the World Series nearly a decade earlier. (He had been pushed back to Game 3 in this series because he had pitched in the season's final game five days earlier, a division-clinching, 5–1 victory over the Padres in which Marichal went the distance for his 18th win.)

Naturally, it was a must-see game for me but one that presented an immediate challenge by being on a Tuesday afternoon, a school day when I was in the 10th grade. After a moral tug-of-war with my mother over the matter, the sanctity of baseball won out over my educational advancement, allowing me to perch myself on the couch in front of the television while having no regrets over missing a day of school.

My mother felt otherwise but let it go with the hope that this would be an outlier and not a trend.

As the game evolved, it became clear that both Hebner, the Bucs' young third baseman, and Marichal, nearly thirty-four and in the actual twilight of his career, were going to be key players. After a second inning Bob Robertson homer had given the Pirates a one-run lead, Hebner paved the way for the Giants' tying run with a throwing error in the sixth. Hebner regained a bit of dignity with a single in the bottom of the inning, but Marichal, in dominant mode, cruised through the first seven innings allowing only three hits and no walks.

The eighth inning was more of the same, with Marichal easily retiring the first two batters. Up to the plate stepped Hebner. Norwood vs. the Dominican Dandy. Tie game. I was rooting for ... whom? In anguish, I wondered how such ethical dilemmas even happen. I still remember clearly what I was thinking, pretending to be fair-minded while trying to figure out how to give Marichal the edge. Hebner already had a base hit, one-third of Pittsburgh's total. If he made an out here, he had nothing to be ashamed of. Even if he had hit another single, as long as it was harmless, I wouldn't have minded.

But Hebner apparently was not thinking single anymore. Marichal made a mistake, and Hebner didn't miss it, blasting one over the right field wall. My heart, somewhat guiltily, sank. The Giants were only down by a run, but the San Francisco Giants of my short lifetime had not had a history of coming back to win anything. Even being in the playoffs was an unfamiliar experience for them. Their last gasp came in the ninth inning. With two outs and Marichal due up, all-or-nothing pinch hitter Dave Kingman strode to the plate. Predictably, on this occasion, it was not all but nothing—a popup to first base, and a final score of 2–1. The Giants had wasted a gem by Marichal, their ace, and went down in elimination flames the following day. Norwood had triumphed, but I wasn't feeling good about it at all, and still don't.

But fate is fickle, and when I had an opportunity to meet Hebner a couple of years later, I jumped at the chance. In the summer of 1973, two Norwood friends of mine, Fred and his younger brother, Peter, asked if I wanted to go down to New York and watch the Mets and the Pirates play at Shea Stadium. A local sportswriter had contacted Hebner on their behalf, and Hebner graciously agreed to meet us outside the park at the team bus. To say it was a thrill to have the possibility of talking to Hebner and seeing the Pirates' players would be an understatement. Yet I have no recollection of what we discussed—I imagine that I was in such a cloud of dizzy adulation that I probably sputtered some baseball statistics at him that he diplomatically faked an interest in before fleeing to the bus. Regardless, the chance to meet a major leaguer was not something to be taken lightly, and I didn't.

Besides seeing Hebner play, we also saw Willie Mays, back home in New York but now with the Mets. Of course, this was not the vintage Mays of a decade or two earlier. At forty-two, it was his swan song, and it wasn't always pretty to watch Mays in that labored season. Still, for a baseball fan to be able to say he saw Willie Mays play had meaning that transcended the moment. Sadly, though, the chance to see Roberto Clemente and Mays together had passed, as Clemente had been killed the previous winter in the tragic plane crash off the coast of Puerto Rico. Truly, a golden era of baseball was coming to a close.

Several years later, when I worked for the *Daily Transcript*, a Norwood newspaper, a close friend of mine there was an advertising manager named Frank Alward, who knew Hebner. Many times I heard Frank tell me what a "great guy" Hebner was. Through Frank, I soon met Frank Wall, the weathered, opinionated, cigar-loving sportswriter of local fame who had covered Hebner's spectacular sports career at Norwood High School—as a hockey player, Hebner had been drafted by the Bruins, but chose a baseball career instead—and had initially set up the 1973 meeting with Hebner. Whenever the three of us were together in the office, the name of "Richie" came up often, usually with Frank Wall blowing yet another cloud of smoke in the air and muttering, "hell of a hitter, *hell* of a hitter."

And when Turnpike Joe Morgan, who lived just outside Norwood, in Walpole, became the Red Sox manager in the late 1980s, he soon named as his batting coach—Richie Hebner. So, I saw Hebner play at Shea, coach at Fenway, and (from my couch) destroy Juan Marichal at Three Rivers. It was a memorable major league journey for me that might have been rather more memorable had it not been for that Tuesday afternoon in Pittsburgh.

Getting back to Norwood and my own days of playing, I grew up on Monroe Street, in a residential area, and my neighborhood was well-populated for the sport of baseball. While some houses had retired couples living out their golden years, a good number of others had families with kids roughly my age, and there were often three or four kids, or more, in each house.

In my own case, my family lived in one side of a duplex, and with five children—three boys and two girls—living on the other side, there were a total of eight children just in that one house. And in nearby neighborhoods, the same pattern held true, so I had plenty of boys to hang out with as a child. Some were close buddies who I saw nearly every day, others passing friends, but what almost all of us had in common was a wish to play baseball, which certainly was fulfilled.

The time and place of playing changed with the years, but the birthplace of my baseball "career" was my own backyard, and my father was my first "teammate," dragging bat and glove out the back door to teach me a sport I was most eager to learn. The neighborhood houses were close together and in a straight line, which I always considered a very good thing when I was delivering newspapers on my paper route, as the load of papers went down fairly quickly from under my weary arm. It also had a very beneficial effect on the local baseball games, at least from the kids' perspective. The backyards of each house followed a straight line, with no barriers between several of the yards, meaning that the yards stretched out unobstructed for a pretty good distance. It was enough space for an infield and an outfield for boys of a certain young age, which is naturally how we envisioned the proper use of the land. The people who lived there and owned the yards, including an elderly couple and an equally elderly widow, may not have appreciated our sporting view, but I looked upon baseball as a serious enterprise, and, in any case, we were simply participating in the national pastime. Who could criticize that?

The main challenges, space-wise, of our backyard diamond were deep left field and the foul territory around first base. Medium left field was not a problem, as that was just a couple of backyards over from mine. Beyond that, however, was a yard that had been turned into a large garden by the family who lived there. This was not an issue when we were small, as we couldn't hit the ball that far. But as we grew, it became a real temptation to try to hit one into the garden, as that was a true blast, and eventually we could do it, even on a regular basis.

The mother who worked in the garden, not surprisingly, was not impressed by our batting prowess. When she was toiling away in the garden as a ball sailed in, she would return it to us in a friendly enough manner. When she wasn't in the garden, however, we would sneak in and try to find the ball ourselves, which was usually a tricky endeavor, attempting to tiptoe between the cornstalks and rows of tomatoes without destroying the garden or being seen by the mother. The kitchen of her house faced the garden, and if she saw us there from the window, she would shriek, "Wait! Wait!!" before scurrying out in her apron to fetch our ball. I will go out on a limb and say that this was probably not one of the pleasures she envisioned when she went through what must have been a lot of labor to get that garden planted and growing each year.

The foul area around first base was far more problematic, and we tried as much as possible to keep the ball in play on that side. The reason was because the neighbor on that side, an elderly man, was much less patient with our ballplaying. His yard was unmowed, so the grass was tall, more like a field of weeds than dreams. Any ball that went there was going to be hard to find under any conditions. But if the neighbor found the ball himself, my memory is that he did not return many of them to us. He kept them. Rumor had it that he put them in his garage, and I remember one occasion when we gave each other ten fingers to try to get up to the window of the garage to see inside. I think someone claimed that they saw a basket full of baseballs, but, given our imaginations at the time, it may have been a basket of apples, or no basket at all.

I never saw that man smile, especially when we were playing baseball and he would stand there and glare at us from across the yard while leaning on his cane. I used to deliver the newspaper to his house, and rake his leaves in the fall, but I don't think he ever spoke to me. His gregarious wife did all the talking and paid me the money. He was a kind of Boo Radley in my life, and I was always slightly afraid of him.

The three brothers who lived on the other side of our two-family house—George, Kevin, and John—were my most immediate and reliable neighborhood friends, particularly where baseball was concerned. (I also inherited the newspaper delivery route from them.) George, four years older, was so much better than the rest of us that he seemed already well on his way to some kind of baseball success. He had a very impressive Rawlings glove which I loved borrowing, as it was rather difficult to drop a ball using that glove, an experience that gave the name "Rawlings," in my mind, a god-like elevation in the dictionary of baseball lingo. Kevin, a year younger than me, was also very talented and, being near my own age, a closer friend personally. On summer days, we were likely to be hanging out morning, noon, and night, usually playing baseball. John was the youngest by a few years and missed most of the salad days of baseball played behind our house, although he, too, had his own moments in the backyard sun. Regardless, "incalculable" would not begin to describe the number of hours I spent playing baseball with all of them.

In fact, when their family took their station wagon on a cross-country trip to San Francisco in 1966, they sent me a postcard that, not surprisingly, did not feature the Golden Gate Bridge, Telegraph Hill, Fisherman's Wharf, or Alcatraz, but Candlestick Park. And, most appropriately, I still have that iconic postcard, safely stored in one of the boxes. Dated 7/18/66 and mailed with a 4-cent stamp featuring a profile of Abraham Lincoln, the card said, "Having a great time and hope to attend Giants-Mets game. Be at Disneyland next week and then home. George & Kev." The 1966 Mets (66-95, and pre-Seaver, Koosman, and, really, Ryan—3 innings, 6 K's total) didn't entice me too much—I was having enough trouble willing the Red Sox to their own infrequent victories every year. Even a trip to Disneyland could not have matched seeing the Giants of that year, with their Hall-of-Fame laden lineup, which was just about the perfect recipe for jealousy.

Years later, in the early 1980s, I would make my own trek to Candlestick, but it was decidedly different from a 1966 visit—I wasn't going to see Willie Mays one year removed from a 52-homer season (he still hit 37 that season), or Juan Marichal on his way to his second 25-win season. That would have been a treat beyond special. At least I could be sure that if George and Kevin did go to the game, they would appreciate what they were witnessing. After all, they were fellow backyard baseball players.

Our games in the yard were played in many forms. One of the more intriguing was a version involving merely two or three players, with an invented variation of baseball in which we used a broom stick for a bat and a jelly jar cap for a ball. The cap was tough to throw for a strike, as it sailed toward the plate with a break like a frisbee, and was difficult to hit at all, but if you connected, that cap would shoot off the stick and sail a good distance. I'm not sure how we came upon that game, and we didn't play it all that often, but I remember it as one of my fondest "baseball" memories.

Other times we would get up close to a nine v. nine extravaganza of actual baseball, pitting neighborhood against neighborhood, which might last a whole afternoon, with subs, relief pitchers, argued calls, and similar trappings of professionalism. Always, we played hard, or at least thought we did, and the next day would most likely bring more of the same.

Our backyard baseball produced a surprise one day that had a rather unfortunate boomerang effect. A man who drove a large beverage truck would sometimes park his truck in the lot out in right-center field, after making his delivery to the loading dock in the rear of the nearby Star Market, and eat his lunch while watching us play. On that day, there were only a few of us in the yard, as it was pretty hot, and we were shagging fly balls when one of the balls rolled near the truck. The man took the opportunity to speak to us, and asked us if we could use some refreshments. Of course, we readily accepted. I think I had a can of 7 Up. Whatever, it was an unexpected and very welcome boost on a long summer day.

But, boys being boys, the Pandora's box had been opened, and the next time that driver showed up, he was surrounded by a bigger gang of suddenly thirsty boys. He begged off that time, and I don't recall that he ever came around again. That was too bad, as having an audience, even of one person, gave the games a bit more authenticity.

My neighborhood friends were around all summer—the San Francisco trip provided a rare exception—so finding boys to play with was usually not a problem even when school was out. On the days that I was by myself, however, I would sometimes play games that I made up on my own. This was not a trivial exercise but, I can see in hindsight, a form of personal therapy.

While I had very much an "outdoor" life as a boy and grew up in a house with a backyard that at times saw a dozen or more boys trying to hit home runs or throw touchdown passes, I also harbored a deep-rooted (and very unwanted) shyness that I tried to conceal, probably not very successfully. This often drew me toward the separate peace of solitude and, at times, still does.

Mine, though, was not a separation of loneliness. I sought it out for the satisfying freedom it offered for me to be my own friend. In this private bubble, while alone, I was never lonely. And, in those days, baseball was frequently the reason. Like Walter Mitty, I could leave behind my own very mortal talent and retreat into an imagined baseball universe, entertaining myself as Bob Gibson tossing a shutout or Tony C nailing a runner at the plate. These interludes of isolation, free of all stress, brought great pleasure at the time and remain a cherished memory decades later.

My favorite version took place right outside my back steps. On the side of my house facing the driveway, the foundation was about a two-foot-high perimeter made of stone. One of the stones, luckily situated in the middle of the wall, was roughly the size of a plate, so I used that as the strike zone of the "opposition."

I would stand back as far as I could from the wall—which wasn't too far, given that my house and the neighbor's house were sandwiched around the narrow driveway—and pretend to be the pitcher, throwing to the "strike zone" on the wall. I used a white rubber ball shaped like a baseball, including imitation threaded seams, which was popular in those days, particularly in the spring, when so many kids would have to play baseball in parking lots until the snow melted. My father at times stood in the living room window and watched, possibly to enjoy seeing me play his favorite sport or to make sure that I did not break any windows. Likely both were on his mind.

This game had the attraction of being *totally* up to me. I would pretend to be whatever right-handed pitcher was on my mind that day—it generally ranged from Earl Wilson to Dean Chance to Mudcat Grant to, of course, Juan Marichal (until I got tired of almost falling over while trying to wind up with my leg over my head)—facing any lineup that I chose. I was familiar with the batting orders of teams in both leagues, but it was

107

more interesting to choose a National League team, since I did not see them as much, and preferably the Dodgers or the Giants, as each had lineups that seemed to be full of All-Stars. I would "pitch" to each batter, with a strike being any pitch that hit the corners of the stone, and a hit being any pitch that I judged to be a meatball. If I threw too many balls off the plate, or too many meatballs, I could take a break for a few minutes and make a call to the bullpen, to bring in Dick Radatz or Hal Reniff or Eddie Fisher (it was very tough to get a knuckleball to hit the stone, so I didn't bring in Fisher too much) or Moe Drabowsky, among many others. And as the ball ricocheted back to me, I could be Frank Malzone starting a double play or Pete Ward stabbing a line drive.

The games went until dinner time, or until it started raining, or, most often, until I was missing the strike zone so frequently that I either had to cheat or admit that my pitch count was out of control, so to speak. There was also the problem that if the pitch hit the rock in a certain way, it would shoot over my head and ricochet off my neighbor's house right behind me, making quite a loud bang in the process. Although my neighbors, an elderly couple, were very patient with my driveway antics and the white paint that I was inexorably chipping off the side of their home, I understood that after a few such line shots back through the box, it was time to call it quits for the sake of continued neighborhood harmony. In that case, I could throw pop-ups to myself for practice, or just go in and lie on my bed and study the statistics on the backs of the baseball cards. Players like Smoky Burgess, Bob Friend, Roy Sievers, and Cal McLish had played so many years that you could spend ten minutes on a single card.

Another game I played alone was a lot more tiring, but far more exciting. Unfortunately, I could play only on Sundays. In this game, my "field" was the Star Market parking lot adjacent to my backyard, and Sunday was the day that the lot was empty, as most people were in church and observing the Sabbath.

Near the rear of the Star Market store was a very high and wide part of the wall that faced the parking lot. I would throw my rubber ball off the wall and try to catch it. What made the game exciting was the size of both the parking lot and the wall. I could throw the ball hard off the top of the wall, and it would go sailing over my head, meaning that I would have to run back at full tilt and try to make an over-the-head catch, and then turn and fire the ball to the catcher to cut down the runner trying to score after tagging up at third. If my throw was low and hard and looked pretty good from where I was standing, the runner was definitely out at the—wall.

However, there were two considerable drawbacks to this game. One was that if I missed the ball, it would roll all the way to my backyard, which, distance-wise, was practically in China. At the beginning of the game, I would chase after each missed ball, eager to get it back and try again. But after enough misses, I chased the balls less and less energetically, until I got to a point where I would say to myself that, on the next miss, I would just let it go and pick it up on my way home.

The other challenge came when I was trying to throw fly balls off the top of the wall, sometimes my reach exceeded my grasp, and I threw the ball *over* the wall and onto the roof of the store. That was a problem, as I had only one ball.

As the boys in my neighborhood knew, though, there was a way to get up on the roof by going around to the back of the store. You could hoist yourself up onto the top of a small, corrugated metal storage area, the metal being blistering hot on sunny days, as I painfully recall. From there, you could pull yourself up over a low-level roof, where a ladder led to the top roof. Sometimes, the climbing was the easy part, as the roof surface itself was so vast that it wasn't always easy to locate the ball, which could roll rather far from where it went over the wall.

Once I found it, I would toss it back down to the parking lot, as I needed both hands free to get back down again. It was a little tricky going up and down, and if you fell from one level to the next, that would be painful. (If you fell all the way from the top roof to the parking lot, that would be absolutely your last fall. No one ever had that experience, I'm happy to report.) The view from above was certainly panoramic, spanning several neighborhoods and the parking lot. I had never been in an airplane, but this was more than an adequate sky view for a young and very curious boy.

With such roof-climbing activities in mind, this is one of the ways by which I measure the path of civilization: I haven't seen any boys scaling supermarket walls in a long time, thankfully. Maybe we can attribute the change to the fact that Sundays went from being a day of rest and worship—and baseball in empty parking lots—to one of nonstop shopping and television sports.

In a similar vein, bike-riding may be a useful judge of social evolution. Nowadays, if you see a 7 or 8-year-old suburban child riding a bike, most often the child will be wearing a helmet, and a watchful parent will be riding, jogging, or walking close behind. In my early biking memories, there were no helmets or nearby parents. Fathers were at work, and mothers were hanging the laundry on clotheslines. We rode freely from neighborhood to neighborhood, through parking lots, across busy streets, up and down hills as fast as we could pedal, one or sometimes two kids to a bike (the second one sitting on the crossbar), in sun, rain, and snow. It was all fun and all unquestioned—that's just how it was, especially when you had to get to a certain baseball field for a game. My own bike came from the town dump—my father picked out a discarded bike frame there one Saturday morning, brought it home, painted it red, put two new tires on it, and, transportation-wise, I was good to go. Times certainly have changed.

7. House of Cards

When I wasn't contemplating anti-gravitational pitching deliveries or careening down the street on my bike headed toward a ballfield, I was pursuing baseball along other lines, particularly those of what are now called "collectibles," which at times involved some personal creativity. I didn't like bubble gum, for example, but when I saw that Bazooka was offering free team pennants in exchange for Bazooka Joe comic strips, I was on the case. Whenever friends bought packages of Bazooka gum, I asked them for the comics (they were happy to oblige), and even when I saw comics laying on the ground, if they were salvageable, I scooped them up and added them to the pile. The result was that most of the pennant collection that I had hanging on my bedroom wall was Bazooka-issue, and it was always a happy day when I saw a package in the mail from Bazooka.

Of course, outside the lines, the true joy of baseball for a boy my age was collecting baseball cards, a hobby that made cards a daily sight in my bedroom and that had a direct, even vital, influence on my view of the Red Sox and of all other major leaguers. The story of baseball, past and present, had started coming to me around the time I began school.

Through my father's tales and my own reading, baseball early on was very much a piece of American history and culture to me. A lot of what I understood about subjects ranging from geography (Brooklyn was in New York, Cleveland along Lake Erie) to race relations (Tom Yawkey was a racist, Branch Rickey was not) to power (Kenesaw Mountain Landis, whose severe photos always intimidated me a bit—did that man ever smile?—had the authority to kick players, even potential Hall of Famers, completely out of the game), came to me through the prism of baseball. Of course, when I was five, most of that knowledge was still in the exciting future that lay ahead. But from my earliest baseball cards I did know that Yaz played for the Red Sox, Billy Martin for the Reds (with his hometown of Berkeley, I later noticed, misspelled as Berkley on the card), Leo Posada (future uncle of Jorge) for the Kansas City Athletics, and Gerry Staley (who was *really* old) for the White Sox, and that was more than enough for starters.

I have no idea what the present situation is regarding kids and baseball cards, but back in the 1960s, for many boys who were baseball loyalists, buying and opening a pack of baseball cards was often the highlight of the day. Any pack might contain a card of Willie Mays, Pete Rose (I still have trouble thinking of him as a vilified cheater—when he played, his name was synonymous with an unsurpassed dedication to baseball, but now "Charlie Hustle" has taken on a whole new meaning), or, if you were really lucky, Yaz.

For me, baseball cards had their own very specific ritual that involved choosing a pack, opening it, and using what came inside. First, the pack had to be inspected carefully before actually being chosen and bought, especially if you already had many cards on the current checklist and wanted to minimize the chances of getting doubles of bad players. I would hold the pack up to the light, or even slightly tear an edge of the pack open, to see if I could determine which cards were on the top and bottom. This was never easy, particularly if an annoyed (and annoying) cashier was staring at you, but the goal was to get a new Red Sox player, or a superstar, or a double that could be traded for one of the above. This was important, as the cards on sale came only from a specific checklist. There was a total of seven checklists, with nearly one hundred cards on each list. After the cards for any checklist had been available for a while, doubles were inevitable—sometimes the *whole pack* was doubles, or even triples, so a sneak peek to avoid that dilemma was almost vital.

Possibly the most impatience I have felt in my life were the times I was waiting in line at a supermarket or a variety store to pay for my cards, wondering whether I held Hall-of-Famers or utility infielders in my hand, often while staring at revolving metal racks of paperback books and wondering why so many of them seemed to be written by either Erma Bombeck or Harold Robbins.

Once I had passed the cashier and the register, I got down to business. I opened each pack slowly, I guess mainly to savor the experience and, in my childish mind, to bring some good luck as to the contents. There were five cards in each pack. If the first card or two was bad, I looked at the rest with even greater deliberation, hoping to change my luck and come upon a much better one. But if a good card turned up right away, I tended to race through the remaining cards, knowing that I had already found a successful pack and was playing with house money the rest of the way. Either way, there was romance in opening a pack of baseball cards, and to a young fan, it never got old.

The cards were not the only things in the pack. There were also other baseball items, such as coins, rub-on tattoos, and various special cards. These were certainly worth saving and trading, and some had quite a bit of value when the crazy days of collectibles later set in. The cards also came with a stick of gum which, to me, was worthless. It was rectangular-shaped, very hard, and had the properties of plastic. If you broke it, it either separated in two sharp-edged pieces, or shattered into small, similar pieces. I had no interest in putting plastic in my mouth, so I rarely ate baseball card bubble gum. However, I think I was in the minority on that point. Plenty of kids seemed to like chewing baseball gum, and often some friends eagerly took the pieces that I was about to throw away.

The next thing was what to do with the cards. The kids who bought the cards just to be part of the sporting scene would commit such heretical acts as putting them in their pants pockets and then sitting down, attaching them to the spokes of their bikes so that the cards would make a firecracker sound when they were riding—the faster they rode, the more firecrackers went off—or just throwing their doubles in the trash.

In my case, I kept every card, carefully divided by team, in shoeboxes, and arranged alphabetically except for Boston, which came first, ahead of the Baltimore Orioles. (When the Milwaukee Braves moved to Atlanta in 1966, my system was thrown even further off.) I didn't keep the cards in good shape because I suspected they would be worth thousands of dollars when I became old and gray. I had no idea about that. I took care of them because, at the time, they meant a lot to me. Much of my childhood earnings went into purchasing packs of baseball cards, and I always considered it money well spent.

For the serious card collectors, doubles were prized and turned all of us into youthful general managers of baseball teams. This was fantasy baseball before the advent of computers and bored grown men sitting in their cubicles at work and secretly checking out their fantasy lineups online while supposedly working on spreadsheets for the boss. Baseball cards were for boys, and we knew what to do with them. A Hank Aaron double could be traded for practically the entire Kansas City Athletics team.

But the most valuable doubles were Red Sox players. A Wilbur Wood card, even the year he was an embarrassing 0–5 (he never did win a game for the Red Sox but went on to win 164 games, including more than 20 games four times with the White Sox, after the team sold him), could be easily dealt for, say, a Floyd Robinson card, especially if someone needed Wood to complete their Red Sox collection.

So doubles, particularly of the Red Sox, had high market value in the horse-trading of boys under a tree in the backyard on a hot summer day. Those, however, were safe trades, unlike the real-life trades of actual general managers, who in the backs of their minds always had to fear that they were trading Lou Brock for Ernie Broglio. Who can forget—or should that be who can *remember*?—Brock, following the trade, going on a three-month, .348 tear in leading the 1964 Cardinals to the pennant and a World Series victory over the Bombers, while the pathetic Cubs were saddled with Broglio, an 18-game winner just the previous season, destined to win a grand total of seven games over three injury-plagued seasons with Chicago before retiring at the age of thirty. Brock merely went on to play his way into Cooperstown. No, you definitely did not want to be guilty of trading Lou Brock for Ernie Broglio.

Sometimes, though, successful teams, even the Cardinals, made poor trades and got away with it, as was the case with a multi-player trade in the fall of 1965 when the Cardinals sent Bill White and Dick Groat to the Phillies for Alex Johnson and Art Mahaffey. White (.276, 22, 103) and Groat (.260, 152 hits) went on to have fine seasons for the Phillies, while Johnson (.186, 2, 6) and Mahaffey (1–4, 6.43) were invisible in St. Louis. But the Cardinals were able to shrug off their talent giveaway and went on to reach the World Series in both 1967 (most unfortunately for the Red Sox) and 1968. The Phillies, meanwhile, were on their way from being pretty good to pretty bad over the next few seasons, a trajectory that their hardened fans, painfully, had seen before.

One player I had on a number of cards was pitcher Frank Baumann of the White Sox and Cubs. Baumann, though, had spent his first five years with the Red Sox and earned his own moment of fame in a botched trade. Baumann had pitched somewhat sparingly (218 innings) but not poorly for the Red Sox, with a 13-8 record. Following the 1959 season, in which the Red Sox went through three managers, the team decided to ship Baumann off to the White Sox for first baseman Ron Jackson. Almost predictably, Baumann then had a one-season awakening in Chicago in 1960, winning 13 games and leading the American League in ERA, while Jackson lasted barely a month in Boston, hitting .226 in 31 at-bats before being traded to Milwaukee, where he never played a game. And for Jackson the Red Sox received infielder Ray Boone, a fine player in his prime, later becoming a rather significant footnote in Red Sox lore as the grandfather of Tim Wakefield's nightmare, Aaron Boone, but now on his last legs at 36. Boone went on to hit .205 in limited action before being released in September. So the Red Sox had traded Baumann for—not much.

On the topic of risky trades, I was not averse to trading a *single* Red Sox card, one that I had no double of and that might never be replaced, if I could work out a highly advantageous deal in terms of baseball talent. Usually that meant trading for a player on the San Francisco Giants, who were my favorite team after the Sox. I got to see Giants players only in All-Star games or on an occasional Game of the Week on television, but I watched them whenever I could. I believe that I did once trade a Red Sox card for Orlando Cepeda and Tom Haller, probably shocking my trading partner. Who would give up a Red Sox for a Giant? In fact, I might have traded almost anyone other than Yaz for Juan Marichal, had the need arisen. I would have traded almost anyone for Yaz, too, if I didn't have his card. Trading was an intense and practically intellectual activity among boys.

Concerning the Giants, over the years I have noticed that a good number of other Red Sox fans have had a special liking for the Giants of those days, despite being three thousand miles removed from the scene. *Why* is an interesting question to ponder. It is true that any team featuring Mays, Cepeda, McCovey, and Marichal is going to attract attention from baseball fans of any city. (The Giants also had an annual Mendoza candidate at shortstop, Hal Lanier, a player who, my father liked to remind me, was the son of southpaw Max Lanier, a two-time All Star for the Cardinals. The elder Lanier was probably most famous for bolting the Cardinals in 1946 for the controversial Mexican League of Jorge Pasquel, who used wads of cash in a sometimes-successful attempt to lure major league stars, including Ted Williams, to play south of the border.) But other teams, most obviously the Dodgers, had plenty of talent as well. Koufax and Drysdale were to the Dodgers what Lennon and McCartney were to the Beatles. From 1962 to 1966, either Koufax or Drysdale personally got the victory in 46 percent of the Dodgers' wins, leading the team into three World Series. The Yankees, until 1965, had a stacked lineup, but a Red Sox fan could not admire the Yankees unless it was done in the strictest privacy and with great courage.

Another possibility is that Boston and San Francisco have often been thought of as sister cities, although I don't know how prevalent that notion was a half-century ago. One odd point is that Boston, fairly or otherwise, was considered somewhat of a racist city at the time (and very racist a decade later, when school busing began), yet a good number of the Giants' stars were black or Latino, which didn't quite add up.

On a different San Francisco-Boston note, all three of the DiMaggio brothers—Vince, Joe, and Dom—attended Galileo High School in San Francisco, and two of them went on to have strong connections to Boston, as Dom had an outstanding 11-year career with the Red Sox, while Vince played with somewhat less success in his two years with the Braves.

Whatever the reason, the Giants seem to have had plenty of support in Massachusetts. For me, it was 80 percent Marichal, 20 percent Mays, and that was more than enough reason to pay close attention to them and get as many of their cards as possible.

With the Giants in mind, I will devote a paragraph or so to their one-time archrivals in New York, the Brooklyn Dodgers, a team that did not exist past my first birthday but was one that my cards brought to my attention and that I often thought of as a Red Sox fan. I'm not sure exactly how this came about, but in its initial form it probably started early on, in 1961 and 1962, when I began getting the Post cereal baseball cards.

I didn't have many cards in those sets—my family could eat only so much cereal—but for whatever reason, I got an unusually high number of Los Angeles Dodgers cards, including Duke Snider, Don Drysdale, Larry Sherry, Sandy Koufax, John

Roseboro, Wally Moon, Charlie Neal, Maury Wills, Jim Gilliam, John Podres, Tommy Davis, Willie Davis, and Norm Larker. It's not clear what specifically appealed to me about those cards—maybe it was how blue everything, including the sky, seemed to be—but I grew partial to them. Later, when I had Topps cards with the entire career records printed on the backs, I got many of the same players and saw that before they had played for Los Angeles, they had played for "Brooklyn." That got me started on the hunt for the story of the Brooklyn Dodgers.

What I found was that while they certainly had had more success over the years than the Red Sox, they had also failed at a level that gave them a certain star-crossed identity that a Red Sox fan could empathize with. The Brooklyn Dodgers had no trouble getting to the World Series on a regular basis, but they had an impossibly difficult time trying to actually win one, not breaking through until the magical year of 1955 against the Yankees, after having lost *five* World Series appearances to the same dreaded Yankees.

Just two years (and one more Series loss to the Yankees) later, Walter O' Malley, after threatening to move the team to, of all places, Jersey City, saw the future in the sunnier—and more profitable—climes of California. The baseball map had already been shaken considerably by the moves of the Braves to Milwaukee in 1953 and the St. Louis Browns to Baltimore and the Philadelphia Athletics to Kansas City in the succeeding years, leaving only Chicago and New York as multiple-team cities. (The Cincinnati Reds underwent the interesting change of remaining in the same city but, as a result of the Red Scare during the McCarthy era, switching the team name, in place since 1890, from the uncomfortably suggestive Reds to the Redlegs before sanity prevailed in 1960 and the name reverted to the Reds.) Now O'Malley, after convincing Horace Stoneham and his New York Giants to join him, emptied New York of two of its storied baseball franchises in 1958 and headed for the West Coast, leaving behind infuriated and unforgiving fans at Ebbets Field and the Polo Grounds.

After reading Roger Kahn's fabled account of those Brooklyn teams and watching the increasing futility of the post-1966 Red Sox, who were looking more and more like the Brooklyn Dodgers in finding ways to lose when everything was on the line, I settled on the Brooklyn Dodgers as my National League version of the Boston Red Sox. And their abject failure against the Yankees only strengthened my pity for the Dodgers and my dislike of the Bombers.

I could write a separate book on the various baseball cards that I remember well, including cereal box cards from that very first year, 1961, of Chuck Cottier, Alex Grammas, Pancho Herrera, Pete Burnside, and other mediocre players whose names I nevertheless learned by heart. My favorite Red Sox card was from 1965—the first full card of Tony C. It was a great photo of him, showing him only from the chest up. The striking thing about the photo was the totally serious, focused, intelligent expression on his face, captured as he gazed out at— what? I had no idea, but as a nine-year-old baseball purist, I imagined that that was how he must have looked in the on-deck circle, staring out at the pitcher, trying to gauge his velocity, whether his fastball or curveball was more effective that day, and whether he should take a pitch or two or go after the first one. His hat looked slightly big for his head, but that was probably just because an intense player like Tony C didn't have time to worry about things like hat sizes. The game was more important. At the time, I didn't know much about the fun-loving, spotlight-seeking side of Tony C. I just knew that he was a terrific hitter, especially at Fenway, and the card reflected how seriously he took the game of baseball. Every player should look that way, I thought. Of course, the shiny rookie trophy featured on the card did nothing to tarnish Tony C's image as a baseball hero. I don't know how many times I looked at that card, but it was never enough.

Aside from members of the Red Sox, a workhorse Twins starter named Camilo Pascual was another favorite. I had Pascual on cards nearly every year that I collected them, which stretched from 1961 to 1968. But it was my first two cards of him, from 1961 and 1962 Post boxes, which were somewhat troublesome to my young mind. His name alone was problematic, as he had both a first name and a last name that were different from all other players, and how to pronounce either one was a challenge. The fact that the names on his first card (Camilio) and the second card (Camilo) were not even spelled the same only added to the task. And the second card said that he had once struck out 15 Red Sox in a game, which obviously did not help his cause with me.

When I got Pascual on a Topps card in 1964, and I could see his year-by-year history, I began to have more of a change of heart toward him. Being a Red Sox fan, I was well accustomed to rooting for the underdog, and I saw that Pascual had underdog qualifications that would have made him a perfect fit with the Red Sox. In his first five seasons in the big leagues, from 1954 to 1958, his win-loss numbers were 4–7, 2–12, 6–18, 8–17, and 8–12, meaning that his career start of 28–66 was embarrassingly competitive with that of the Mets' prolific loser (12-34) Jay Hook. And Pascual had been pitching for the old Washington Senators, who were at least as pathetic as the Red Sox teams that I cheered for. (For the record, the Senators of those years managed to lose 88, 101, 95, 99, and 93 games, giving their fans about the same quality of baseball that the Red Sox were providing to their own long-suffering supporters in the 1960s. Senators fans must have uncomfortably remembered the "First in war, first in peace, last in the American League" refrain given to the Senators' teams of "The Big Train," Walter Johnson, who endured *twenty* 1–0 losses toiling for the lowly Nats.)

But the most interesting thing was that Pascual's career win-loss record on that '64 card was 113–120, almost .500, including back to back years of 20–11 and 21–9 in '62 and '63.

120

In some way (most unlike Jay Hook), he had roared back from oblivion, and I was finding Pascual on a number of "Pitching Leader" cards as well. He was now worth my attention, and getting a Camilo Pascual card in a pack was a good acquisition. The fact that he was from Cuba, as was Minnie Minoso, another of my favorite baseball card players, gave him an additional boost. (Politics was a sport I knew nothing about at the time, so the Cuba connection did not bother me.)

In 1964, there were two other cards that certainly got my attention. The cards of Ken Hubbs of the Cubs and Jim Umbricht of the Colt .45s were noteworthy because of the tragic fact that both players had recently passed away, Hubbs in a plane crash and Umbricht from cancer, and their deaths were noted on the cards themselves. I remember feeling surprised and confused at reading the news, expecting to be looking at the players' statistics and instead finding out that they had died. In my mind, baseball players dying wasn't something I had ever imagined. That year was probably the first time I understood what the expression "in memoriam" meant. Fortunately, no Red Sox players had "in memoriam" cards that I knew of.

Another card I did not expect to see was the 1964 issue of Bob Kennedy of the Cubs, which identified him on the front as the team's "head coach." Head coach? Weren't basketball coaches "head" coaches? Wasn't Red Auerbach a head coach? Baseball teams had managers, not head coaches. But here was baseball-card proof that a team had a head coach. When I sought an explanation, what I found was an absurd situation that fit the Cubs perfectly in those days and might have suited the Red Sox as well. Cubs owner Phil Wrigley, apparently in a flight of fancy, had decided that his consistently unsuccessful team needed better leadership, and what better way to improve direction than to dump the idea of having a mere single manager and instead use the collective wisdom of a rotating system of "head" coaches.

Starting with the 1961 season, the Cubs instituted what became known as the "College of Coaches," rotating as many as eight or nine "coaches" as leaders of the team throughout the next two seasons. Unfortunately for Wrigley, when the past proved prologue and the Cubs went an inglorious 123–193 during that stretch, he reluctantly adjusted his image of greatness for the Cubs and named Bob Kennedy the lead "head" coach (but not manager!) of the various coaches. Kennedy did a modestly successful job of righting the ship, bringing in the Cubs at 158–166 over the next two seasons, but a 72–90 finish in 1965 doomed the experiment. When Leo Durocher was hired the following November, there was no longer any doubt as to who would be running the club in 1966.

One player I seemed to get every year on a card, and who became one of my favorites, was Willie Kirkland, a left-handed hitter with decent power. There were several reasons why I was partial to him. I believe that the closest I ever came to getting a foul ball at Fenway was off a shot into the right field seats by Kirkland that landed a row ahead of me. Baseball-card wise, I had him on an impressive 1963 Jell-O card on which he looked absolutely poised to hit one out of the park. I also had him on a 1963 Topps card in which he appears to be pondering the universe, but I gave him a pass on that one. The fact that he played for the new Washington Senators in the mid-1960s, who were just as bad as the old Senators (and as the Red Sox, of course), may have increased my sympathy for him. Finally, in 1960, he had been traded with Johnny Antonelli by the Giants to Cleveland for Harvey Kuenn, two of the great names from the 1950s, and three years later was sent to Baltimore for Al Smith, elevating him in my childhood accounting of baseball history. Interestingly in the case of Antonelli, he began his career with the Braves in Boston (1948) and ended it with the Braves in Milwaukee (1961).

So, Kirkland was one of those players I hoped the Red Sox would get, although I understood that the idea of him replacing Tony C in right was absurd. Maybe he could have played center.

Before moving on from Kirkland, he had his own Red Sox-like moment of improbability that deserves mention. One of the most bizarre baseball stories I ever heard concerned a sacrifice bunt in a game between the Cleveland Indians and the Chicago White Sox in 1961. Playing for the Indians, Kirkland had three home runs and a walk when he got a final at bat in the ninth inning with runners on first and second and the Indians trailing, 9–8. Manager Jimmy Dykes, who the Indians had traded for in a managerial swap the previous year, sized up the situation and had Kirkland, in line to possibly hit his *fourth* home run of the game, put down a bunt to advance the runners, which he successfully did. But the baseball gods immediately punished Dykes for his lack of imagination, as a walk and a double play sealed the victory for the ChiSox. One wonders what would have happened if Albert Belle or Milton Bradley had been given the bunt sign in that situation—the manager may have needed a bat for his own protection.

A card that was slightly unnerving, especially to a very young boy, was the 1962 Post cereal issue of Ryne Duren of the Angels. In the photo, Duren is holding his glove up to his chest as a pitcher might do while in the stretch, a pose that looked natural enough for a pitcher. The problem with Duren was his eyes: you couldn't see them. He was wearing sunglasses, and not just any sunglasses but very dark, almost sinister-looking sunglasses. I collected thousands of baseball cards in those years, and I don't recall any others in which a player was wearing sunglasses. When I later learned that Duren had significant problems with both his vision and his control—he averaged 6 walks per 9 innings—his glasses seemed even more ominous, especially for any batter facing him. As I think about it, I imagine that Pete Mikkelsen's rather prominent, coke bottle-ish eyeglasses may have distracted hitters a bit as well.

Perhaps the final word on eyeglasses should come from Willie Mays. When a prolonged slump once had some questioning Mays's eyesight, Charles Einstein, a San Francisco journalist and friend of Mays, approached him about it, noting that Frank Howard now wore eyeglasses. "He ain't hittin', either," was Mays's dismissive response. Fans must have held their breath when Howard faced Duren.

Of most importance regarding my own baseball cards, I learned the countless, assorted statistics that are the lifeblood of the sport to many fans. I was five years old when I got my earliest baseball cards, and my parents helped me with the reading part on the backs of the cards. The numbers I figured out pretty quickly on my own, as that was the actual meat on the bone for a baseball fan. And comprehending the statistics was hardly an idle effort, as those youthful hours spent calculating batting averages, earned run averages, and winning percentages honed the basic math skills that I still have today. That 2/7—or a batter going 2 for 7 in a doubleheader—equals .286, and countless such statistics, have a permanent place in my memory.

Admittedly, the backs of the cards did not list anywhere near all of the stats that are tallied today, like WHIPs and OBPs, but the essentials were there, even individually, year by year, during some issues. In certain cases, for devoted fans and probably even for some casual types, the numbers had a kind of magic, to the point that they became etched in your memory. That was certainly the case with me. Numbers like 44, 121, and .326—Yaz's triple crown numbers—should be as familiar as the alphabet to any Red Sox fan of a certain age, as should 15–6 and 16–9, Dick Radatz's win-loss numbers as a relief pitcher in his prime.

As a boy, my father had had his own interest in statistics and owned baseball cards of some of the best of his time, such as Frankie Frisch, Goose Goslin, Larry French (who in one remarkable 18-win season threw 274 innings but got by with just 72 strikeouts), and one of his favorites, the Giants' Carl Hubbell—how many times he would later mutter, "If I still had those cards, they'd probably be worth a million bucks." They would have been worth a lot to me at that time, not to sell them but just to *have* them. I did get a decent collection of 1961

Golden Press facsimile cards of old-timers, including Dazzy Vance (197 wins, all coming after the age of 31), Hank Greenberg (331 home runs), Pie Traynor (.320 batting average), George Sisler (2812 hits), Al Simmons (1827 runs batted in), and others, and I studied the statistics on the backs of those cards as if the players were still active.

Among players I knew, the numbers 25–8, 21–8, 22–13, 25–6, 14–10 (injuries), 26–9, and 21–11 were special, as they belonged to Juan Marichal in his own golden years that were not quite as golden as they could have been for him. He started his career with a lights-out, one-hit, 12-strikeout shutout of the Phillies in July, 1960. His superlative performances went on to include one season of 30 complete games, 16 of them in a row, another year with 10 shutouts, and a now well-documented 16-inning, 1–0 complete game victory over Warren Spahn (who, at forty-two, amazingly also went the distance). He won more games in the 1960s than any other pitcher.

Yet, all of his success earned him no Cy Young awards—in fact, there was only one year, 1971, when he received even a single vote. His bad luck was to be pitching during the same years as Koufax and Gibson, not unlike the earlier plight of Shoeless Joe Jackson, who hit .356 over his career yet never won a batting title, thanks to the 12 titles that Ty Cobb won.

Worse, Marichal's Giants had the unwanted distinction of finishing in second place four consecutive years (1965–1968) in the pre-division days, winning more games than any team during that stretch, and then second again the following year in the NL West. Marichal made it to the World Series only once, in his third year, and even in his prime seemed to be most well-known for his unfortunately iconic and nearly tragic moment of smashing John Roseboro over the head with a bat, an act that is obviously difficult to forgive, although years later, Roseboro did just that, allowing Marichal to finally garner enough votes to enter the Hall of Fame. At Roseboro's funeral in 2002, Marichal, reflecting the poignancy of their unlikely friendship, told the mourners, "I wish I could have had John Roseboro as my catcher." Sandy Koufax, in his own speech, turned to Marichal and said, "You would have loved pitching to John Roseboro." Ironically, Marichal did finish his career in a brief stint with the Dodgers, but long after Roseboro had left the team.

As far as cards go, Marichal's 1964 card was undoubtedly his best. After all, it doesn't get much better than 25–8, and the glittering photo of him impressively highlighted his stardom. To show the extent of my fixation with Marichal, when *Sport* magazine published an article on Marichal that included a full-page photo of just his face, I asked my father to paint a portrait from it, which he agreed to do. The result was not museum quality—my hopes were a bit too high and unfair to my father—but I nevertheless hung the painting on my bedroom wall for years. (He also did a painting for me of Wilt Chamberlain—same quality—from the cover of a Wilt biography that I had read several times during my initial NBA crush, which hung next to Marichal. Why I didn't choose Bill Russell, I have no idea.)

To digress a bit more on Marichal's odd pitching style, what made it so baffling, as hitters often lamented, was that from behind his absurdly high leg kick, he could throw the ball from nearly any angle, including straight over the top, submarine-style, and every possibility in between. And he could do so with a variety of pitches, including a fastball, curve, change-up, and a devastating screwball. "The best pitcher I ever batted against was Juan Marichal, because he threw so many goddamn different kinds of pitches against you," was Pete Rose's take on it, and Rose faced some of the best.

Perhaps worst of all to batters, he did all of this with pinpoint accuracy. The middle of the plate was a stranger to Marichal, who in 1966 walked a grand total of 36 batters over 307 innings, an average of barely one per game, while allowing a mere 228 hits. Over the past century, only seven pitchers in either league have had a better single season WHIP, a heady list that includes Sandy Koufax, Bob Gibson, Dave McNally, Greg Maddux, Pedro Martinez, and, most recently, Clayton Kershaw and Zack Greinke. In fact, Martinez, Kershaw, and fellow Giant Madison Bumgarner are the only starting pitchers since World War II who have a better career ranking than Marichal, and Martinez became the second Dominican player to enter the Hall of Fame, the only other being Marichal.

I should acknowledge, though, that I am aware that while statistics may fill the minds of baseball enthusiasts, such an avalanche of numbers, understandably, does not excite everyone, even some of those who made a living from sports. Old-time San Francisco sportswriter Abe Kemp, who started his journalism career more than a century ago and was a contrarian even on a good day, left no doubt where he stood on the matter of the beauty of numbers. "Statistics I detest," he wrote. "They're the scourge of the American sports page. The fifteenth time he wiped his ass; the sixteenth time he rubbed his nose. You're writing a story and you say he's six foot seven, he's four foot two, or his earned run average is —that's a lot of crap."

Well, such was the crap that I sought out nearly every day of my childhood, especially on my cards, and Kemp was right—there certainly was a lot of it, which suited me fine. And to finish the story on Kemp, who was never less than entertaining on sports or any other topic, he once related the story of a cub reporter's interview of a Berkeley student who had won a scholarly prize and claimed that she regularly ate beans to aid her intellect. When the next day's headline read, "Coed Eats Beans to Make Her Astute," Kemp noted that "torrents of letters poured into the *Examiner*. Hell, it was a blizzard." No doubt it was.

One item from my collection box, a yellow, hand-sized "memo book" (priced at 15 cents), provides another nostalgic glimpse of the influence of baseball cards—and other sports cards—in my life. The book is filled with page after page of handwritten major league lineups and statistical lists of all-time leaders in wins, hits, home runs, and other categories, as well as NFL rosters (the AFL was also on my radar—I had nearly all of the AFL cards—but evidently not yet on a par with the NFL in my young mind). The year for one particular entry must have been 1964, as my Red Sox lineup read:

> Felix Mantilla
> Tony Conigliaro (spelled Coniglaro)
> Carl Yastrzemski (spelled Yastremski)
> Dick Stuart
> Lee Thomas
> Frank Malzone
> Ed Bressoud
> Bob Tillman
> Dick Radatz

With Radatz as the pitcher, this was obviously never the starting lineup. I probably just couldn't bear to leave The Monster off the list. But knowing the names of big league lineups each year was a rite of passage for me, aided immeasurably by the ever-present cards. (Just flipping through the pages of this memo book now is a walk through sports history—for instance, the first four names for the Cleveland Browns are Jim Brown, Ernie Green, Lou Groza, and Gene Hickerson. A team could do worse.)

A final point about the beauty of scrutinizing the backs of baseball cards—and baseball history in general—is the "What if" speculation that inevitably occurs. Countless barroom patrons over many years have gone long past last call in animated debates on such questions that present both compelling human stories and, in a game dominated by numbers, great statistical teases.

These questions certainly were on my mind many times when I looked through my stacks of cards and the *Baseball Encyclopedia*. What if Pete Reiser had not run into outfield fences so hard? What if Herb Score had not gotten smashed in

128

the face by a line drive? What if Jackie Robinson could have made it to the majors at twenty, instead of twenty-eight? What if the tormented Steve Dalkowski could have put every second or third pitch in the strike zone? What if Sandy Koufax had had a healthy left elbow? (Or, for that matter, what if he had just been able to find the plate during his first six years in the majors?) Not to compare in any way the significance of baseball to that of war, but what if Ted Williams, Bob Feller, Joe DiMaggio, Warren Spahn, and Willie Mays had not lost multiple seasons, some in their prime, to military service? In the case of Williams, what if he had just been a nicer guy? When DiMaggio beat out Williams for the 1947 MVP, the inimitable Red Smith wryly noted, "It wasn't the first time Williams earned this award with his bat and lost it with his disposition." And, of course, what if Tony C had seen that pitch from Jack Hamilton a second sooner? Or, still from a Red Sox point of view, what if Boo Ferris, winner of 46 games, with 52 complete games, in his first *two* big league seasons, had not injured his shoulder at the youthful age of twenty-six in that fateful third season of 1947? The name of local hero Harry Agganis, the Golden Greek, has to be brought into the conversation as well, at least by Red Sox fans.

Last but not least is what I think of as the Cesar Cedeno syndrome, which affected players with great "potential" who started out with a bang and went on to have long and what seemingly could have/should have been Hall of Fame careers but, for various reasons ranging from injuries to the inexplicable, fell short, in some cases far short. The club would include Ralph Garr, Rico Carty, and Vada Pinson, along with a good number of others from later years, such as Don Mattingly and Nomar Garciaparra. Even the much-maligned Carl Crawford would belong—after all, by the age of 29, Crawford had accumulated 1480 hits, 105 triples, 409 stolen bases, and a .296 average.

What would the statistics of all these players look like, and how would that affect some of the great records of the

129

game, had their personal circumstances been different? We'll never know, which just guarantees that heated barroom and talk radio debates among baseball fans will endure.

8. The Impossible Dream

The year of 1967 may have produced the Summer of Love in San Francisco, but much of the rest of the world was enduring quite a different reality. Vietnam continued to be a quagmire that sucked in American soldiers by the hundreds of thousands, more than 11,000 of them destined, tragically, to return to their country that year in caskets. On the other side of Asia, in another Cold War conflict, Israel routed Arab forces in the Six Day War, with the conquered areas of East Jerusalem, Gaza, the West Bank, and the Golan Heights still in territorial dispute to this day, and perhaps to remain ever thus. In Africa, civil war broke out in Nigeria, where a food blockade became the weapon of choice against the people in Biafra, with emaciated children, dying by the thousands, being the haunting face of that depravity. Closer to home, the city of Detroit burned for nearly a week in July as race riots left 43 blacks and 10 whites dead. With racial and political strife intensifying, Martin Luther King Jr. was reaching mythic heights as the conscience of the country, a single year before he would die a martyr at the still-young age of thirty-nine, although King may have felt he had already lived several lifetimes in his defiance of racial hatred. And for much of the nation's youth, as their hair grew along with their loathing of anything their parents did (except sending in the college tuition checks on time), a generation gap gripped the country and split many families apart while nearly doing the same to the nation itself.

But on my eleven-year-old island of innocence, 1967 had nothing to do with such momentous affairs. My thoughts, as usual, were on baseball, and the Red Sox, as usual, were expected by most people I knew to do the same as they had done year after year: not much. The arrival of the 1967 season did not seem to herald any dramatic change from the previous years of bottom dwelling finishes for the Red Sox. They had the usual stable of can't miss prospects, which was no different than any other year since I had started following the team. My baseball cards gave me a thorough statistical understanding of the game, but the Red Sox team card always lacked the one statistic that mattered: wins.

Yet, in the depths of the mid-60s darkness, and largely unnoticed by most Red Sox fans, including me, seeds that had been planted were starting to grow. Lonborg had come up to the big club in 1965, with George Scott, Joe Foy, Reggie Smith, and Mike Andrews joining him the following year. Of course, Yaz, Rico, and Tony C were already fixtures in the lineup. There was also a take-no-prisoners new manager in Dick Williams, who clearly was not going to follow in the footsteps of his immediate predecessors. And the 1966 team, once they were a comfortable 25 games out of first place, had played .500 ball over the last two months of the season. *Sports Illustrated*, in its baseball preview, acknowledged the past but found reasons for Red Sox fans to keep hope alive. "Dick Williams promises not to tolerate the traditional Red Sox traits of individualism, inattention and ineptitude," *SI* noted. "If he can find some pitching, too, the 1967 Sox may revive baseball in Boston."

But hope, especially for a baseball fan, always springs eternal in March, and to me at that time, every year could be "The Year." Still, there was certainly no reason for a rational, adult Red Sox fan to dream about baseball in October. The fact that the Yankees were as bad as we were, and had been for a couple of years, provided some reassurance while looking ahead to the upcoming season.

The 1967 Red Sox went from laughingstock to contender in striking fashion. Early in the season, a young pitcher who would have an otherwise entirely forgettable career managed to electrify Red Sox fans—and his own teammates—with a near no-hitter in Yankee Stadium in his very first major league game. Although Billy Rohr finished with a one-hitter, the game seemed more memorable than the *actual* no-hitters that had come fairly frequently from Boston hurlers during the dark days of the early and mid-1960s. Maybe it was a harbinger. After all, in April, almost anything could be a harbinger to a Red Sox fan. We had nowhere to go but up.

And the team was winning. They were not tearing the league up, but they were winning at least as much as they were losing, which had rarely happened in my young lifetime. They were, as sports analysts like to say, hanging around. Maybe most surprisingly, the young players looked like they could genuinely play the game. Foy was a decent-hitting third baseman, and Petrocelli and Andrews were solid up the middle.

For me, most entertaining in the infield was George Scott, the lovable Boomer, who had grown up picking cotton in Mississippi with his mother. In fact, as a rookie in 1966, he was so thrilled to tell his mother that he had been named an All-Star that he shared the story, undoubtedly with great enthusiasm, with the media. Mickey Mantle, who worshipped his own father, read about Scott's elation in the newspaper and was impressed enough by his devotion to his mother that he made the classy gesture of praising Scott when he reached first base that day against the Sox.

As a slugger, a slick-fielding first baseman, and a spirited, good-natured soul who breezily dropped F-bombs in conversation like snowflakes in a blizzard, Scott rarely lacked for recognition. A budding star in Boston, Scott could not only hit home runs and strike out in spectacular fashion, but, for a baseball player who was built like an offensive tackle, he was the most graceful first baseman in the league. A ball in the dirt was nearly the same as a perfect throw to Scott, who had such soft hands that no bounce seemed particularly challenging to him. He could scoop an errant throw out of the dirt and start trotting back to the dugout in the same motion, as if he had no doubt that the ball would settle in his glove, the ump would come up with the right hand, and that was that. Truly, it was baseball magic. I used to almost hope for bad throws to first on occasion, just to see Scott lean down and pluck the ball from danger.

His swing reflected his supreme confidence. He would stand at the plate, staring out at the pitcher, and point his bat slowly and squarely in the direction of the mound each time as he cocked it, as if to dare the pitcher to throw him a strike. The Boomer undoubtedly missed many more strikes than he ever hit, but either way the entertainment factor was very high when he was up at bat. It was hard to dislike The Boomer. And it might be appropriate to add that, like Jim Rice later, Scott could get around the bases remarkably well. He ended his career with 60 triples—one more than even Yaz had. Not bad for a 200+-pound slugger.

The outfield was impressive as well. Yaz was a complete player now on a respectable team, rather than a lone star. He claimed that his most enjoyable year in baseball prior to 1967 had been his last year in the minors at Minneapolis, and no one could doubt him. Reggie Smith emerged as the center fielder of the future, a player who was solid in the outfield and who could hit for average and power from both sides of the plate. Smith's choice of batting stances always intrigued me. From the left side, he would hit with a totally closed stance, but from the right side, he used a totally open stance, waving his bat impatiently in each case. Tony C, always a fan favorite, continued to send rockets over The Wall on a regular basis and, with his movie star looks, be the darling of most female fans.

And the pitching staff, amazingly, was coming together. Lonborg was winning games at a dizzying clip, getting unexpected help from Jose Santiago and mid-season pickup Gary Bell, with John Wyatt saving them. This kind of good fortune had not often smiled down on the Red Sox.

The catching, miraculously, also improved. It had been a position of mediocrity since All-Star Rick Ferrell had played there three decades earlier. But the Red Sox received a shot in the arm with the August arrival of the estimable Elston Howard from the Yankees. The transaction gave me my first understanding of the timeless sports fact that no matter how much fans may dislike another star player on a rival team, when that star player from that dreaded team lands on your own roster, you are likely to become a big supporter. I never actually hated Elston Howard. In fact, I grudgingly liked Howard, Freehan, Earl Battey, and Johnny Romano, I think, just because they were much better catchers than anyone on the Red Sox.

But with Howard, we had someone who had been a star, and I was thrilled when I heard that the Red Sox obtained him. Never mind that he was old, on his last legs, and clearly near retirement. He couldn't do much at the plate anymore, to put it politely. A player who had once hit .348 for the 1961 Bronx Bombers, he hit for less than half that average with Boston. But, more importantly, he had played in and *won* World Series championships. Only people as old as my grandparents could hope to remember any connection between the Red Sox and World Series championships. Yes, Howard had been a legitimate star, a winner, and, as it would turn, a valuable addition to the Red Sox down the stretch. He played nearly every day because, as they say, he had been there before.

Even the Red Sox role players made lasting names for themselves in Red Sox lore. In an early June trade with the White Sox, the Red Sox swapped an aging Don McMahon for hard-nosed infielder Jerry Adair, who had had some solid years earlier in Baltimore that impressed teammate Dick Williams. With the Red Sox, Adair came up with clutch hits and gaudy fielding of the kind that make fans clamor for a player who they may have barely heard of the previous winter. Dalton Jones, a lifetime .235 hitter, had 13 pinch hits. In a key late season game against the White Sox, Jose Tartabull, a speedster with few other baseball skills, made a memorable and extremely unlikely throw to the plate from right field, erasing a run at home in another unmistakable sign that the Red Sox may be a team of destiny. Of course, Tartabull was in right field at the time because Tony C had been beaned. Even the tragedy of Tony C, it appeared, couldn't derail the Red Sox.

135

Nearly every player on the team, it seemed, was notable in some way, and one who certainly fell into that category for me was little-used Norm Siebern, a three-time All-Star now finishing up his fine career on the Red Sox bench. Siebern gained his moment of Impossible Dream fame with a pinch-hit, bases-loaded triple off Jim Coates to help the Red Sox win a key August game, 12–11, against the Angels at Fenway, a single swat that accounted for nearly half of his RBI's (7) that year with Boston.

As a player I had on cards every year since 1961, Siebern also was a familiar face who was connected to baseball history in a big way in my mind, mainly because he had been traded by the mighty Yankees to Kansas City for Roger Maris in a seven-player deal in 1959. As I collected cards in those early years and pored over the information printed on the backs, it was curious to see how many Yankees players had come over from the Athletics in the late 1950s. Clete Boyer, Ralph Terry, Bobby Shantz, Art Ditmar, and Hector Lopez, along with Maris, all had arrived from Kansas City. Years later, when I read of the rather shady relationship between the owners of the two teams and how the Yankees used the Athletics almost as a farm team, I had yet another reason to dislike the Bombers. Fortunately for the Red Sox, their own pick-ups from the Athletics—Santiago and Wyatt—provided key help, while the lowly 1967 Yankees were comparable to the Kansas City Athletics of almost *any* year.

One of the biggest reasons for the improved play of the Red Sox was Dick Williams himself. As with many other players and managers, I had my own past with Williams, and it was not encouraging. My card collection included a 1962 Post card of Williams when he was with the Orioles, and his numbers indicated that he would not be out of place with the Red Sox, which was not a compliment. With a .206 batting average and a total of 64 hits for the previous season, Williams was in Mike Ryan/George Smith territory. How many guys on the Red Sox, a team that seemed to need a psychologist more than a manager, were going to listen to someone with Williams's limited achievements on the field? At least Pesky and Herman had had the proper credentials statistically—both had been All-Stars, and Herman would later be voted into the Hall of Fame. Williams, on the other hand, had actually played on Pesky's moribund Red Sox teams in 1963 and 1964, fitting in nicely by hitting a robust .224.

But while baseball is a game of statistics, statistics was not baseball for Williams. His game was effort and discipline, both of which had been alien concepts to the Red Sox for longer than anyone cared to remember. He referred to himself as "the chairman of the board," with the other board members being coaches, not players. There was no longer any team captain. Players who didn't perform well were benched. Players who did perform well could expect little applause from Williams. He played no favorites, barking at everyone equally and often, including umpires and sportswriters. Watching Williams squawk with umpires was one of the memorable highlights of those years. He was not lovable, and he was not apologetic. He had promised that the Red Sox would win more than they would lose, and he focused on that one goal: winning. He was just what the team needed.

Most impressively, the Red Sox had stocked the 1967 team largely through its own scouting efforts. The entire outfield (Yaz, Reggie, Tony C) and infield (Foy, Rico, Andrews, and The Boomer), as well as the best pitcher (Lonborg) all had been signed or drafted by the Red Sox. With Neil Mahoney in charge of the farm system through most of the 1960s and O'Connell willing to bring up young players, black and white, with talent, a culture shift had occurred at Fenway. And O'Connell had an instinct for shrewd deals, such as purchasing or trading for Santiago, Wyatt, Tartabull, Adair, and Howard early on, and later pitchers Ray Culp, Dick Ellsworth, Sonny Siebert, and Gary Peters, drafting Carlton Fisk, Dwight Evans, Cecil Cooper, Bill Lee, Jim Rice, and Fred Lynn, and picking up Luis Tiant from the scrap heap of released players. He also had the courage to bring in a manager tough enough to change the team from a well-funded circus act to a hustling group of players focused on what was happening on the field.

Blessed by the facts that the Yankees were now a doormat and that no other dominant team had stepped up to replace the Bombers, the Red Sox not only were competitive but contenders by mid-season. Playing before increasingly large crowds and fighting with the Tigers, Twins, and White Sox for the top spot, the Red Sox, in one of the great stories of local lore, found themselves still in contention on the final Sunday of the season. What they needed was a win at home against Dean Chance and the Twins and a Tigers' loss in a doubleheader against the Angels. In "Impossible Dream" style, the Red Sox got both, with Yaz getting four hits ("Yaz Sir, That's My Baby") and Rich Rollins popping out to Rico Petrocelli before, as Ned Martin famously declared, there was pandemonium on the field. When Dick McAuliffe, who had grounded into exactly one double play all year, grounded into a double play, the dream was no longer impossible. The Cardiac Kids, with Yaz going 23 for 44 in a torrid stretch run, had vaulted from the ninth place to first in one season, heading into a showdown with the Cardinals in the World Series, a historical rematch of the 1946 World Series, as all of the old-timers, including my father, reminded us every chance they got. And not insignificantly to Red Sox fans, they had finished *twenty* games in front of the hapless Yankees.

Boston was swamped by championship fever, which showed how much of a baseball town it was, as the Red Sox had barely made it to the Series at all that year and hadn't actually won it in nearly fifty years. The Celtics, on the other hand, had put up nine championship banners in the previous eleven years, but no one would have used the word *fever* to describe anyone's feelings toward them, inside or outside of Boston.

The likelihood of the Red Sox defeating the Cardinals four times in less than two weeks was, well, very unlikely. St. Louis had beaten the last of the great Yankees teams in the

World Series just three years earlier, and with Orlando Cepeda coming off an MVP season and Bob Gibson ready to start three of the games if necessary, the situation was not heartening. Still, the Sox could counter with their own MVP in Yaz and 22-game winner Jim Lonborg, along with a youthful lineup that had shown that it would not wilt under pressure. The fact that the team was even *in* a World Series gave me a level of excitement that might be detrimental to my health at my present age.

In those years, the All-Star and World Series games were played under the sun, so how to actually see, or at least hear, the games was a legitimate hurdle facing many fans, including me. In fact, one of my main memories of the World Series from those years was being in the car as my family drove back from my grandparents' house on a Sunday afternoon in October 1964 and hearing the dramatic call as Ken Boyer hit a grand slam to beat Al Downing at The Stadium (in a game that took a tidy 2:18 to complete).

The Fall Classic, though, had not been an issue for the Red Sox, as they previously had never been a threat to be playing in October, at least in my brief lifetime. In past years, I had grown accustomed to watching other teams play in the World Series, which almost always seemed to feature the Dodgers, a team that was sort of unreal, nearly exotic, to me. (For most of 1965, they used an infield made up entirely of switch-hitters.) I rarely saw them play a regular season game, as they were in the National League. Also, they often played late at night, so scores of their games were never available until the next day, and even then, the newspapers just said "late game" instead of a score. Adding to the Dodgers' legendary status, many baseball experts agreed that Koufax could throw faster than anyone since Walter Johnson—"you can't hit what you can't see," was Ty Cobb's take on Johnson's fastball—Willie Davis and Maury Wills could both run faster than the wind, and almost no Dodger could hit a home run. I knew the last one was true myself because the stats on the backs of my baseball cards verified it. They had no power, and runs were always at a premium. Once Don Drysdale, with a night off, was told that Koufax had just pitched a no-hitter. "Did he win?" Drysdale asked. But as familiar as the Dodgers were with the World Series in my youth, the Red Sox were strangers until 1967.

Missing some of a Dodgers-Yankees, or a Cardinals-Yankees, or a Dodgers-Twins, or a Dodgers-Orioles World Series game was very annoying but survivable. Missing some of a Red Sox World Series game against *anyone* was unthinkable. But all of the World Series games would be played in the afternoon, most of them when I was in school. That was a true dilemma.

Luck was shining upon me, though, in that fateful fall. I was in sixth grade at the time, in my last year of elementary school, and my teacher, a kindly and evidently influential man, was able to snare what may have been the only television in the school—black and white, of course—and allowed his students, and himself, to watch under the guise of learning about "current events," or some such excuse. We did get to watch some of the early innings before it was time to race home to see the end. The results of the Series to the old-timers should have been pre-ordained—the Red Sox would lose in seven because they were the Red Sox and not the Cardinals. But experiencing the thrill of the chase apparently was irresistible, in school or at home, to all of us.

The Series had the potential to be a classic, and it did not disappoint. Lonborg threw a one hitter in the second game, Yaz was immense in the field and at the plate, and it all came down to the seventh game at Fenway. The fairy tale came crashing to a halt, though, with the right arm of Gibson, who won for the third time, all complete games, outpitching Lonborg, who had to go on short rest and just wasn't up to it. Even in the bullpen warm-ups that day, Lonborg "couldn't break a pane of glass," reliever Dan Osinski noted.

As is often the case in these situations, the batting hero in the Series for St. Louis was not the marquee player but the supporting cast. The bat of Orlando Cepeda was silent. It was

Julian Javier, Lou Brock, and old Yankee nemesis, Roger Maris, who did the Red Sox in. They got the hits and scored the runs, while Gibson took care of the rest. For the Sox, there was no shame in losing to such a talented group, and the team's best years seemed to be ahead. Even Yaz, the veteran, was only twenty-eight. For me, it was extremely disappointing but hardly a disaster.

Still, to get all the way to the seventh game—it had been tantalizingly close, and with the Red Sox, you never did know when the chance might come again. With his usual style and grace, Roger Angell described the ambiguous sense felt by Red Sox fans, certainly including me:

> The laurels all are cut, the year draws in the day, and we'll to the Fens no more. A great baseball season—the most intense and absorbing of our times—is over.... Hundreds of thousands of New Englanders must winter sadly on a feast of memory. The autumn quiet that now afflicts so many of us has almost nothing to do with the Red Sox defeat in the last game of the World Series, for every Boston fan has grown up with that dour Indian-pudding taste in his mouth. New England's loss is not of a game or a series but of the baseball summer just past—a season that will not come again, not ever quite the same.

It was a gnawing loss that had taken less than two and a half hours to unfold on the field but required days and weeks afterward to absorb, even if we admitted, however reluctantly, that the Cardinals were the superior team. Still, for Red Sox fans, "wait till next year" had a much more optimistic sound to it in the fall of 1967, and it was true that I could hardly wait for the next season to begin.

For me personally, the team's success had unintended and unfortunate consequences that I had not foreseen. Red Sox fans, long accustomed to failure but still hopeful at heart, had taken up their usual support posts next to the radio or in front of the TV as the early season unfolded. They were not, predictably, at Fenway. There were still few bragging rights in saying that you were going to a Sox game that night.

My father had brought me to five games each year from 1963 through 1966, and we started out in 1967 with the same intention but never got to the finish line. In previous years, we had had no trouble getting tickets, buying them right at the window, sometimes twenty minutes before the first pitch. Yet, as the Red Sox kept on winning that summer, or at least not losing so much, fans started showing up for games. Suddenly, there *were* bragging rights to having Sox tickets.

When things really heated up around mid-July, our easy trek in and out of Fenway became a challenge that my father had not expected and was in no mood to deal with. The crowded trolley cars, the wait at the ticket line, the constant getting up and down from your seat as someone went to buy still more refreshments, the crush of people jostling to get out of the park at the end of the game—all were an unwanted hassle to my father. A somewhat wobbly patron who spilled a sizable amount of his beverage on my father's shoes as he stumbled past us along the aisle may have sealed our fate at Fenway. What had been a relaxing night out for us morphed into a baseball version of rush-hour mayhem. His heart never having quite been won over by the Red Sox—his abiding love for the Braves of his youth was proof that the first cut is the deepest—my father's patience was limited, headed toward extinction.

It was great that the team was winning—there were no complaints on that end. But my father and I got to only four games that year, and I recognized that the Fenway party, and a large part of my childhood, was suddenly on very shaky ground. All I could do was hope for the best, both for me and for the Red Sox.

142

A final memory of note from that improbable season involves the matter of what makes a no-hitter a no-hitter, and what makes a complete game a complete game. Dean Chance brought this to mind when he hurled five perfect innings against the Red Sox on August 6 before the skies opened up and rain cancelled the remainder of the game, giving the Twins a 2–0 home victory. Chance was credited with a complete game but not a no-hitter. ("Believe me, boys, I'm glad it rained," Chance, happy for the win, told reporters after the game. Two weeks later, Chance did pitch a legitimate no-hitter in a 2–1 win over the Indians.) At the opposite end of the spectrum, Reds ace Jim Maloney, in 1965, pitched 10 hitless innings (in which he struck out 18 and threw 6 wild pitches) but lost, 1–0, in 11 innings to the Mets on a Johnny Lewis homer. Officially, it is a complete game but is no longer considered a no-hitter, although it was called a no-hitter under the rules at the time.

According to the present rules, a no-hitter is not an official no-hitter if the game does not go at least nine innings, even if the pitcher does go the distance in the shortened game, but is also not a no-hitter even if the pitcher does pitch nine hitless innings (or more) but does not go the entire game. On the other hand, a complete game *is* credited to the pitcher if the game itself goes a mere five innings yet is *not* awarded if the pitcher goes more than nine innings but not the entire game. Maloney had the same official result—a complete game but not a no-hitter—against the Mets as Chance had against the Red Sox. Yet if Maloney had not given up the Lewis homer and had been replaced by a reliever in the twelfth inning, he would have been credited with neither a no-hitter nor a complete game despite having pitched twice as many innings as Chance, and no-hit innings at that. And in the case of Chance, one could ask the nearly impenetrable question: how is it possible for a pitcher to lose credit for a no-hitter because it was not a complete game and still receive credit for having pitched a complete game in the same game? I'm not suggesting that this is an issue that anyone should ponder at length, but it does seem to be a contradiction, or at least a bizarre inconsistency, in the rules of baseball.

9. Yaz

While there would have been no Impossible Dream without Carl Yastrzemski, his rock star popularity that year was far more the exception than the rule over the course of his lengthy career. Even with the hyper-coverage of Red Sox teams in recent years, it is not an exaggeration to say that Yaz received scrutiny, including plentiful doses of criticism, fair or otherwise, that rivaled the attention received by the most controversial players today or probably of any era. Year after year, Yaz was *the* lightning rod among all Red Sox players, and one of the biggest in the major leagues.

Everything—his actual ability, his batting stance, his base running smarts, his effort at running out ground balls, his relationships with fans, teammates and owners, his enigmatic moods, his selfishness/unselfishness, his family life, his fishing, even his postgame cigarettes—all came constantly under the microscope of journalists, talk show callers, and barroom experts who were eager to give their own version of how to "explain" Yaz. Who knows how Yaz himself felt about the undying attention? Perhaps his enduring silence, which has now become legendary but respected, says it all. As a boy in the 1960s, I loved watching him play and finding his baseball card in a pack—the rest was all background noise. Still, in a book on the Red Sox, Yaz must be "explained," certainly a well-trodden path in the city of Boston.

From a baseball perspective, a question that raged in the day and continues to flare up even now on occasion is whether Yaz was a legitimate Hall of Famer or just one of the "statistical" members, a player who hung around so long that he had to make it just because of his staggering career numbers.

Yaz does not owe anyone an apology for being in the Hall of Fame. He is where he belongs. Still, he was not Joe DiMaggio, so there is at least room for discussion. His talents were impressive, but not equally so across the board. His MVP/Triple Crown year of 1967 was really what made Yaz a baseball legend. Still, two areas of his game that were truly stellar were his peerless fielding and his consistently high level of performance over more than two decades.

Regarding Yaz's fielding, he was as talented as any of the elite outfielders of the day, a group that included Mays, Clemente, Kaline, Curt Flood, Paul Blair, Ken Berry, Jim Landis, and Mickey Stanley. Had any of them played left field at Fenway Park, it is not likely they would have been better than Yaz.

Yaz would get an A+ in any fielding category, a genuine accomplishment considering the park he played in. For decades, The Wall has wreaked havoc on outfielders and on baserunners, offering ample proof that an unusual level of anticipation and instinct is necessary to avoid embarrassment or worse for most players once a ball sails out toward left field in Fenway Park. Yaz could instantly judge if a fly ball was gone, going off The Wall, or playable on the warning track. If the ball was a bomb, Yaz sometimes didn't even turn around to look, keeping his hands planted on his knees and simply waiting for the next batter. If a ball was not gone but was going to be close, Yaz was brilliantly effective at decoying by trotting back to The Wall and looking up at the net lackadaisically, acting as if the ball were out, and then suddenly bare-handing the carom and throwing a strike back to the infield, often catching a bewildered runner jogging toward second base or even fleeing back to first base. If the ball was going to hit The Wall within ten feet of the ground, Yaz would go back to the base of The Wall and calmly time his jump, stealing many extra base hits from frustrated batters. And Yaz could charge a base hit, scoop it up on the dead run, and make a strong, accurate throw to any base. He was not a flashy player, and there was seldom any wasted motion with Yaz, but if he needed to leave his feet to make a catch, he would do it, sometimes in spectacular fashion, as Tom Tresh once found out when his shot to left field looked like it would break up Billy Rohr's no-hit effort. Very rarely did Yaz drop a fly ball—actually, I don't *ever* recall seeing that happen—misjudge a carom, or throw to the wrong base. His fielding was unsurpassed—he was as solid an outfielder as there was in baseball.

The numbers testify to his performance: Yaz won seven Gold Gloves and led American League outfielders in assists seven times, including five consecutive seasons of leading all leftfielders in the league. Years after he retired, Yaz remarked in an interview, "It's funny. I remember defensive plays as much as offensive. Probably better." To those who witnessed Yaz patrolling left field, his statement was not hard to understand.

In his years before reaching superstardom in 1967, Yaz was an excellent example of a solid, pure hitter. He hit for both average and at least decent power, and used the entire field at Fenway. He led the league in doubles three of his first six years in the league, and many of those were balls on the outer half of the plate that Yaz just went with, sending either a line drive or a lofty fly ball, well-directed, toward The Wall. There was no overshift on Yaz in those days, as he was not definable as a dead-pull hitter.

At the same time, if he got a misplaced fastball from the middle in, he absolutely could turn on it and send a rocket over the bullpen in right field. The point was that you could not pitch Yaz a certain way, as he had no glaring weaknesses at the plate. High fastballs were always a temptation difficult for him to lay off, but woe to the pitcher who attempted to throw a high fastball past Yaz but instead didn't get it quite high enough.

In most other areas, Yaz fell somewhere between good and very good, but, as a credit to his dedication to the game, he remained in that range for twenty-three seasons. Yaz's longevity enabled him to amass the gaudy numbers well-known to his supporters—3419 hits, 452 home runs, 1844 RBI's—while maintaining a .285 average. True, his prime as a power hitter consisted of only three exceptional years, but one of those was among the greatest seasons in modern baseball history, in which he won both the Triple Crown and the MVP, and he went 7 for 8 on the final weekend when the Red Sox absolutely needed to win both games. His postseason play—a .352 average in 14 World Series games, and numerous gems in the field—was praiseworthy, and he was chosen for eighteen All-Star games. Yaz may not be a no-discussion Hall of Famer to some, but it would be a tiny Hall if Yaz and his peers were left out.

To me as a fan, Yaz also had the admirable quality of being someone who conducted himself with dignity on the field, not unlike, say, Al Kaline. When he hit one out, he ran around the bases and into the dugout in good stride—it was almost never his goal to show up a pitcher. As a fielder, he earned many ovations, acknowledging them with a wave that could be interpreted as "Thank you very much, but now please stop, as I'd rather just be playing left field than receiving so much attention." He certainly never encouraged applause of any kind to be directed at himself. While off the field he was a cutup at times with his teammates, fans never saw that side of Yaz between the lines. He did argue at times with umpires, a popular target being Ed Runge, a pitcher's umpire. Yaz reportedly once said to Runge, "Ed, you're the second-best umpire in the league. The other twenty-three are tied for first." He also sometimes dropped his bat at the plate after a called third strike and, on one memorable occasion, covered home plate with piles of dirt. Still, Yaz didn't erupt often, and like many stars, he probably had good reasons when he did.

When he was at the plate, the look of intense concentration on his face made it clear that Yaz was doing what he had always labored so hard to master: the act of hitting a baseball. His ritual in the batter's box remains etched in my mind. After walking up to the plate, Yaz would give his pants an instinctive tug at the waist, scoop up some dirt, dig his back foot firmly in the box, studiously look out at the pitcher and the alignment of fielders, and deliberately set himself in his stance, his body bent just a bit forward, his hands up near his head, with his bat cocked high and waving slightly in anticipation until the pitch was on its way. In his home-run hitting days, when he swung and missed, sometimes the power of his swing would cause his left knee to buckle and drop to the ground, his whole body momentarily contorted in a spasm of failure, with a flashing grimace on his face, before, in his dignified way, he would right himself and start the process all over again.

But while his determination to excel at playing baseball was unquestioned, his on-the-field hustle was, on occasion, lacking, a criticism aimed at him by managers and fans and not always without merit. Like many players before and since, he did not run out every routine ground ball to second base, and this at times absolutely did bother Pesky, Herman, and Williams. In fact, in 1969 Williams once fined Yaz $500 for not running hard enough to home plate on a close play, an opinion Yaz disputed. In *Ball Four*, Jim Bouton famously noted that Yaz "has a bit of dog in him," adding that when he asked Yaz's teammates about the validity of the fine, they replied, "He deserved it all the way." (Given the state of affairs with the Red Sox clubs of those days, that opinion may have said as much about the teammates as it did about Yaz.)

Willingly or not, Yaz was looked upon as the leader of the team, and his lapses in hustle were hard to justify, even on those pre-1967 clubs when lack of hustle was practically a team requirement. Yet, even Pesky marveled at Yaz's love of the game and his fierce determination to improve and compete. If Yaz could get out of bed in the morning, he was likely to be in the lineup. It was that simple. The consistency with which he played in almost every game, every year (at the age of forty, he was in 147 games and hit .270), is a testament to his respect for the game and for himself. It is hard to imagine Yaz asking out of a game or taking a day off. I'm not saying it never happened— maybe he did duck some tough southpaws, but if so, it was very rare. More likely was that most managers would take twenty-five players with the dedication of Yaz, one notable exception being the irascible, and former Boston Brave great, Eddie Stanky, who foolishly saw Yaz as an All-Star "from the neck down." Yaz worked diligently on his game, up to his final season, and he stayed in shape.

It wasn't always his play on the field that brought attention to Yaz. The Red Sox for many of his years on the team were like a traveling carnival, and, for better or worse, he was the face of the franchise. Fans loved to heap criticism on the team, either for losing constantly before 1967, or for not winning enough after, and Yaz, with his bounteous salary, took much of the blame. Through most of it for fans, fact was hard to tell from fiction. How much did Yaz really go to Yawkey and complain about losing, or blame other players or the manager? Judging by their record, not often enough.

Yaz was especially pilloried on the radio talk shows, much to my youthful consternation. After a while, the rant was predictable and indiscriminate: no flaw of Yaz's went unnoticed, and more than a few were invented along the way. "Yaz is a prima donna," "Yaz dogs it," "Yaz is selfish," "Yaz is a clubhouse lawyer," "Yaz only swings for the fences," "Yaz won't bunt," "Yaz has no baseball IQ," "Yaz loves his own stats," "Yaz is a manager-killer," and on and on. Generally, these comments came from middle-aged men who may have resented Yaz from the day he "replaced" Ted Williams. Or maybe they just resented his six-figure contracts, or his aloofness that was interpreted as a kind of snobbery.

Whatever—if there was criticism to be leveled at the Red Sox, Yaz was the first, and often the main, target. Undoubtedly the memories of these years of being under verbal and printed assault influenced Yaz to some extent. In September of 1977, Red Sox rookie Ted Cox set a major league record when he collected six hits in his first six at bats over two games, leading a reporter to ask Yaz, then thirty-eight, if he would like to be in Cox's position and starting out again as a big leaguer. "Oh no. No thanks," Yaz replied. "I'm glad to be my age." To Yaz, much of his Red Sox past may have been an impossible dream, for better and worse.

The negativity toward Yaz softened considerably in his later years with the team, as his longevity provided him with a kind of iconic status among many, particularly the die-hard Yaz fans, but the resentment of Yaz never disappeared entirely.

Regarding how Yaz himself felt about the fans' unflattering views, it is interesting to compare his situation with that of another favorite target of Sox fans (and writers), Ted Williams. Entering the major leagues with a chip on his shoulder after a difficult upbringing in San Diego and a determination to become the greatest hitter who ever lived, Williams demonstrated throughout his career that his focus at the ballpark was on what happened on the field—his job was to hit a baseball, not to go out of his way to please the fans, and he was not shy about expressing that sentiment, whether he was spitting at them, refusing to tip his cap, or offering any other of his myriad antics from a well-stocked arsenal of animosity. (This is not in any way meant to take away from the considerable time that Ted Williams generously gave in supporting the Jimmy Fund. His comment, "Look, it embarrasses me to be praised for anything like this…. It's only a freak of fate, isn't it, that one of those kids isn't going to grow up to be an athlete and I wasn't the one who had the cancer," shows the sincerity and empathy that Williams truly felt toward the stricken children.)

Yaz, on the other hand, did not react to the criticism in the visceral way that Williams had. Largely, he simply endured it. In truth, Yaz, in his solitary way, seemed to feed off of his own professional pride far more than the cheers or jeers of the fans. After a disappointing 1971 season in which Yaz, troubled by a nagging thumb injury, saw his average drop 75 points and his homers fall from 40 to 15, he made a telling comment to Jimmy Cannon the following spring. "Sure you play for money," he told Cannon. "But you look for recognition from your fellow players. That's why this year is so important. You want to get back that admiration from the players." It is no surprise that Yaz referenced *the players*. Before his peers, Yaz had enormous determination to excel. It probably should be understandable that, given the public vitriol he often faced, Yaz was rather less focused on pleasing the fans. In good conscience, who could fault him?

Still, when Williams, in 1960, and Yaz, in 1983, faced their own swan songs in their final games at Fenway, their approaches to the fans were revealing. Williams, not surprisingly to anyone, remained a model of consistency. In the ceremony at home plate prior to the game with the Orioles, Red Sox announcer Curt Gowdy introduced Williams as the greatest hitter who ever lived, and after some additional comments from Mayor John Collins and a Chamber of Commerce representative, Williams stepped to the microphone. Unable to resist the temptation, Williams, in Trump-like style, took aim at the "Knights of the Keyboard"—the scribes who had been his nemesis since the start—and noted the "disagreeable things" they had said about him as he nodded his head toward the press box. Then, shifting gears, Williams praised Yawkey as the greatest owner in baseball, stating that Boston was the one place he would choose to play baseball and, in a magnanimous and unexpected gesture, declared that the Boston fans were the best in the country.

Such a thawing of the ice between the hater and the hated was unlikely to last, even in such a typically sentimental moment, and didn't. In the eighth inning, after receiving a standing ovation, Williams hit his fabled home run off Jack Fisher in his last at bat, rounding the bases quickly and heading into the dugout, all the while failing to tip his cap or make any gesture to acknowledge the relentless cheering of the fans. Rather than pulling Williams from the lineup in the top of the ninth, manager Pinky Higgins sent him out to left field for a cameo appearance, giving the Splendid Splinter a chance, at least in a small way, to make amends with the sparse crowd of 10,000.

But Williams would have none of it. When Higgins took him out a moment later, Williams strode back across the field and into the dugout, head down, defiant to the end, despite the applause raining down on him from the hardy faithful in the stands. In the clubhouse afterwards, Ed Linn, reporting for *Sport*, asked Williams if he had had any wish at all to leave on a positive note with the fans. Williams replied, "I felt nothing." When asked again, he repeated himself: "I said *nothing*. Nothing, nothing!" Linn characterized the whole of Williams' career by writing, "When he walked out of the park, he kept his eyes to the front and never looked back."

Yaz, on the other hand, did choose to look back in his final moments at Fenway, and in a most heartfelt way. In front of a sellout crowd in an otherwise meaningless afternoon game against the Indians, Yaz, full of emotion, took the high road, and no one could say it wasn't sincere. At the pre-game farewell ceremony, Yaz stood silently, waving repeatedly to the crowd, while for six minutes a torrent of cheers cascaded from the stands. And in a very un-Williams-like moment, Yaz addressed the crowd with humility and grace, closing with, "New England, I love you."

Following the ceremony, Yaz, forgoing a drive around the field to show his gratitude to the delirious fans, instead chose to jog around the perimeter of Fenway, touching as many outstretched hands as he could. When asked later what the screaming masses had said to him, Yaz replied, "They just kept saying, 'We Love You, Yaz,' over and over. I'll never forget it." During much of his eventful career, he could hardly have imagined such a culmination to his years at Fenway.

What I never forgot in my own Yaz-world was the thrill of getting Yaz on a baseball card, and I had him on a card every year that I collected them. Oddly, he had the same photo on his 1964 baseball card as he had had on his card the previous year. Why, I have no idea, but the photo is intriguing because of the

153

inscrutable expression on Yaz's face. It's not exactly a Mona Lisa look, but the effect is certainly one of mystery, reflecting the actual nature of his personality, as far as most fans were concerned.

In the photo, Yaz is staring ahead but slightly off to his left, his look more pondering than focused, his eyes slightly sad or perhaps just impatient with the whole picture-taking process. His mouth is barely short of what may be called tight-lipped. The "not's" in the photo are easier to describe. He is not happy, he is not welcoming, and he is not about to share whatever his thoughts are with anyone. That, to many fans, was Yaz: a great ballplayer on the field, otherwise tough to figure. I had the 1964 card, and, as much as I rooted for Yaz, that photo bothered me in some way. I much preferred looking at my 1962 rookie card of Yaz, from the back of the cereal box, where he had what might be called a smile on his face—at the very least, he looked like he was into the whole thing, even raising his glove in a hint of enthusiasm.

Yaz was an enigma when he played, and to some extent will probably always remain so in Red Sox lore. One day in the spring training camp of 1968, following a busy winter of banquets and speeches, Yaz, as he often did, was taking extra batting practice. Observing Yaz's fixation on his craft, Roger Angell wrote, "It came to me that all this was not just preparation for what was to come but that here, strangely, was a place where he could find privacy. Inside the cage, inside the game, he was alone, approachable only by his fellows and subject only to the demands of his hard profession."

For fans who wanted Yaz to share himself in a much more public way, such behavior was at least highly questionable, if not unacceptable altogether. But for those who took their disenchantment with Yaz to something bordering on hatred, for whatever reason, I believe they missed the point. For while Yaz was not Willie Mays, he brought a level of grace and determination to the game, every day for over two decades, which was a joy to watch on so many occasions. A perfect throw from the left field corner to second base, a decoy on a ball off The Wall, a shot hit over the bullpen area, a ten-pitch walk—all contributed to the pleasure of watching Yaz play on a daily basis. Most importantly, the Red Sox were a better team because of Yaz. People who found reasons to criticize Yaz to the point of anger had issues other than Yaz to deal with. That was my simple explanation for the worst of the Yaz-bashers.

One point that members of the anti-Yaz crowd tended to have in common, not surprisingly, was a strong resentment of his mega-salary, which hit $100,000 following the Impossible Dream season. And the fact that the money reminded people of Yaz's cozy relationship with Yawkey had effects other than just annoying working-class fans. It irritated players as well, one being Curt Flood, who was a star on two World Series winners with the Cardinals (one, of course, over the Red Sox) in a stellar career, capturing seven Gold Gloves, making three All-Star teams, and batting .293 over twelve seasons. Flood, it should be noted, made $90,000 himself.

But in 1969, when the Cardinals traded Flood to the Phillies in a multi-player deal that included, among others, Tim McCarver (going) and Richie Allen (coming), Flood, who deeply resented having his place of employment being a matter entirely in the hands of team owners, sued Major League Baseball over the soon-to-be-famous "reserve clause" and refused to play for Philadelphia. In a letter to Commissioner Bowie Kuhn, Flood came right to the point: "I do not feel I am a piece of property to be bought and sold irrespective of my wishes."

In interviews, Flood went so far as to compare his situation to that of a slave, which did little to enhance his bargaining power in the court of public opinion or in actual courts of law. "A well-paid slave is nonetheless a slave," was Flood's view. A sportswriter retorted, "Flood may become the first petitioning slave in the history of the Republic to have a Swiss bank account." Flood, understandably, may have come upon his sense of slavery while playing in the minors in the

1950s and hearing southern fans call him a "goddamned nigger son of a bitch." And the slavery analogy was not new: twenty years earlier, in 1949, Federal Judge Jerome Frank had observed of the owners' stance, "Only the totalitarian-minded will believe that high pay excuses virtual slavery."

Flood sat out an entire season and took his case all the way to the U.S. Supreme Court, where he lost in 1972 but ultimately paved the way for the "10-5 rule" that gave at least veteran players their first chance at economic liberty.

But what clearly bothered Flood in addition to his lack of freedom in baseball was the yawning gap in the attitudes of his fellow players toward what he saw as their own servitude to the owners. Some players, including Bob Gibson, Vada Pinson, Jim Grant, and Richie Allen (who was himself, as mentioned, traded for Flood) shared Flood's frustration, but others, Flood was not shy about pointing out, did not. He cast his eye particularly on stars who had gaudy salaries and very comfortable connections with the same owners who solely determined their fates, for better or worse. In his autobiography, Flood was especially impatient with teammate Stan Musial. After acknowledging that Musial was "exceptionally talented, popular, and durable," Flood went on to say that Musial "not only accepted baseball mythology but propounded it," labeling him "unfathomably naive" and too full of comments about how "wunnerful" it was to play for the Cardinals and about "his own good fortune" in St. Louis.

Flood felt much the same about Yaz. Again, he did not mince words. "The most vociferous champion of the *status quo*," Flood wrote, "is Carl Yastrzemski, a go-getter for whom a bright future is predicted in the upper reaches of baseball administration." (Apparently Flood did not realize how much Yaz preferred going fishing over sitting at a desk.) Referring to Yaz following the Red Sox loss in the 1967 World Series, Flood mocked him as "the glamor boy" who "rebounded from defeat with about $200,000 worth of contracts" for product endorsements.

156

For his part, Yaz was indeed vocal about Flood's actions and their effect on baseball. After the player representatives from each team voted unanimously to back Flood, Yaz told Marvin Miller, executive director of the players' association, that all of the players, not merely the team representatives, should have been allowed to vote. "That backing should never have been given to Flood," he insisted. And no matter who voted, Yaz made it clear where he stood: "Personally I am against what Curt Flood is trying to do because it would ruin the game," a view that perfectly reflected the owners' thoughts as well.

Miller informed the players of Yaz's comments, not only not sympathizing with Yaz's outlook but going so far as to clearly illustrate the personal connection between Yaz and the opposition management. He noted that prior to the 1969 season, Yaz, in Miller's view, had tried to damage the union's pension negotiations, and that American League President, and former Red Sox General Manager, Joe Cronin, who was close to Yaz, had attempted to foist a weakened pension proposal upon the players. Joe Torre, the Cardinals' team representative and obviously a teammate of Flood's, conceded that Flood "is not an easy person to get to know." But he sided with Flood and felt that Yaz's comments were ill-advised. "If Carl Yastrzemski would come to our meetings once in a while, take time to find out what's going on—take time out from his busy personal schedule—he may not have made some of the statements he has," Torre asserted.

To be fair to Yaz, he was in esteemed company regarding Flood's decision to test the reserve clause, and while many of the players were (like Flood) already in the stratospheric salary brackets, skin color was not a factor. Harmon Killebrew, Frank Howard, Ron Santo, Gaylord Perry, Frank Robinson, Hank Aaron, Billy Williams, Ernie Banks, and Willie Mays all either disagreed with Flood or were noncommittal. Even retired greats, including Joe DiMaggio,

Bob Feller, Robin Roberts, Gil Hodges, and Ralph Kiner, rejected Flood's arguments about baseball as a form of slavery.

The likely truth with Yaz was that he spoke honestly but probably had, in fact, formed many of his views after discussions with Yawkey and others in management, and in any case would have felt extremely uncomfortable opposing Yawkey on such a key issue. And just to put a human face on the matter, Yaz, like many players, had not come from money and undoubtedly did not take his financial largesse for granted. Following his first batting championship in 1963, Yaz himself had to fight management for more money—when General Manager Pinky Higgins told Yaz that Frank Malzone was the highest paid player and would remain that way, Yaz replied, "Well, give him a raise." So Yaz was not always a lackey of ownership. But he was hardly feeling like a slave, either.

In fact, the beginning of the end for my father's interest in baseball may have come with Yaz's first $100,000 contract, an amount that was, I'm guessing, easily more than twenty times what my father was making at the time. Baseball, as has often been said, always accurately, is a boy's game, and for a grown man to get paid that much money to do what boys had been doing cheerfully and for free for a century—it must have seemed too absurd to a blue-collar worker, and probably even to much better paid workers as well. Not surprisingly, my father started with his "what would Johnny Mize be worth today?" soliloquies around that time, and as salaries spiraled ever higher over the years, his questioning of the money did as well.

My father and I standing next to one of our unreliable cars.
But with the dawn of baseball in my life, those were happy days.
(Personal Collection)

I was 12 years old in 1968, my last year of Little League. I'm standing behind my house, near
the clotheslines—our backyard ballfield, just out of view, was to the left.
(Personal Collection)

159

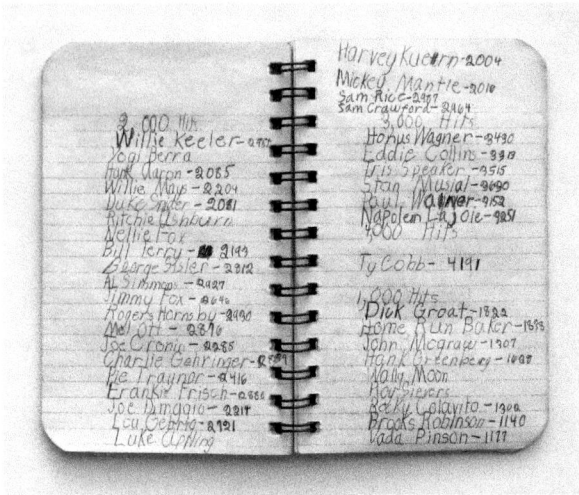

No matter how far back they went, baseball statistics never got old to me,
as these typical pages from my notebook illustrate. Based on the numbers, this entry was
written following the 1964 season, when I was 8 years old.
(Personal Collection)

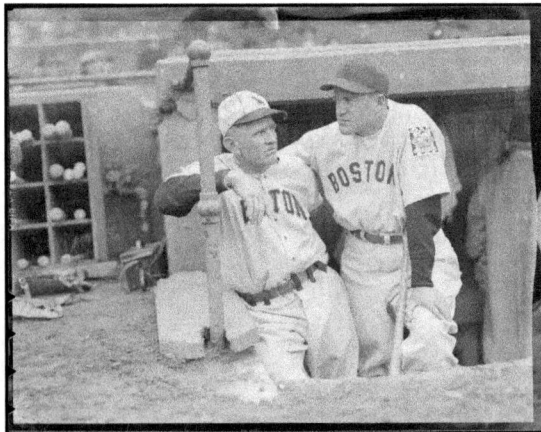

Bees manager Casey Stengel and Red Sox manager Joe Cronin chatting on April 15, 1939 at
Braves Field (known as National League Park or "The Beehive" at the time). The game took
place during the annual City Series prior to the opening of the major league season. My
father, 13 years-old at that time, would certainly have been cheering for Stengel's team.
(Courtesy of the Boston Public Library, Leslie Jones Collection)

My oldest baseball card, appropriately one of Teddy Ballgame.
(Personal Collection)

The 1959 Red Sox infield (L-R) of Frank Malzone, Don Buddin, Pumpsie Green, and Pete
Runnels, which was strong at the corners but decidedly weaker up the middle. I had all of
these players on baseball cards in my earliest days of collecting.
(Courtesy of the Boston Public Library, Leslie Jones Collection)

For one brief, shining moment, the career of Don Schwall (R) was on a par with that of
Warren Spahn, as they compared notes on the mound before the 1961 All-Star game at
Fenway Park, played on July 31, the second of two All-Star games that year. Schwall gave up 5
hits and a run in 3 innings, while Spahn had gone 3 hitless innings in the first game, played on
July 11 at Candlestick Park in San Francisco.
(Courtesy of the Boston Public Library, Leslie Jones Collection)

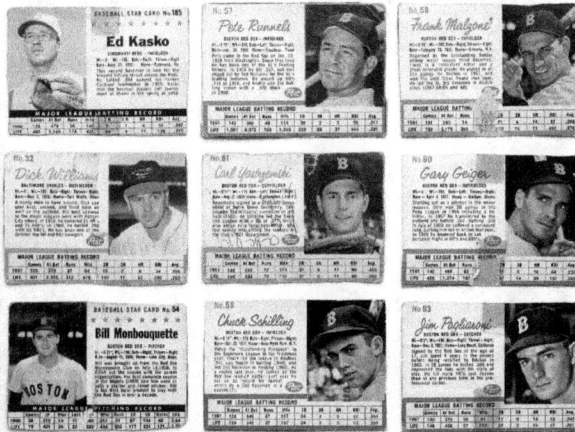

The Red Sox, present and future, were well represented among my first baseball cards, the
rookie card of Yaz being the highlight of the well-used collection, cut out from the backs of
Post cereal boxes.
(Personal Collection)

Thanks largely to Roger Maris, Mickey Mantle, and the other sluggers who cleared the fences on a regular basis in the 1961 season, Major League Baseball decided to enlarge the strike zone by the 1963 season. And as the numbers show, just before the close of that season, the rule change did indeed aid pitchers in both leagues.
(Personal Collection; Phil Bissell illustration)

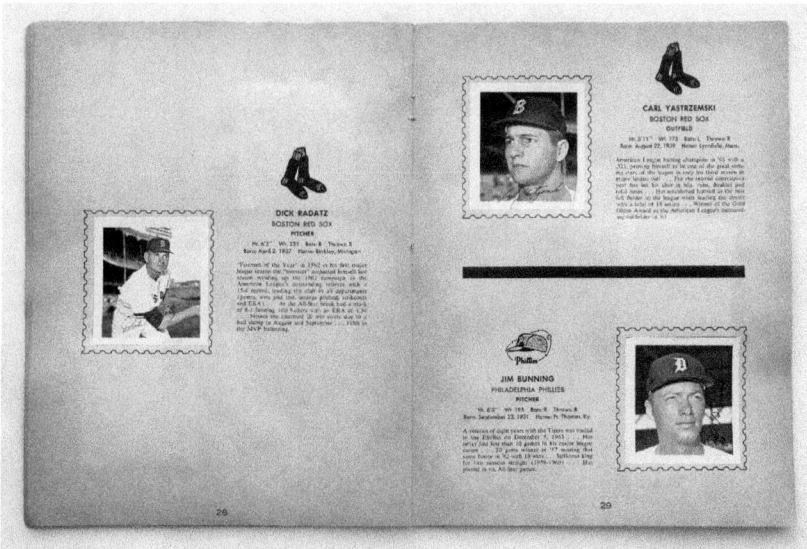

In a 1964 Wheaties pamphlet of stamps featuring major league stars, including Dick Radatz and Yaz, these were obviously my favorite pages.
(Personal Collection)

163

Dick Stuart loved the feel of a bat in his hands during his two years with the Red Sox, but
using a glove at first base was a far less comfortable experience for him.
(Personal Collection)

On the mound and at the plate, Earl Wilson was a success, but in a poor reflection on the
organization, he was also well-known for simply being a black player on those Red Sox clubs.
(Personal Collection)

Yaz had a batting title, Gold Gloves, and All-Star appearances to smile about in those early Red Sox years, but his postseason glory had to wait until 1967.
(Personal Collection)

JAMES LONBORG - Red Sox

The first Red Sox pitcher to win the Cy Young Award, Jim Lonborg had a season for the ages in 1967.
(Personal Collection)

165

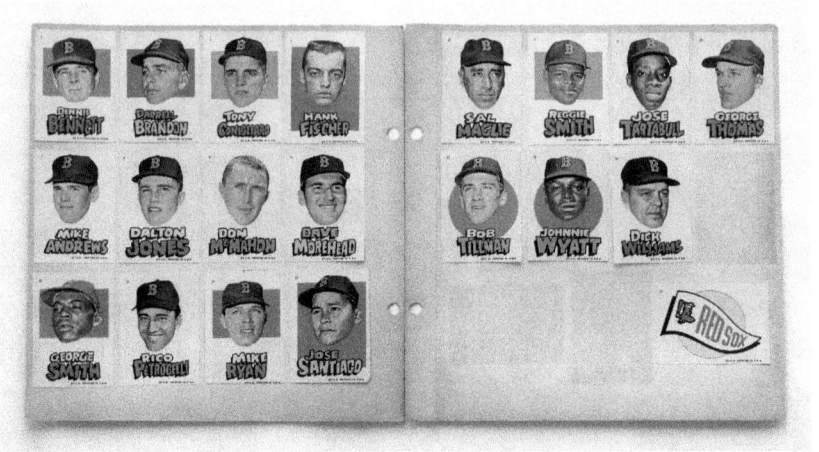

Two pages from my Impossible Dream scrapbook.
(Personal Collection)

Home runs came easily and often to Rico Petrocelli in 1969, when he hit 40 out of the park,
the most homers in his 13-year career, all of it spent with the Red Sox.
(Personal Collection; Larry Johnson illustration)

Giants' players (L–R) Felipe Alou, Jim Davenport, Willie Mays, Juan Marichal, and Orlando Cepeda were feeling good about going to the first All-Star game of 1962, in which Marichal got the first of his two All-Star victories, his second coming over Dick Radatz two years later. Cepeda (1973) and Marichal (1974) would go on to play for the Red Sox. (Courtesy of the San Francisco History Center, San Francisco Public Library)

Marichal's signature high-kick. (Personal Collection)

Many believe that this photo should feature two Hall-of-Famers, with Luis Tiant (L) deserving to be alongside Marichal in Cooperstown. (Courtesy of the Boston Red Sox)

167

10. Fields of Dreams

Viewing a Red Sox game back then was no simple matter. Certainly newspapers, magazines, books, and the radio were essential to the effort of following baseball in my early days as a Red Sox fan, as having an opportunity to see the Red Sox play was not something to be taken for granted. Young fans today might have some difficulty imagining the reality of it all. If you wanted to watch the team play in person, particularly before 1967, you could simply walk up to the gate before the games started, buy nearly any ticket in the park, and get to your seat easily. Fighting through the crowd was not something you ever had to worry about at Fenway. But if you were a child, the hitch, unfortunately, was that you needed a persevering parent, almost certainly a father, to bring you to the game, and judging by the attendance figures of the time and what I could see with my own eyes at Fenway, there was a distinct shortage of such parents.

And if you could not get to the park, television coverage of games was limited, to say the least. Forget about HD, cable, or even daily telecasts. There was none of that. For some people, including me, you could forget about seeing the games in living color, too. Black and white was as colorful as it got. Weekend games at home were televised, and those were always day games. Away games depended on how far "away" was. Some weeknight games were televised, but not most. I watched the games on a television in my living room, and the picture was reasonably clear when the rabbit ears were working well. When they weren't, the frustration level of trying to get them to stay in just the right position for an hour or so was not a memory I savor.

Nevertheless, I did watch as many games on television as possible. And one of the beauties of the baseball season was that it never ended with the last out of the World Series. At least, that's how it was from 1967 on in Boston. Baseball in Beantown had a connection to every season in that fans, young and not so young, were either playing, watching, or talking about it all year round. But if you lived in New England, the arrival of spring was special, as many young boys resumed their annual dream of one day hitting a home run or making a diving catch at Fenway. And the beauty of spring to many locals is that it is not winter.

Spring in New England, however, does not actually start when the calendar says it does. The first calendar day of spring often looks depressingly similar to any day in mid-winter. But a young New England boy who loves baseball can't be deterred by these vagaries of nature. The Red Sox themselves were already back on the diamond in late February, although they had the enviable advantage of playing in the sunshine of Arizona or Florida. For a couple of years during World War II, when the major leagues joined the national effort to conserve energy, the Red Sox did endure some genuine winter conditions during "spring" training by remaining in the local area and practicing daily at an indoor cage at Tufts College, with the players staying at the Hotel Kenmore in Boston. The Braves trained amidst equally intellectual surroundings, spending two springs, 1943—under the "old perfessor," Casey Stengel—and 1944 at the elite Choate School in Connecticut before relocating to the ivory towers of Georgetown University in 1945.

So, with the Red Sox already in action, waiting until April to play in the backyard or at the local playground was not an option. If snow still covered the ground in mid-March, then a plowed-out parking lot was the best bet in terms of finding a place to play. Of course, my friends and I froze almost as soon as we "took the field," and if we happened to hit the ball off the end of the bat, our frigid hands felt like they had touched the third rail on the train tracks. And there was certainly no sliding into bases or diving for line drives. But it was baseball of sorts, good enough for March.

More commonly, some of the ground was bare, with patches of snow here and there interrupted by vast stretches of mud, which meant that the field was eminently usable. Every attempt to run, or to field a ball, was an adventure, usually landing the player in the muck, and by the end of the game we couldn't tell anymore where the mud ended and the snow began. It was a fine mix of mush that covered our pants and undoubtedly put many washing machines to the supreme test. But it was all worthwhile. Baseball was the national pastime, and playing in the spring mud was one of its finest rituals for young boys.

Inevitably, and fortunately, the ground hardened, actual green grass appeared, and we could take the turn at first base after getting a hit without fear of slip slidin' away into short right field. What this meant as a practical matter at my elementary school was that, from spring to the last day of school in mid-June, the boys would throw down their lunch with the greatest possible speed each day in the cafeteria in order to get out to the baseball diamond.

These boys, I should note, were a separate crowd from the baseball-playing boys of my neighborhood, some of whom were older than me and in a number of cases attended the local Catholic elementary school, St. Catherine's, not that I recall their Catholic education resulting in behavior that was any more civilized than what I experienced every day in the public school. (The girls at my school, from what I remember, lingered in the cafeteria before going outside and jump-roping or playing four-square, or hanging out in small, generally boisterous groups and talking about things that boys probably didn't talk about.) The best part of the lunch break was the free time on the playground, where we were allowed to play baseball until the bell rang and brought us back to the cruel reality of multiplication tables, flash cards, and Weekly Readers.

Boys would quickly choose up sides, the last boys being the most insulted by their late selection in those days of no appeal. Time was not wasted shifting defenses, grooming the mound, choosing bats, or any of that. We had only a limited number of minutes to play until the dreaded bell brought all fun to an end, and those minutes were spent playing. The pitcher got the ball from the catcher and threw the next pitch. Batters did not work the count unless they had a death wish, often expressed by their own teammate waiting impatiently on deck. Players ran on and off the field between innings. The majority of boys in that elementary school were never better at time management than they were during those pleasurable hours of lunchtime baseball.

Again, one of the highlights of these games for me was the fantasy aspect to it. I had my own well-thought-out strategy of facing some of the imposing pitchers in my elementary school. For the first strike, and usually the second as well, I would use my best Frank Howard or Tony C stance at the plate and absolutely swing for the fences. We had no actual fence, so the best you could hope for was a solid gap shot that would roll forever in the vast field.

Some stances were too ridiculous to even try. Dick McAuliffe, for example, had a left-handed stance so open that he was practically facing the pitcher, and a swing that resembled someone chopping wood while choking up considerably on the axe—it was not a batting style he learned from Ted Williams. Results are results, though. McAuliffe ended with 197 home runs and more than 1500 hits in a distinguished career that, unfortunately, finished up very quietly in Boston, the result of another Red Sox deal gone wrong: sent out in 1973 was a young Ben Oglivie, who went on to make 3 All–Star teams and hit 225 home runs over 13 years for the Tigers and the Brewers, while the aging McAuliffe batted a paltry .206 over parts of two seasons in Boston.

One stance that always intrigued me was that of Roberto Clemente, and I tried my best to duplicate it. His body relaxed and his eyes focused, with his hands gripping the bat around the handle and about letter high several inches apart from his chest, holding it still as the pitcher entered his windup, Clemente would gauge the pitch before lifting his left leg and taking an assertive stride toward the oncoming ball and, in a swing that started with a decided hitch around his belt and then whiplashed across the plate at the last possible second, could send a pitch on the *inside* part of the plate rocketing toward the gap in right center, with Clemente ending up on second or third base. I don't know how he did it, but it was a compelling swing that I always wanted to try just one more time, no matter the result.

Anyway, once the count got to two strikes, I would switch to my best Cesar Tovar or Bert Campaneris stance, just trying to make contact and get on base. All of this meant that I had no stance at all, which probably was a bad idea for my own "career," but in a child's baseball mind, fantasy trumps reality, and I was quite happy in making no attempt to change that fact.

The seriousness of those baseball games produced an unlikely event that should be a kind of blemish on my life, but instead is a rather warm if somewhat fuzzy memory that reminds me of the importance of being earnest, especially when the subjects are baseball and youth. The great enemy of our games was the school bell, which brought all action to a halt and had students streaming toward the school doors to line up before heading back to class. Teachers, unfortunately, were there to add some haste to the proceedings, some with great enthusiasm. Those were the teachers you never wanted to get in class.

But one day, the bell brought a different outcome. It was a sunny, warm afternoon, most likely in May or June, perfect for playing baseball, not for studying grammar. Our game was at some critical juncture—maybe the tying run was on third, or the go-ahead run was on second, or some such drama—when the bell sounded. Who knows if it was the interrupted game itself, or the beautiful weather that

172

practically demanded that everyone be outside on such a day, or just some excited boys who were far more than ready for the freedom of summer to come and school to end—the reason probably was a combination of all of the above. In any case, the result was perhaps the first student sit-down strike in the history of the school.

We trudged reluctantly from the diamond to the school steps facing the playground, complaining all the way about the unfairness of the elementary school universe. Some kids were gathering around the stairs before heading in. The exact beginnings of our nonviolent protest are a bit vague in my memory. Probably one of the ne'er do well student-athletes, of which we had a few, said something to the effect of "I ain't going back to class." And a friend joined him. And quickly there was a group of kids—it may have been only five or six, but in my heroic memory it was at least fifteen—who were sitting on the steps, refusing to go in.

Against the entreaties and threats from the teachers, we sat there, unwilling to budge. Whether it lasted a few minutes or many minutes I can't say for certain (naturally, I prefer to believe the latter), but eventually we did achieve some notoriety by causing the principal to come out and see what all the commotion was about. The principal actually was a likable man who happened to be the husband of my second-grade teacher, who was also very likable, so I felt a twinge of guilt over the matter as it unfolded. But, justice was justice, so we stood our ground.

No reader will be shocked to know that the principal was not agreeable to letting us take the field again to finish the inning. We finally did go back to class, and as I can't recall what our punishment was for such impudence, it may be that there was no punishment at all, perhaps a reflection of a wise principal. I certainly remember other punishments meted out to various students, such as having to stay in for recess for any of a dozen or more minor infractions that teachers seemed to have a sixth sense in detecting, or actual suspensions from school for some of the more mischievous students. So, there was no rule against punishment in my school. But I do know that I felt a certain amount of satisfaction over the whole affair. Placing baseball over schoolwork was natural in my elementary school mind.

Although it may be unnecessary to make this point, I will note that the elementary school of my childhood bore no resemblance to the academic institutions that children, at least those growing up in leafy suburbs, now attend. There were very few standardized tests to stress out over, no daily homework assignments in nearly every subject, no backpacks full of textbooks, calculators, planners that could double as doorstoppers, and other SAT-improving paraphernalia to be dragged back and forth from home every day, no individual parent-teacher conferences to monitor Junior's march to the top, no after-school activities to keep you from falling behind in the CV-building competition, and no weekly newsletters from the school principal assuring concerned parents that their school is focused, laser-like, on producing students fully prepared to ultimately attend an elite, private, four-year college. All of that lay somewhere off in the future of the global economy.

My school, I think, was typical of an elementary school in a working class/middle class neighborhood of that time. In my classes, there were some well-behaved and attentive students who had a clear focus on doing their best academically. The majority of students were somewhere in the middle, not budding scholars but certainly intelligent enough, and easy to get along with. However, the far end of the academic spectrum was represented among students, too. It was not unusual for unruly or uncooperative students to be told to stay after school, or to stand in the corner, or to wait in the hallway, or to simply go straight to the principal's office. By fifth grade, the school had separated an entire group of students, including a few girls, who to that point had unfortunately learned more from the streets than from any books, and placed them in a basement

174

room with a young male teacher who, the hope went, could "relate" to these troubled children and, more importantly, physically keep them in their chairs and in the room.

My own situation ran the gamut. Academically, I did very well at that age. I got mostly A's throughout elementary school, finding the work not very difficult. I liked to read—certainly baseball books gave me an encouraging start in that direction, and other books I remember fondly from childhood included the Hardy Boys, the Power Boys, and the Three Investigators of Alfred Hitchcock, as well as all of the inexpensive Scholastic paperbacks that we could order several times a year through the school. Nothing heavy, but enough to send me off in the right direction and, from my parents' point of view, provide hope that I would one day be able to earn a paycheck.

I should add that a helpful factor in all of this was the lack of homework in those times. I'm sure there was some, but the fact that I spent so many days playing sports after school suggests that I wasn't lugging home too many books. It was a good balance that probably helped me both in and out of school.

At the same time, I had friends in each of the groups, high to low, and was influenced by all of them to some degree. I wasn't uncomfortable about either befriending some of the smarter kids or sometimes hanging out with the rougher crowd of boys. There was good and bad on all sides—that was how I looked at it, and I didn't worry about too much of it when choosing friends. My memories of those days are mostly happy ones. And baseball often was a strong connection between my friends and me, but not always the only one.

Examples are plentiful, and point to the long and winding road we all follow in our own lives. From my elementary school, unfortunately, the road did not always lead to the promised land, at least for the boys. The lives of two of my best elementary school friends come to mind.

One, an easygoing boy named Mike, was in my class almost every year through elementary school, so we knew each other very well. (I still recall that our birthdays were only a couple of weeks apart.) He was an excellent student who didn't give much thought to his high grades and a very good athlete who wasn't too impressed by that side of himself, either. If we were playing baseball and he hit a single, he was just as likely to strike up a chatty conversation with the first baseman as he was to concern himself about how many outs there were or whether he might score on a double. One year he made the Red Sox team during tryouts in Little League, which meant that he was in the "majors," in Little League parlance. If I had made the Red Sox, I wouldn't have been able to sleep for a week from the excitement, but Mike took it quite in stride. He was always quick with a smile and a good joke, and we spent many enjoyable hours together in those days.

Later, as the junior high and high school years went by, we saw less of each other, and his interest in education diminished significantly before high school graduation brought it to an end at 18. Yet I always thought of Mike as one of the best friends I ever had on a baseball field. When I recall our countless days spent on that playground, so often laughing together, not a care about our futures, I doubt that he has any regrets over that time. Neither do I.

Most unusually, another school friend, named Terry, almost never played baseball or any other sport unless a team was desperate for another player, when he would join us good-naturedly. Decidedly unathletic, which was almost a kind of social handicap for a boy in those days, he had the additional challenge of serious vision problems that required him to wear rather thick eyeglasses. But he was an excellent student who did not take himself too seriously and had a very dry sense of humor that I always appreciated. In elementary school, we spent many days just hanging out and laughing over things long since forgotten. Sadly, in later years, he turned away from school and the mainstream, living an increasingly aimless life until he died tragically of a brain aneurysm in his late twenties. He has now been dead more years than he was alive. I had known him since kindergarten, and his story made me wonder why things go as they do in life. I wonder still.

Other boys in my school went on to varying degrees of academic success or lack thereof, with the balance tipping somewhat more toward the latter than the former. I expect that most of the girls managed their school lives more ably, although that is not an expert opinion. In any case, I learned that baseball was a pathway to friends of all stripes, and it served me well throughout my childhood.

The stress on all of the teachers in my school to educate/ride herd on the students they faced each day in class must have been intense, and sometimes resulted in scenes worthy of Tom Sawyer. I vividly remember the times that one of my teachers, a tall, imposing man of German descent and normally mild-mannered, would turn red with anger, wave his finger pointedly at the class, and blast us in what was probably fluent German for taking more than two Ritz crackers apiece out of the big, red, Ritz box during our morning milk and crackers break.

And if he caught an actual perpetrator committing an even worse crime, he would back you up against the wall and perform the same ritual right in your face. As the year went on, he succumbed to more and more such outbursts, and for us students to suppress giggles, which surely would have brought on the elementary school equivalent of the death penalty, was a supreme challenge. I never heard him talk about baseball, something that might have reduced his stress load considerably.

Some teachers tried a lighter approach to pacifying students, which, at least in my classes, proved more effective. The school's two fourth-grade teachers, both very young and quasi hippie-ish women, would often combine their classes during the last hour of the school day, and one of them would get out her guitar and teach us whatever subversive song was in her arsenal that afternoon, with all of us eventually singing along in some crude form of unison. I can still recite many of the lyrics from songs such as "Sloop John B," "Where Have All the Flowers Gone," "This Land Is Your Land," "Tom Dooley," "If I Had a Hammer," and "Michael Row Your Boat Ashore." On less musical days, they would read us stories, with great animation, from a large book of Winnie the Pooh tales, which was my introduction to Christopher Robin and Hundred Acre Wood.

The overall approach seemed to work, judging by the lack of complaints from students. On the other hand, it didn't make us any more eager to return to our geography lesson the next day, either. That classroom faced the playground, and even during the Winnie the Pooh readings, I gazed longingly out at the empty baseball field, my own Hundred Acre Wood. That land was my land.

Sometime before the end of elementary school life, my neighborhood friends and I had outgrown our backyard baseball field, presenting the dilemma of finding another field that was unoccupied. For any children living in a suburb now, this story may be hard to imagine. But I suspect that the situation in many other neighborhoods in Norwood and in other towns was not so different. For in my boyhood days of the 1960s, every boy I knew played baseball, and talent had nothing to do with it. Absolutely everyone played. In my neighborhood, there were no exceptions. There were some very good players and some very mediocre players, or worse, but all played at least occasionally. Even in my elementary school, obviously including boys from many neighborhoods, it is hard for me to think of *any* boys who simply did not play baseball, ever. Not even one case comes to mind. Baseball was clearly the favorite sport of boys at the time, and perhaps it should have been equally clear to Red Sox management that even the slightest hint of a decent Red Sox season would have brought fans out in droves to Fenway, which is precisely what happened in 1967 and has been happening ever since.

Anyway, boys were on baseball fields in those days, so the taxpayers could rest assured that they were getting their money's worth in terms of usage of the public playgrounds. There were several fields for my friends and me to choose from, public and private, with the challenge at times being to find one that was empty.

Each field had its ups and downs. My elementary school, the Callahan, had the baseball field that I knew well from recess. The advantage of this field was that it was huge, giving it a kind of major league feel just because of the size. But that was all it had—size. And there was no fence, so if a well-hit ball got by you in the outfield, there was almost no point to run after it. Even the screen behind the plate was so far back that retrieving the ball took up half of our free time and was more exercise than running the bases. To solve this problem, a spare player would often stand in front of the screen to catch errant pitches or fouls and quickly throw the ball back to the pitcher.

Another field, in a wooded area near a company called Mason-Neilan, went by the same name to us. Mason-Neilan was a Little League-size field but one that had a wooden fence all the way around, and wooden dugouts and a screen close behind the plate. There were always some interesting graphics or messages carved or painted on the wood by older boys with active imaginations, but having a fence gave the field the huge advantage of being a legitimate home run park. If you hit one out, it was an official home run, and no one could say otherwise, unless a fight broke out over whether it was fair or foul.

In the middle of town was the best field of all, the featured part of a town civic center, known to everyone simply as "The Civic," that had tennis and basketball courts, a swimming pool, and the spacious, beautifully (I thought) kept baseball field. There I occasionally watched games of the Legion baseball team, whose players carried themselves with such self-confidence and had the on-field chatter down to such a science ("throwin' strikes, Chuckie, throwin' strikes, you got this guy, Chuckie, you got 'im, nuthin' good, nuthin' good, it's

179

all you, Chuckie, all you....") that it appeared certain they were on their way to some sort of diamond greatness.

I didn't play much at The Civic until I was out of elementary school. My two strongest memories were that there seemed to be almost no bad bounces on the infield, and that the hippie house just beyond the right field fence was a major point of attraction for fans, sometimes even more appealing than the game itself. It was a big box of a house where young men with long hair and young women with even longer hair hung out, sometimes sitting on blankets in the front yard, the guys wearing no shirts and the girls wearing barely more, all of them always laughing and happy and evidently living in endless summers of love. Their prized possession, without a doubt, was their VW bug. It was generally parked out front, positioned like a monument to the era, with bumper stickers that probably said something like, "Let It Be," or "Feelin' Groovy," although the words are now lost to history, maybe blessedly so. Also lost to history is the house itself—and even the street—now replaced by a hospital parking lot, a real-life example of Joni Mitchell's "they paved paradise, and put up a parking lot."

But all of these were the better fields that were sometimes taken early in the day in the town-wide competition among boys to seize a good place to play. If all else failed, the last resort for my friends and I was an area in our neighborhood that was just a clearing in the woods, and not even particularly flat, that we used only in desperation. On that field, a good hop was any ball that didn't come up and hit you in the groin, and it was very possible to run into a tree or step into a rabbit hole while chasing a fly ball. It was one of those fields where, if for any reason we couldn't play any longer, few complained too much.

The game of wiffle ball had a short but noteworthy interval in my neighborhood baseball life around this time. The beauty of wiffle ball was that you didn't need a large field, and you could still swing the bat as hard as you liked. Our "home" field for these games was located behind the nearby house of another friend named Mike, whose backyard had an interesting configuration of having no center field (too many trees) or right field (an unmowed expanse). Each pitch had to be hit to left, which is where his house happened to stand. The quality of your hit was measured by whether the ball hit the house (a double or a triple) or sailed entirely over everything, settling softly in the front yard for a well-earned home run. We used a fungo-like bat, bright red, and occasionally could launch a majestic shot up into the sky, clear over the roof.

One of the conveniences of our system was that you needed only two players—a batter and a pitcher—for a game. But even when it was only Mike and myself, we often had eighteen "players", as we would each choose a major league lineup to emulate. Obviously this presented certain challenges, such as when I was the Pirates and had Willie Stargell trying to hit a home run to left field. These games could last for hours, stretching into doubleheaders and even tripleheaders, but it rarely seemed long enough. And on the topic of fathers and sports, Mike's father was one of the best—with great sincerity (and a booming voice of encouragement), he was like a father and a teammate for practically every kid in the neighborhood in all four sports.

There were certain truisms of slow pitch, pickup baseball games back then that, unfair and cruel as they were, held firm. Of course, real games, such as in Little League, were quite different, as there were coaches and rules and a hint of dignity to the process, and *all* players on the field were supposed to have some level of talent.

But in a typical slow pitch, pick-up game, with players of all skill sets, reality ruled. Assuming there were nine players on each team, if your team put you out in right field, you were almost certainly the worst player on the team. If you were told to pitch, you had to be able to put the ball over the plate often enough to keep the batter and your own fielders from complaining too much—that was about it. (One friend in my elementary school days often had a cigarette hanging out of his mouth when he pitched, apparently trying to lend a little Bogart-like toughness to the position. It did have the effect of distracting some batters, as the cigarette was more intriguing to watch than was the ball.) If you were the catcher, you were likely to be not considered the most active player on the team. If you were told to play a different position each game, you were probably allowed to play because your team needed bodies on the field. If you played any other position, especially on a regular basis, you were fine.

And there was no appeal. If you questioned the reasoning of the decision, the answer was likely to be a variation of "Because you stink." The world of children's baseball, or any children's sport, for that matter, could be cold. Perhaps that is why some of today's parents, survivors of right field or some other humiliating banishment, protect their kids from all but the most organized of sports. Whatever the explanation, the taxpayers are no longer getting their baseball money's worth—many fields of dreams are now just fields of memories, good or bad, rarely used except when teams with full uniforms play a game in front of cheering, ever watchful parents.

My own memories of playing organized baseball, in Little League, are mostly positive. My Little League career had many memorable moments. Admittedly, they are memorable only to me, but, like the memories of most people, that doesn't make them any less important. In general, I remember how much I enjoyed each day of practice and wondered how some kids could find shagging fly balls or taking infield grounders boring. Now, from an adult point of view, when I see a baseball field where a Little League practice is taking place, and I notice how many kids are just standing in one place, I realize how baseball practice could be construed as the ultimate boring experience. Maybe I just wasn't overly perceptive, but I never saw it that way.

Despite his diminishing enthusiasm for family affairs, my father continued to attend just about all of my games, along with many other fathers. I'm sure that mothers were there, too, but certainly not in equal numbers. With many families having at least three children, mothers had more than enough work facing them at home to keep them away from the ballfield. That was true for my own mother, although she did get to see me play once in a while.

Anyway, my father was a regular at the games, although never a particularly vocal one during the action. High praise from him after a game was a brief comment on something that I had done well. On the other hand, if I had screwed up, I heard about that in rather more detail, usually with a "god damn" thrown in somewhere for effect. Even if I had had a couple of hits, if there was a strikeout mixed in, he growled at me about protecting the plate and going with the pitch. But I didn't mind any of his comments too much—if he hadn't chosen to come at all, that would have gotten much more of my attention, as he was still my main link to baseball, in spite of my growing unease with his overall disinterest. I did suspect that if I had been performing in a school play instead of a baseball game, he would have found reasons not to come, but I tried to block out such thoughts and focus on the reality that he *was* there.

On a few nights when the umpires did not show up, my father was drafted into umpiring duty, which was definitely not his cup of tea. I think he agreed to do it only so the game could go on. When facing a field full of 8-year-olds, he had a decided handicap of not liking to call strike three on a batter or ball four on a pitcher, so a 3–2 count was practically an existential crisis for him. The result was that both teams tended to have equal gripes with him. One balmy night at the Callahan School field, he umped when I was pitching, a predicament that signaled a truly desperate need for an umpire. In my own very biased view, I felt that he gave the hitters the calls in an understandable effort to appear fair, which may have been mostly a rationalization for my own poor performance that night, and our car ride home was silent with annoyance on my part over the loss and probably gratitude on his part that the ordeal was over.

Plus, as all parent-umpires must regret, they can't watch the action on the field in the same way. In the stands, you focus on your own kid. On the field, you have to watch the ball and move around on each play, and then sometimes catch grief at the same time. But he did his duty, and the games went on. I do believe that it was always a relief to him to see the umpires arrive at the field before each game.

In my own case, two Little League stories come quickly to mind as I think back to those halcyon days of imagined stardom. One involves a memorable manager. Most Little League managers back then looked like they could have been anyone's father, and they generally were. My first two managers fit the bill solidly. Kindly, unassuming, encouraging sorts, fathers with their own sons on the roster, they didn't make any enemies, and I enjoyed playing for them. Little League wasn't quite like the gentleman's sport of golf, but most managers of the youngest boys tried to keep the emphasis on the kids and there was rarely much grousing with umpires over balls and strikes or with parents over why their kid was getting splinters sitting on the bench. (Some of the benches actually were made of wood and looked as though they could have been there since Tinker-to-Evers-to-Chance, so getting splinters was often a hazard of the trade, and taking them out was sometimes a bloody affair.)

But my third manager, Mr. R, was not cut from that cloth. A man with hair modishly long, befitting the time, and a personality that kept him, and his vocal cords, in perpetual motion, he was a genuine character. Mr. R played to win, which was an ongoing and perplexing problem, as we rarely even came close to winning many games that year. No matter—after each loss, regardless of the margin of humiliation, he was quick to encourage us with his usual, "We'll get those bastards next time, boys!"

And therein lay a large part of the issue, for Mr. R had the vocabulary of a truck driver in a job normally filled by church-going men. He was Leo Durocher, Bill Parcells, and

Ozzie Guillen in charge of a motley crew of mediocre (but motivated!), pre-adolescent baseball players.

I had a particularly advantageous view of his entertaining behavior, as I pitched on occasion and sometimes gave up enough runs to necessitate numerous visits to the mound by Mr. R. While the catcher, a friend named Rick, and I looked on in both amazement and trepidation, Mr. R would hustle out to the mound—no slow, Walter Alston walks to the mound for him—put his arms around both of us, and yank us toward him as if we were in a football huddle. His breath suggested odors that boys my age were not supposed to know about. "Okay, let's get this next f---ing kid out and then get back in this f---ing game! So don't give him any good sh-- to hit!" Or words along those lines, the variations being not worth mentioning, while Rick and I wondered what would happen if, as was likely to be the case, we didn't get the next guy out.

But I have good memories of playing for Mr. R precisely because of his undeniable passion for the game. He made us practice like we were undefeated. He hit ground balls and fly balls to us without end, and he expected every one to be fielded cleanly. If you screwed up, he would curse you to pieces and then give you a hug. If he didn't like your batting stance, he would jump in close behind you and move your hands on the bat and push your butt this way or that and change the position of your feet, and if it didn't work he would do it all over again, often cursing the whole way. And he wasn't concerned about who we were playing or what their record was or what *our* record was—it was all about getting better and playing well so that, some day, we might find ourselves on the winning side of the score. We certainly were not winners in the standings, but Mr. R did give value to the experience, and that year I felt that I was playing for something real. Many parents undoubtedly felt otherwise, but everyone could agree on one thing: Mr. R cared.

Another baseball episode of mine, a year or so earlier, was far less inspiring. As Terry Francona likes to say about the sport, "This game can humble you." I remember, not fondly, when it did precisely that to me, and I have not forgotten the experience, five decades later.

It happened in a Little League game when I was about ten or eleven. I hit a ball that got between the center fielder and the left fielder and rolled to the fence. As I approached second base, I saw that the center fielder, in a hurry to get the ball to the cutoff man, was having trouble picking up the ball, so I kept on going to third, where I was waved around. About half-way home, I saw that the catcher looked as though he wasn't expecting a throw, so I let up before reaching the plate, no longer running hard, probably barely trotting. All of a sudden, the catcher had the ball, I was tagged out, and the play was over.

But the moment was not over. My manager, a very nice man, knew what had to be done, and he benched me on the spot. I deserved it. I had disrespected the other team, I had disrespected my own team, and I had disrespected the game. It was completely humiliating, and obviously, I remember it to this day. Baseball is a game, not significantly important, but what that game told me about myself that day *was* important. I had put myself above others, not given my best effort, and been punished accordingly. In life, you cannot simply click on the "undo" icon, and sometimes that is a very good thing. I guess I should be grateful that I never pulled a stunt like that with Mr. R....

Despite my love of baseball, however, somewhere around the time that I was ten or eleven, the sinking feeling that all was not well regarding my future playing career with the Red Sox began to grip me. This did not happen in a particular flash of illumination but more gradually, over games and seasons, in an inexorable march toward the common sense part of my brain.

There were distinct warning signs, the biggest by far being the fact that not only was I more and more aware that some other players in Little League were better than I was, but it was becoming increasingly clear that a *lot* of other players were better than I was. And that was just in my town. My basic math skills were getting better each year, courtesy of my hours spent figuring out batting averages, winning percentages, and earned run averages in my head, and I was starting to understand that if I wasn't even close to being among the best players in my own town, and there were many thousands of towns in the country, and there was a growing number of big leaguers who were from *other* countries, and there were only twenty teams in the entire Major Leagues, then my future at Fenway seemed something less than a sure thing. In fact, it was beginning to look like a catastrophe. My plan had been Fenway or bust, but I had never seriously considered the latter, which now stared me in the face.

11. The End of the Innocence

Not quite ready to concede that I might have to work for a living when I grew up, I took up basketball. The initial signs were somewhat encouraging, as I was a little tall for my age, and the ball went in the basket fairly easily if no one was guarding me. Playing conditions were often a bit challenging in my neighborhood, as two of the baskets I used most frequently were simply net-less rims nailed to backyard trees, with the tree itself serving as a backboard, and the court was not a paved area but Mother Earth.

But it was all fun and did go well at first, so the Celtics, naturally, became a possibility for me and a reasonably acceptable alternative to the Red Sox. I could get used to playing at the Boston Garden, I thought, even though I had never actually been there and, truth be told, had not seen more than a few professional basketball games on television. I had some catching up to do, but no matter. Dreams die hard for children. Mine, unfortunately, were about to die hard—and fast.

But first came my new flirtation with the Celtics. I don't know if it was love at first sight, but if it wasn't, it was pretty close. It was easy to like the Celtics in those days, as they were the defending NBA champions on a regular basis. As absurd as the story of the Red Sox often was, the Celtics, through no fault of their own, frequently found themselves in equally ridiculous situations. At the time I just accepted things as they were, but from a modern vantage point, the examples are comical and plentiful.

The Celtics, despite having won championships nearly every year since I was born, got almost no love at all. Few people ventured to Boston Garden to watch them—even playoff games were no guarantee to sell out, and that sad fact continued for years. In 1973, for example, I went to a Celtics playoff game against the Atlanta Hawks in which John Havlicek shot the lights out, scoring 54 points, and there absolutely were empty seats at that game, and quite a few of them. Ever in search of fans, the Celtics at times took the show on the road, out west to Springfield, Massachusetts, to play some "home" games there. The outrageous "Sports Huddle" radio talk show, in search of its own fans as well, would rent a bus and transport people out to the game in what must have a been a zany road trip. One imagines a "Sports Huddle" bus as having at least two flat tires and no brakes. So, unfair as it was, the Red Sox by 1967 were getting lots of fans but no championships, while the Celtics had decidedly fewer spectators but plenty of rings.

I first followed the Celtics largely in passing in 1966-67 (the year Wilt finally broke through for a championship, ending the Celtics' run at eight straight), and then seriously the next two seasons. At the same time, I started watching college games and never got tired of seeing Lew Alcindor, Pete Maravich, Bob Lanier, Rick (Mr. Indiana, before Larry Bird) Mount, and Calvin Murphy on Saturday afternoon telecasts. My favorite college player was Mike Maloy of the (pre-famous) Lefty Driesell, Davidson College Wildcats, who was drafted by the Celtics before playing in the ABA. Along with the championship play of the Celtics, those college games were a most memorable introduction to the game of basketball for me.

I listened to many Celtics games, watched the ones that were on television, and read the Celtics' articles in the *Boston Globe*, cutting out many of the articles and photos as I had done with those of baseball players practically since I could hold a pair of scissors. They won the championship both years, and I remember listening to the playoff finals against the Lakers, late at night, on my transistor radio in bed.

In the tale of the tape for the 1969 clincher in Los Angeles, Russell's final game, Russell, Havlicek ("he's as good as any forward we have, and as good as any guard we have":

189

Russell), and Jerry West went the full 48 minutes, with Russell pulling down 21 rebounds and Chamberlain 27, but Wilt making only 4 of 13 foul shots in a game decided by 2 points. West, who poured in 42 points while playing on one good leg, said afterward of the Lakers' annual loss in the Finals to the Celtics, "Every year it gets more difficult to sit here and talk about it.... I don't think I can take it much longer." Lakers' coach Butch van Breda Kolff was more blunt: "It's nice to have Jerry West to go to, but it would be nice to have four guys with him." Even Red Auerbach, in his one postgame television comment, praised West. Russell summed up his own team's success: "We see each other as men, and we judge a guy by his character.... You can see what we have achieved as a group, and it's definitely thrilling." Who could disagree?

After a year of watching Hank Finkel struggle mightily (but always with his best effort—he knew what it meant to be a Celtic) with the impossible task of replacing Russell, I was pleasantly surprised to see how well a rambunctious but undersized draft pick from Florida State was filling the bill. Dave Cowens became a nightly sight to behold, and I mention this only because amid extremely stiff competition, he remains my all-time favorite Celtic.

His immense talent was almost underappreciated simply because his fearlessness and determination were so overwhelming that it was hard to focus on much else about him. It was truly Celtics basketball to see Cowens, usually pounding on someone a head taller, rip down a defensive rebound, fire the outlet pass, race down the floor like his pants were on fire, and then take a return pass for a foul line jumper or for a maniacal drive to the basket, where at least 99 percent of the time there was, not surprisingly, no one waiting to take the offensive charge.

His battles in the post against the Bucks' Lew Alcindor in particular, who towered nearly half a foot over Cowens, were epic, and while Alcindor did score (as he did against everyone), it took every ounce of his estimable skill to get the job done against Cowens. And sometimes even that wasn't enough, such as in the seventh game of the 1974 Finals, when Cowens came up huge (28 points, 14 rebounds) against by-then Abdul-Jabbar (26 points, 13 rebounds) in leading the Celtics to the championship, their twelfth, and the first of the Cowens era. My own favorite battles of Cowens occurred against the Baltimore/Capital/Washington Bullets' center Wes Unseld, who was equally undersized and almost equally motivated, but it was the legendary showdowns with Alcindor/Abdul-Jabbar that captivated NBA fans, and rightfully so.

But what I most admired about him was that the biggest critic of Dave Cowens, by far, was Dave Cowens. Off the top of my head, I can't think of any athlete who took losses or poor personal performances harder than he did. And when he believed that he could not give his teammates the superlative level of support that they expected from him, night in and night out, when exhaustion finally had taken its toll, he not only considered walking away, he *did* famously walk away, temporarily, just months after winning his second NBA championship. "Seeing him lying on a trainer's table," Leigh Montville wrote at the time, "still exhausted two hours after a game against Jabbar, there never has been any doubt about how hard Cowens has worked." Amen to that.

While following the Celtics became my new quest, the trouble was *finding* them. On the unusual occasions when their games were televised, they were on channels that provided a grainy, snowy picture that must have driven anyone over thirty toward blindness. An intrepid sports announcer named Bob Fouracre, who seemed to be a one-man production and announcing crew for Celtics' telecasts, made a valiant attempt to disguise the fact that the technical presentation of a Celtics game was roughly on a par with a junior high school audio/visual production. And this was for a team that had won half the championships in NBA history!

Radio contact with the Celtics was no sure bet, either. The disrespected Celtics shared a radio station with the Bruins, and their radio broadcasts wandered from AM to FM back to AM, depending on the Bruins games and other factors that I never understood. FM at the time was akin to radio purgatory, as many cars had no FM dial, and portable, transistor radios were the rage but mainly had AM dials. So, a Celtics game on FM virtually guaranteed that only diehard listeners, including me, would bother staying home and tuning in.

Although he had only a passing connection to the Red Sox, the name of Johnny Most has to be included in any discussion of Boston sports. Most gained fame—notoriety is probably a more appropriate word—as a chain-smoking, coffee-addicted, raspy-voiced, unrepentant, and totally partisan announcer for the Boston Celtics. In doing research for another book years ago, I came upon the interesting fact that Most's grandfather was the noted anarchist Johan Most, as dedicated to promoting anarchy as his grandson was to screaming at referees in pursuit of victory for his beloved Celtics.

And when Most called a basketball game, anarchy always seemed to be the state of affairs on the court. In the basketball world according to Johnny Most, every call went against the Celtics, every opposing player guarding a Celtic was committing a foul on every play, every Celtic playing defense never committed a foul, every Celtic starter was an All-Star, every starter on the opposing team was a hired thug who played dirty (that included Bill Bradley, he of Princeton and Oxford, whose crime was to play for the detested Knickerbockers), every Celtics coach was a genius, every opposing coach was a crybaby, and on and on. Most, high above courtside, as he always reminded us, saw his own very personal game unfolding below him, and called it that way, making it obligatory for fans who actually wanted to know what was happening to either have a fertile imagination or a TV, for the rare televised games, to accompany Most's unstoppable voice.

Most had his own language as well that he used to call the game. Before each game, the teams were "getting set to do basketball battle." When Sam Jones made one of his patented bank shots from the wing, it was "too late!" When an opposing player committed something other than a garden variety foul, the player immediately became a "cheap, dirty, gutless" bruiser in Most's view, and stayed that way for the rest of his career unless, of course, he was traded to the Celtics.

Most, being practically a Celtic family member himself, used a nickname for almost everyone. John Havlicek, one of the true gentlemen in the game, was nevertheless known as "Jarrin' John, the bouncing Buckeye from Ohio State." Larry Siegfried was "Siggy," Bailey Howell, was "Buckshot," Tom Sanders was "Satch," Don Nelson was "Nellie," Wayne Embry was "Wayne the Wall," and Don Chaney was "The Duck." They were all brothers-in-arms to Most.

Yet, Most was a fan favorite, and deservedly so. His allegiance to the team was unquestioned, and even though the game itself did not often reflect his creative description of it, the entertainment factor was so high with Most that you couldn't turn him off. Any play could send him into an ever-higher pitch of verbal agitation, entering what would be considered heart attack range for most people. I sometimes wondered if the Celtics kept Most perched up in the rafters to prevent bodily harm that would certainly be inflicted by opposing players if they could hear his screaming taunts, but it was always music to the ears of his Celtics listeners.

Before I knew about any of that, though, I knew Most from his gig as an announcer of baseball scores on the "Wheaties" scoreboard following Red Sox games. In those pre-internet, pre-cable TV days, it was not easy to get the scores of other games, so the "Wheaties" program was very helpful. At the time, Most seemed like a pretty calm, normal announcer as he read the scores of the games. His scratchy voice did make you think he was a threat to light up another cigarette at any moment, but, to me, he was just another sports guy on TV. Later, though, he became an unforgettable character. (And when he let his hair grow in the 1970s in a misguided effort to appear mod, he must have been following some very bad advice on personal appearance.) Had he stayed with baseball, it would have been must-listen radio to hear him call the last out of a no hitter, or a home run such as Bobby Thomson's or Kirk Gibson's. Then again, it might have taken years off his life.

But almost from the start, I could see that there was a problem regarding professional basketball that had never been an issue with baseball: the size of the players. The centers were much taller than me, the forwards were much taller than me, and even the point guards were taller than me. All the practice in the world wasn't going to change this troubling fact. I was tall for a normal person my age, but slightly tall people were rarely seen in the NBA. Maybe, for me, it was just as well, as it was less painful to think that I was merely too short, rather than not even remotely talented enough. What was clear was that I would be playing baseball and basketball for fun, not for a living. Like little Jackie Paper, I finally had to move past the dreams of the magic dragons of my childhood—my beloved Red Sox and the Celtics—and grow up.

Around that same time, another uncomfortable realization about my future was that much of it, if not all of it, would be up to me. There were many factors leading me to that daunting conclusion, one of the most consistent being money, or the severe lack of it, in my family. To keep myself afloat financially (meaning that I would be able to buy baseball cards and books), I worked at various jobs in the neighborhood as a young boy, including delivering newspapers, mowing lawns, raking leaves, shoveling snow, and selling, door to door, cans and jars of blueberries that I had picked in a nearby wooded area (my neighbors bought them with a smile on their face, although I doubt they had an urgent need for recycled cans full of blueberries).

I kept the money that I made in a jar on a shelf in the kitchen pantry. At any given time, the jar held from $5 to $50, depending on how much work my neighbors, many of whom were elderly and happy to have a neighborhood boy doing their yardwork, were offering me. In my family, that amount of actual cash was like a Brink's haul, and events followed accordingly. One day when I went to get some money from the jar, I noticed that there were only $1 dollar bills there, yet I was certain that there had been a $5 dollar bill as well. Sensing the likely source of the problem, I asked my father if he knew anything about the money. Not too sheepishly, he replied, "I meant to tell you about that. I just needed it for gas. Don't worry—I'll get it back to you next week." Whenever my father said, "Don't worry" about anything, particularly money, it was time to worry.

Money "disappearing" from my jar became a scenario that happened with increasing frequency (and silence), the result being that I began working more hours to make up for my mounting financial losses. In school I never took any academic courses in finances or budgets or balance sheets, but my experiences with that jar taught me all that I needed to know about money: it's hard to make it and easy to lose it. Five decades later, that principle persists.

The most glaring reminder of the dearth of money was the family car, always a very used, often rusted, seldom reliable piece of machinery. The good news was that we generally had one, mainly because if our car died unexpectedly, which was a very predictable occurrence, relatives would put up the money for a replacement of the same quality. The bad news was that it was just a matter of time before the "new" car would die as the old ones had. The places of expiration were diverse, ranging from the driveway to the church parking lot to a supermarket parking lot to the breakdown lane on a highway to any back road on the way to somewhere.

In most cases, my father's reaction was the same: he would come unglued, with obscenities pouring forth—"God damn it! God damn it!"—while he tried to form a plan of action in his utterly confused mind. And when the car had conked out anywhere other than our driveway, the challenge of finding a phone to call from was often immense. When no phone booth was nearby, my father more than once had to knock on doors and rely on the kindness of strangers to use their phones, although I suspect that generally he was so flustered that he could barely dial the number, probably making the benevolent homeowners wonder if seeing was believing.

The bad luck of the car and the Red Sox combined, unfortunately, on one memorable summer night after a game at Fenway. My father and I took the Green Line trolley back to the Newton station from Fenway, but when we got off and returned to the car, we saw that a window, unbelievably, had been smashed in. I don't remember all the details, but enough damage had been done that, in some way, my father was unable to start the car. Even in my childish mind, the thought that a person of sound mind could have looked at that car, another in a long line of clunkers, and determined it to be suitable for theft was laughable.

But my father had to make an anguished—and angry— rescue call to one of my uncles, after which I waited in the lot with my distressed father, who kept kicking the poor car's tires in frustration, as if the car itself were somehow responsible for the debacle. And looking at it from my uncle's point of view, I'm sure he quickly imagined yet another car bill landing in his lap once he heard my father's story on the phone.

Along with the money woes, my father's lack of judgment formed a perfect storm of personal ineptitude. He not only had little money, but had even less idea of how to use it. Saving for the future was a foreign concept to him, partly because, to be fair to him, there was not much to be saved. But thinking about the future in any practical way was not within his mental grasp. As a boy playing Little League and not thinking much about my future, either, I was not too worried about this. But as time passed, it did begin to dawn on me that if my father had very little grip on his own life and no reasonable idea of what might lay beyond tomorrow, I had better develop some survival skills. Relying on advice and guidance from my father was a path to oblivion. Like father, like son was not an option for me.

196

Another uncomfortable personal issue involved the pronunciation, or mispronunciation, of my last name. My father pronounced it Harts/horn. For whatever reasons, this pronunciation proved to be quite challenging for many people, I realized. At various times, teachers, neighbors and, perhaps most frustratingly, my baseball coaches pronounced it as Hartson, Hartsen, Hart/shun, and Hart/shen. Few pronounced it as my father did, and my effort to continuously have to speak up and correct the many other versions brought attention to me that, as a self-conscious boy, I did not relish. Had my name been Jones, I would have been fine with that.

The most common pronunciation was Hart/shorn. At some point in my youth, not wanting to spend my life struggling with such an unnecessary annoyance, I chose the path of least resistance and quietly went with that pronunciation. Subconsciously, I may have also felt the desire to start creating some distance between me and my father. Afterwards, I noticed that the sky did not fall, and my life went on. What's in a name? Ringo Starr is not Ringo Starr. Ernest Borgnine (McHale!) was not Ernest Borgnine. Even beloved Johnny Pesky was not Johnny Pesky. Simplicity has its appeal.

12. Media Mavens

From my home, I relied increasingly on the media to keep me up to date on the team. Even when the Red Sox had fielded poor teams, the media covering them was top notch. That certainly included the radio and television coverage. Baseball had been largely a radio game for decades, which made household names out of the best of the announcers, such as Red Barber and Mel Allen. Television coverage of baseball was still a somewhat recent, and not very common, occurrence when I started paying attention to the Red Sox.

The Red Sox did well on both counts. Curt Gowdy and Ned Martin handled both the radio and television announcing, with Mel Parnell doing the color. Like many fans, what I remember most distinctly about Gowdy was the folksy way he said, "Neighbor, have a 'gansett!" when he was promoting the sudsy pride of Rhode Island, Narragansett beer. My other impressions of him were that he talked mainly about baseball on the air with Martin (as opposed to lengthy discussions of what they ate for dinner in the hotel the previous night) and never missed a chance to mention Ted Williams, his close friend.

I heard much more of Gowdy when he went on to do the baseball Game of the Week with Pee Wee Reese and Tony Kubek for NBC. Televised nationally on Saturday afternoons, it was a special treat for baseball fans, as the mere fact that National League teams were on TV in Boston made it required viewing. Later the broadcasting crew included the gregarious and amusingly self-deprecating Joe Garagiola, whose humorous takes on his old playing days, mainly with the St. Louis Cardinals, when he was a solidly mediocre catcher for about a decade, were always worth a listen. A close second to

Garagiola's baseball tales of yore were his quips about his lack of hair—he would have made a great pitchman for any hair replacement company, but he was ahead of his time, so to speak.

A final memory of Gowdy is that my father, in a deliberate but joking manner, often referred to him as "Hank" Gowdy, recalling the old catcher and, later, coach for the Boston Braves, including the legendary 1914 World Series champions, when Gowdy caught not one but *two* 26-game winners during that season of glory and hit a lofty .545 in the Series. The patriotic Gowdy then went on to become the first player to enlist in World War I, in 1917, and fought heroically in the trenches in France. Remarkably, Gowdy later left a coaching position with the Reds to rejoin the Army during World War II. As an officer at Fort Benning, Gowdy became the only active major leaguer to serve in both wars. With Gowdy and other Braves players, my father did not miss a chance to remind me of their moments in the sun, no matter how far back they stretched.

Frank Deford once observed of the finest radio announcers in baseball, "Sometimes the games we heard from their lips were better than the games we saw with our eyes." This was certainly true in the case of Ned Martin. Like the *Globe's* Ray Fitzgerald in print, Martin was a gift from the literary gods, and I never tired of listening to him. It was hard to tell if he was a frustrated poet whose fate was to announce baseball games, or a frustrated announcer whose fate was to recite Shakespeare and other lyrical passages between pitches. And he was an ex-Marine who had seen the slaughter on Iwo Jima, just to add to the mysterious make-up of the man.

Listening to Martin meant never turning the dial, at least if you had the slightest touch of romance in your soul. He knew baseball, and could analyze the game as well as anyone. And while his affection for the Sox was clear, he was no homer. "Keeping it real" was instinctive for Martin. He gave credit where credit was due, on either club—given the respect, almost in hushed tones, with which he spoke of Mel Stottlemyre, for example, there was no doubt that Martin would have loved to have seen Stottlemyre throwing his masterful sinker in a Red Sox uniform. (And so would I!) And Red Sox errors, wild pitches, missed bunts, and baserunning snafus were described in full, and unfortunately often, sometimes requiring a touch of the poet when the pain or humiliation of repeated miscues became too much to bear. In the worst of circumstances, Martin relied on King Claudius, in *Hamlet*, to aptly assess the damage: "Oh Gertrude/When sorrows come, they come not single spies/But in battalions."

But Martin endured it with the patient resignation of one who understood that such was the predicament for all fans of the beleaguered Red Sox, and the endurance itself, like Sisyphus and his rock, was a timeless fate borne by generations. Martin's heart, though, never lost its passion for the Sox or for the spectacle of baseball, and when a play of unexpected merit or misery transpired, he would describe it fully before aptly summing it up with his trademark expression, "Mercy!" When he later teamed up for several years with Jim Woods, another announcer who described more than what was happening on the field, although a little less poetically, the result was radio bliss for Red Sox fans. Jack Craig himself, the dean of media critics, called them "the finest baseball radio play-by-play ever heard in Boston." About Martin, Craig observed quite correctly, "Martin became more than very popular with his listeners. They felt genuine affection for him." Yes, we certainly did.

Another long-time voice of the Red Sox was Ken Coleman, a Quincy native who had a remarkable career, having done Indians and Browns games in Cleveland for years before coming to Boston. My favorite football team was the Browns, as the Boston Patriots were only in the American Football League, unfairly maligned at the time as a minor league until Joe Namath, in words and deeds, took the National Football League down a few notches in the memorable third Super Bowl. I liked the Browns mainly because of Jim Brown and, soon after Brown's premature retirement, his Hall-of-Fame replacement Leroy Kelly (and, I should add, UMass's own Milt Morin, the outstanding tight end and the Minutemen's first NFL first-round-pick). When I heard that Coleman had seen *every* game that Jim Brown had played, I was astonished and probably jealous as well. Coleman was a polished announcer who was, as they say, a good ambassador for the game. I thought he had the breadth but not the depth of Martin. I don't know— maybe his trademark refrain of "There's a foul ball off to the left, caught by a fan from Billerica" (or any other town in New England) just grew a little tiresome. But Coleman was professional and classy and certainly a popular broadcaster for many years.

In the 1970s came other notable voices, the most compelling being that of former Red Sox outfielder Ken Harrelson, who brought his refreshing candor to the airwaves. With his witty, insightful, and honest commentary on the play of both teams, it was clear that The Hawk loved baseball, life, and himself, possibly not in that order. He was one of those people you turn on a game to hear, and many fans, including me, did just that.

One of the best radio sports talk shows of the time was "Voice of Sports" on WHDH every Saturday evening, hosted by the always unflappable and gracious Don Gillis. A pioneer of sports broadcasting in Boston—I knew he had to be a pioneer because he had already been around a while when I started my radio quest for sports talk—Gillis led an opinionated panel that usually included Tim Horgan and Bill Liston of the *Boston Herald* and Joe Costanza of WHDH. One unique thing about the program was that they took no phone calls. They just sat around a table, as I imagined them, discussing/arguing the latest issues regarding the local teams, particularly the Red Sox and Celtics.

Horgan was the bulldog of the group, not afraid to call Yaz a loafer for not running out a ground ball or any rookie a flash in the pan. Especially when it came to the Red Sox,

Horgan generally, and often aggressively, subscribed to the theory of "whatever is, is wrong." It was must-listening to hear him lambaste a manager for losing control of the clubhouse, a trade illustrating the Red Sox philosophy that it is better to give than to receive (Earl Wilson for Don Demeter, anyone?), or the reasons for optimism for any upcoming season. "Pitching? Oh yeah, the pitching's terrific! Other than the starters and relievers, the pitching's in great shape!" was a typical blast from Horgan, which often came with a very purposeful sneer at the end.

I don't know if he despised everything as much as he seemed to—I tend to think he came across as a curmudgeon just because, in fact, he had personally seen one year after another of ineptitude at Fenway. But Horgan was on top of his game every week, and I wish I could still listen to him now. I regret that he didn't write for the *Globe*—that was the *Globe's* loss.

On almost any other show, Bill Liston himself would have been the resident scowl, but instead he sort of worked as the setup man for Horgan, offering his own dismissive comments on the team before Horgan moved in to utterly destroy the target. Joe Costanza, by contrast, was mild-mannered, opting to take the other-side-of-the-coin approach and gently encouraged in that direction by Gillis to give the program a semblance of balance.

But the show had two strengths that, at least in my memory, never waned: the panelists lived and died with the local teams, which made their comments always heartfelt, and there were no callers, so one didn't have to fear any discussion of a suggestion, probably formulated over months of contemplation, that, say, the Red Sox make Tony C a catcher while moving Russ Gibson to center field and Reggie Smith to the bullpen. On the other hand, the prospect of unleashing the wrath of Horgan on such callers would have sent ratings through the roof.

An underrated and possibly underappreciated show was "Sportscope," with its three hosts, Eli Schleiffer, Teddy Sullivan, and George Bent, which was relegated to a barely audible station on the far-right side of the radio dial. The program had hardly any commercials, which unfortunately was not for want of effort or need. Truly, the marketplace was not sympathetic to Sportscope. What distinguished the program was that the hosts made no pretensions of being professional in any sense. None had a voice of authority like Gil Santos, and I always had the impression that they could truly be any three guys in a bar just sitting around over a few beers and chewing the sports fat of the day. There was no hype, no insider scoops, no attempts at sounding like "experts" on anything. They just had, for the most part, rational observations on the local teams and a sports passion to match. Their callers tended to reflect the level of discourse of the hosts, making it a call-in show that you did not fear listening to.

Their contrasting personalities added to the charm of the show. Schleiffer, the nominal leader of the group, had a voice that sounded like his mouth was half-full of potatoes. Smooth he was not. But he had a quirky sense of humor and was an able facilitator of the show. Bent was the most outspoken, not quite like Horgan but often close, while Sullivan would be the voice of reason unless Bent, for some reason, was taking it easy on the locals, in which case Sullivan would chime in with a tame dig at one player or another. But the show worked, as the hosts and their callers knew their sports and kept the intensity level high throughout. And the intimacy of it all, knowing that you were among a handful of listeners who even knew the show existed, made it seem more special.

The "Sports Huddle," as mentioned earlier, was often hilarious in its off-beat look at the sporting scene, and, like "Sportscope," was initially buried at the end of the AM dial. But very unlike "Sportscope," the "Sports Huddle" eventually gained fame and, in the case of lead host Eddie Andelman, even fortune. I sometimes wished that the "Sports Huddle" had spent more time discussing the ups and downs of the local entries rather than, for example, calling up a Chinese restaurant in Los Angeles to ask an unsuspecting waitress how she thought the Angels were going to do against the Red Sox that weekend, or, later, relentlessly ridiculing Don Zimmer to the point of renaming him Chiang Kai-shek. But I have to admit that I did laugh a lot, which was really the show's aim in the first place: just to have fun.

Providing less fun but pleasurable to listen to nonetheless was Guy Mainella on WBZ's "Calling All Sports" program. Mainella took a more sober and analytical approach to the local sports entities, and the fact that his call-in show, unlike the others, was on the air five nights a week made it quite easy to keep up with the froth and foam being spewed by both young fans and older pre-Yawkeyites in their unabashed assessments of the Red Sox. Mainella covered all the bases and was professional to the core, but somehow, I thought more was possible. I was interested in what he had to say, but not obsessively so. However, that probably just reflects my preference for the barking of Tim Horgan or the musings of Ned Martin—many other listeners obviously felt Mainella did just fine.

I found that radio, particularly AM, had one other very useful value regarding baseball. At night, even on a small radio, you could catch games up and down the dial from cities such as New York, Baltimore, Cleveland, and Philadelphia. I could even get the Expos games of Coco Laboy and Rusty "Le Grand Orange" Staub from Montreal—in French, unfortunately. The reception for all of them tended to fade in and out, with background static a constant annoyance, so it was not something you could listen to for more than twenty minutes or so without starting to lose your mind. But this radio exposure gave the sport a more expansive feel, and helped me to convince myself that I was a legitimate baseball fan and not just a yahoo.

In my own case, though, I often preferred getting my baseball fix of news by reading, and there was plenty of worthwhile material to choose from. One of the great treasures was the sports section of the *Boston Globe*. For reasons unknown to a young boy, no one in my neighborhood seemed to read the *Herald* or the *Record American*, so I delivered about forty copies of the *Globe* each day except Sunday, making me very familiar with the paper. In contrast to all revenue-starved newspapers of today, the *Globe* at that time had no ads on the front page, or on the front pages of any inside section. When people picked up their paper, they saw actual news, not sale prices and bank promos.

In the sports section, I routinely poured over the box scores, studying the Red Sox numbers in particular but always slightly miffed that the West Coast games, played so late, did not appear until two days later, if at all. For those, I had to check the weekly *Sporting News*, which I subscribed to—a highly satisfying investment of some of my newspaper earnings.

But the *Globe* was must-reading for Boston sports fans, and I still remember the writers whose work appeared regularly. Jerry Nason had his column on the front page of the sports section. Nason, given his talent, probably should have been my favorite writer. But, from my young boy's very limited point of view, he had the annoying habit of writing so many columns about marathons, something called the BAA, and the latest fleet of running sensations to arrive in Boston for the April tradition of racing from Hopkinton to Copley Square. At the time, I was certainly not into running, having no interest in a crowd of guys who would run up and down hills for 26 miles, often in the rain. (In a sign of the times, women were not considered—by men—to be physically fit to do the same, even after Bobbi Gibb did just that in 1966.) I only remember thinking, each time that I read one of his running columns, that he had wasted yet another opportunity to write about baseball, a sport he observed with great insight. But I recognized that he had a certain authority, even gravitas, to his writing, and when he did write about the Red Sox, it was always most informative and entertaining. So, I looked forward to reading his pieces on the Red Sox. I just wanted more of them.

Clif Keane's writing was not at all dispassionate—in my memory, he was always quick to point out who was in a slump, who hadn't come through in the clutch, who had missed a steal or a bunt sign, who had overthrown the cutoff man, or who was sleeping in the dugout. For that reason, I liked reading his work. He had an edge to his writing. I'm sure he praised players as well, but that was almost irrelevant in Keane's case.

Two writers I always enjoyed were Roger Birtwell and Harold Kaese. They were from the old school, a couple of experienced baseball writers who could reminisce about the glory days of the sport. To me, it seemed as if they had personally witnessed Napoleon Lajoie (the pride of Woonsocket, Rhode Island) and Three Finger Brown in action, although they actually didn't go back quite that far. But I always loved reading about the history of the game, and Birtwell and Kaese (who wrote a book on the Boston Braves) never missed a chance to dip into the lore of the sport, often writing as if Ted Williams and Vern Stephens had been in their prime just yesterday. The modern game of the 1960s, with its coast to coast travel, higher salaries, national television coverage, and numerous black and Latino players, may have seemed dramatically altered from the game they had grown up on, but it was all baseball, and they covered it with an eye to history. I read their stories not just for enjoyment but to go back to the "once upon a time" days of baseball.

Here is a taste of Birtwell, in his column, "Birtwell's Baseball," from a 1969 article entitled, "Pitchers Have But One Arm."

> There is a great maw—in this land—
> that devours young pitchers.
> Its jaws get their snap from a shiny
> white atom ball. They gain added bite from the

modern bat's spring. And they are whetted by owners who pay off on power.

The days of the Ruffings and Rixeys and Fabers ... men like Ted Lyons ... are passing. In fact, they have passed. Even one of the recent ones, Sandy Koufax, had to quit at 30.

But a great many are gone long before that.

Jerry Stephenson, with an ERA of half a run at Seattle, a month later couldn't comb his own hair; Jose Santiago, a year ago one of his league's best pitchers, now is obviously through; Jim Lonborg, a bright star in '67, has won only six games since.

I'll always remember the words of a lady in the hamlet of Alba, Mo. Her name is Mabel Boyer and she has had more sons in professional baseball, I believe, than any other woman who ever lived.

"When my oldest boy, Cloyd, had arm trouble," said Mrs. Boyer, "I said to myself 'I hope none of my other boys become pitchers.'"

And they didn't. They all, as I remember, became infielders. Two of them opposed each other in a World Series.

Pitching is at least 75 percent of baseball. Pitchers get gold and glory. But also, a pitcher has only one arm.

And the Great Maw awaits them.

Birtwell wasn't Hemingway, and he wrote this as Bob Gibson, Steve Carlton, Mickey Lolich, Ferguson Jenkins, and others were showing no signs of fearing the Great Maw. Still, Birtwell had seen a lot of baseball, which was what mattered most to me.

My favorite *Globe* writer was Ray Fitzgerald. A typical Fitzgerald story undoubtedly left many readers wondering why he was writing about men playing sports rather than composing lines of verse or fiction. He could write perceptively about the key plays of the game, but he was more effective when he was philosophizing on the twisting, turning vagaries of a particular game or season or even a lifetime.

Ruminating in one column on his love of football, he wrote, "There remains about the game the romanticism of autumn, of October homecomings and traditional rivalries in early November, of falling leaves and bonfires. It is still a game that is best when there is a nip in the air and another in your pocket.... A casual Saturday afternoon in a stadium becomes part of the mind's scrapbook, to be taken down from the shelf and leafed through again 20 years later as a remembrance of things past, a reminder of the way we were." He concluded, "Well, enough of that, or I'll be describing the way Red Grange looked the day he ran for five touchdowns. Bring on the season. Bring on the Steelers and the Elis and the Sooners and the Braintree Wamps. Bring on Terry Bradshaw and Tony Dorsett and the high school kid who hasn't been discovered yet. Give me some more memories for the scrapbook."

Something written by Fitzgerald tended toward the sublime, often with humor but not at the expense of the truth. In a 1969 column on the Celtics' dismantling of the Knickerbockers in the playoffs, Fitzgerald, after hearing Bill Russell refer to basketball as an "art form" in a postgame interview, wrote, "If basketball players are the classical dancers of modern athletics, the Knicks last night played with their ballet slippers tied together. Rudolph Nureyev would have sat down and cried." (I should probably add that while the Knicks may not have been sufficiently artistic that night, their forwards rotation of Willis Reed, Bill Bradley, Dave Debusschere, and sub/hatchet man Phil Jackson must easily rank as the most successful frontcourt combination, on and off the court, in NBA history.)

Fitzgerald didn't start writing for the *Globe* until the truly bad days of the Red Sox had pretty much passed, but he saw enough baseball heartache to qualify as a fellow sufferer. It was appropriate for Fitzgerald to be covering the Red Sox because he saw not merely the stats of the game but the strengths and frailties of the human beings who were playing it, and the Red Sox provided a smorgasbord from which to choose. His brand of humor was perfect for a chronicler of the Sox. Like all fans, he needed to be upbeat to survive the 162-game season which, even after 1966, never ended in glory, and fatalistic to accept the inevitable. Anyone looking for a play-by-play analysis of the game was not likely to seek out Ray Fitzgerald's name. He didn't always take a direct route in making his point, but with his irresistible humor and his focus on the human side of both victory and, more often, defeat, he somehow made it slightly easier to accept the failings of the local nine, and probably of ourselves as well.

There were other noteworthy *Globe* writers—Ernie ("Thoughts While Shaving") Roberts, Will McDonough, and Neil Singelais, to name three. Soon, another generation of sports writers, including Leigh Montville, Larry Whiteside, Peter Gammons, Bob Ryan, Dan Shaughnessy, Nick Cafardo, and Kevin Paul Dupont would continue the tradition of excellence for the *Globe*, and I enjoyed reading them as well, but their predecessors were my introduction to the Red Sox and newspapers.

In those days, the *Globe* had the excellent policy of running stories and columns by national sportswriters such as Red Smith, Jim Murray, and Milton Gross. Among the *Globe* items sitting in the boxes at my house is one in particular that deserves mention for anyone interested in Red Sox, and in baseball, tradition. It is a 12 x 7 color photo of Pete Runnels, posing in his batting stance in foul territory at Fenway (with a background of appropriately near-empty stands), under the large title of "Batting Champion." Runnels won two batting titles for the Red Sox, but I know that this photo was cut from the newspaper following the 1962 season, when I was six years old, by what is written on the back.

The 1962 World Series had already been delayed by a three-game National League playoff between the Dodgers and the Giants, and once the Series between the Giants and the Yankees finally got underway, rain on both coasts disrupted play and led to cancellations of games. In one of the strange-but-true tales of baseball lore, the Giants' imaginative groundskeeper, one Matty Schwab, had his crew spray the field with a chemical that would force earthworms to the surface and allow the rainwaters to flow down the escaping worms' holes and help drain the playing area.

Such fun could hardly be ignored by the Series scribes, and it wasn't. On the reverse side of the Runnels photo is an article written by Red Smith, who was evidently, like Schwab, exasperated by nature's repeated interruption of the proceedings. Not to upstage the fine accomplishment of Runnels, but Smith's prose, undiminished more than half a century later, deserves a repeat performance. Below are the first two paragraphs:

> Don't look now, but along about 3 p.m. Monday Eastern Daylight, there may be an Autumn replacement for Bugs Bunny on the television screen. With the help of a few thousand resident worms, it may be possible to revive an archaic, half-forgotten entertainment called baseball which is supposed to have enjoyed wide popularity in antediluvian San Francisco.
>
> There's nothing new about worms in baseball, of course, but in the past they have operated mostly in the front office. The ones recruited to help get Candlestick Park ready for the sixth, and possibly seventh, World Series game inhabit the soil of that peculiar playpen.

It's safe to say that the *Globe* featured two baseball champions on that page, one who did his work with his bat and the other with his typewriter. And to add my own Juan Marichal-touch to the story, Marichal, pitching a shutout through four innings of Game 4, hurt a finger when a pitch struck him while he was trying to bunt and had to leave the game. Manager Alvin Dark questioned the injury to the point of promising that Marichal "will not pitch again in the Series if it rains for a week." Marichal did not pitch again, the rain did continue to fall, and the Giants did go down to defeat, perhaps, in Dark's case, deservedly so.

13. Book Learning

In addition to reading the *Globe*, I had a very organized—possibly maniacal—approach to learning about baseball by reading books in the 1960s. Although there were about fifty fewer years of baseball history to deal with than now, I had no trouble finding interesting books on both the stars of the day and those in the "old" days going back to the turn of the century. I can almost certainly trace my general interest in reading and books back to these early days of baseball reading.

In my bedroom, I had a small bookcase, made by my father, which served as a kind of baseball library, and the books, which grew over the years, were divided according to my own system. In one group were books on players of days gone by, written by authors such as Milton Shapiro, Arnold Hano, Charles Einstein, Tom Meany, and Fred Lieb. They were filled with intriguing anecdotes, photos, and, thankfully, lots of statistics, and I read them over and over. One of the first of these historical books, and one of my favorites, was a thin volume entitled *Stories of Champions*, published by Scholastic in 1966, which had very readable bios of Ruth, Cobb, Walter Johnson, Honus Wagner ("the Flying Dutchman"), and Christy "Big Six" Mathewson, whose local connections included his inauspicious, 2–13 professional start with the Taunton (Mass.) Herrings in 1899, three wasted complete games for the New York Giants against the Red Sox in the 1912 World Series (all losses, 0–2 record, 0.94 ERA), and two years as president of the Boston Braves before his untimely death in 1925. I ordered it from the school book order form, and I think I probably read the whole book before dinner on the day I brought it home from school.

These books presented memorable views of the giants of the past that were masterful in keeping the legends of baseball alive, in all aspects. On Johnson, Meany wrote, "Rarely has there been a baseball hero with the innate modesty and decency of Walter Johnson. He neither smoked nor drank, never beefed at an umpire or argued with a teammate. He didn't swear and he never had the faintest semblance of a swelled head. About the only complaint anyone ever could make of him was that he was stubborn—as witness his insistence on throwing the wrinkle he called a curve every time he had two strikes and no balls on the hitter."

On Ruth, Lieb recalled the Babe's legendary charitable efforts. "He was especially interested in the lame, the crippled, and kids injured in accidents or suffering from serious if not fatal diseases," Lieb wrote. "He visited untold number of boys in hospitals, private homes, even six-story walk-up tenements. He always gave them the greeting 'Hello kid, now you get well.' Usually he closed by saying, 'I'll hit a homer for you tomorrow.'"

But Ruth had another, equally famous, side that Lieb witnessed as well, and it was not one that reminded anyone of Walter Johnson. "Ruth was a big man who did things in a big way," Lieb acknowledged. "He ate big, drank big, hit big home runs, so it is not surprising that Babe had a big sex appetite. And this appetite was unquenchable. Babe was not a one-woman man. One woman couldn't satisfy him. Frequently, it took half a dozen.... His phallus and home-run bat were his prize possessions, in that order."

From my reading, I came away with the impression that Meany and Lieb were almost as much a part of the game as the players. (Lieb, in fact, was an honorary pallbearer at Ruth's funeral. Helping to carry the Babe's casket was Jumping Joe Dugan, who played third base for the 1927 Bombers and in 1982 passed away in, of all places, Norwood.) At the end of his career, Lieb put together his baseball "all-time greats" in lists of twenty-five years, stretching from 1876–1900 to 1951–1975, and he claimed that he had seen all but *six* of the players perform. That's longevity. For the record, Ted Williams and Juan Marichal made it, while Yaz didn't.

The diligent research of Glenn Stout, however, has exposed Lieb as an unreliable source concerning the "buffoonery" of Sox owner Harry Frazee in selling Babe Ruth to the Yankees, an accusation that evidently had more to do with Lieb's anti-Semitism toward Frazee (who wasn't even Jewish!) than with any financial problems on Frazee's end. Frazee did not deserve the decades of scorn heaped upon him. And that Lieb once wrote that a Jew could be a skillful boxer but "did not have the background to stand out in a sport which is so essentially a team game as baseball" cannot be read as anything but anti-Semitic.

Still, Lieb did witness a lot of baseball played by many of the giants of the game, so at least some of his colorful anecdotes, I'm assuming with hope as much as conviction, were based on reality. Otherwise, if Lieb and his journalistic brethren were inventing much of hardball history as they wrote it, then many boys, including me, grew up with more fallacy than fact in our baseball education. That Christy Mathewson was a saint and Rube Waddell a lush were childhood images that endured because of words from scribes such as Lieb and Meany, but maybe they shouldn't have.

I also read insightful books by former pitcher Jim Brosnan, and, yes, a book on those amazin' Mets by Maury Allen. Naturally, there was Al Hershberg's book on Yaz, too. These works prepared me well for two slightly later books, *The Boys of Summer* by Roger Kahn and *The Summer Game* by Roger Angell, which were praised as heavyweights of baseball literature, and rightly so. Years afterward, I continued to read Angell's books of discerning observations, published at five year intervals, for a kind of momentary, nostalgic hit to remind me of the times when it was possible for baseball to matter so much to a young, uncluttered mind.

214

My father took his own trip down memory lane, some years later, when a book entitled *The Image of Their Greatness* came out. He spent many nights poring through the old pictures, often picking out a photo such as the one showing Dizzy Dean and Lefty Grove together and remarking something like, "Christ—you wanna compare Denny McLain to *them*?" Well, from 1965 to 1969 (108–51), there was a case to be made.

Another book that I read eagerly, and one that—unintentionally—illustrates the maddening history of the Red Sox, was *Baseball: The First 100 Years*, published by Major League Baseball in 1969 as part of the celebration of the sport's centennial season. Packed with memorable photos, old and new, a text that recalled the sport's great moments as well as reviewing the present players, and, again, piles of statistics, the book was a page-turner for any baseball fanatic.

For the Red Sox, on page 155, the frustration of fifty years was summarized with painful clarity. For its "look to the past," the team's featured players were Cy Young, Joe Cronin, Jimmie Foxx, and Ted Williams. That may not have been equal to the Yankees' selection of Ruth, Gehrig, DiMaggio, and Dickey, but it was close enough to argue about. Below that (*well* below, one might add), in the "look to the future," were photos and bios of Ken Brett and Jerry Moses. In true Red Sox-style, Brett may have not only been a better hitter than he was a pitcher, but he was probably a better hitter than Moses, a catcher. Even all these years later, one is tempted to cry, like Scrooge before Marley's ghost at the sight of his own gravestone, "assure me that I yet may change these shadows you have shown me, by an altered life!" But more decades would pass before there would be any life alterations for the star-crossed Red Sox.

And for full disclosure, the Yankees' own "look to the future" featured Jerry Kenney and Bobby Murcer, with Murcer alone besting the Red Sox by a considerable margin. Taking the prize overall for the most impressive "look to the future" was the Oakland Athletics, with Vida Blue and Rollie Fingers, who would crank out 191 wins and 138 saves between them for the A's. And with its "look to the past" of Home Run Baker, Lefty Grove, Al Simmons, and Rube Waddell, the A's could gaze back or ahead feeling pretty good about their illustrious organization, and Charlie Finley no doubt was in the habit of doing just that in 1969.

Finally, a most fortuitous development in my own world of baseball reading at this time was the publication of the mother of all statistical collections, that first baseball encyclopedia. Although I needed two hands to pick it up, I was never dissuaded from poring over it, page by page, dwelling even on (maybe *especially* on) players I had never heard of, and on statistics that I couldn't imagine. There are countless examples of such, but I'll just mention one here to highlight the point. In 1886, one Charles "Lady" Baldwin, a southpaw pitching for the Detroit Wolverines in the National League, put up a noteworthy stat line of 42–13, starting 56 games and completing 55 of them, tossing 487 innings and striking out 323, with a 2.24 ERA. Interestingly, those 42 wins would make up more than half of his career total, 73, compiled in six seasons, five of which were relatively uneventful. Lady's luck certainly didn't last for long, but for one year, hitters rarely touched him.

Of course, there were other eye-opening statistics from players I *had* heard of. One memorable example not likely to be repeated soon is Hall of Famer Luke Appling's 1936 line of 6 home runs, 128 RBI's, and a .388 batting average. Only The Iron Horse himself, Lou Gehrig, stood between Appling and the MVP in that stellar season for each. Two years earlier, though, Gehrig had been on the other side of fate, as his 49 home runs, 166 RBI's, and .363 batting average gained him only *fifth* place in the MVP voting, with three members of the pennant-winning Tigers alone (Mickey Cochrane, Charlie Gehringer, and Schoolboy Rowe) and one of his own teammates (Lefty Gomez) finishing ahead of him.

The Red Sox' Walt Dropo had a statistical career that always baffled me. A three-sport star at the University of Connecticut, Dropo was selected in both the 1946 NFL draft and the 1947 NBA (known at the time as the Basketball Association of America, or the BAA) draft but chose to sign with the Red Sox in 1947. While his dazzling rookie numbers of 34, 144, .322 legitimately earned him Rookie of the Year and All-Star honors in 1950, Dropo plunged the next year to 11, 57, .239, spending a stint in the minor leagues before being traded away the following year. And even though he went on to have a 13-year career, he hit over 20 home runs only two more times, and never again drove in 100 runs or hit .300. In my statistically-cluttered mind, I wondered how does a guy drive in *144* runs in his rookie year and then fall off the charts? Countless baseball managers have undoubtedly pondered similar questions at length each time one of their own players has struggled inexplicably—and indefinitely. Players just "losing it" seems hardly an adequate explanation, but it happens.

For a boy my age, there was much more baseball reading than just books. There were numerous monthly baseball/sports magazines, and the photos from these magazines were essential in filling the baseball scrapbooks that I kept and covering my bedroom walls. The weekly *Sports Illustrated* was certainly a magazine that I enjoyed reading. Luckily for me, my father worked with a man who subscribed, and every few months he would collect the back issues, tie them up in rope, and give them to my father to take home. That was like having Christmas several times a year, and the bundles included the swimsuit issues as well. At my young age, I wondered a little about the connection between bikinis and sports, although I went on to learn that women in bikinis had statistics of their own.

My favorite magazine was *Sport*. Although it was certainly close, *Sport* struck me as a more appealing publication than *SI*, one that tackled the stories of players past and present with superb writing and in great depth. Each of the monthly issues featured full-page photos and stories, including a lengthy article, contained toward the back of the magazine, usually on an individual player. By the time I was done reading one of those articles, which often absorbed me from start to finish, I was ready to lie down for a few minutes just to let my brain recover from the experience. The feature on Juan Marichal may have sealed the deal with *Sport* and me. And Red Sox-wise, I still have the June 1964 *Sport* cover of Dick Stuart, lazily holding a bat, with a wide grin on his face, betraying no hint of the calamitous Boston teams he played on or the leading role he played in making them calamitous.

But the true Bible of baseball reading was *The Sporting News*, and all of its myriad publications. First there was the essential item, the weekly newspaper itself. When I realized that each issue contained the box score for *every* major league game played the previous week, I ordered a subscription, which I kept up through my childhood. The idea that I could now see the box score for every West Coast game, even if it was a week after the fact, was amazing to me in those very pre-internet days. There were also weekly updates on each team by local writers, and the full statistical roundup of both leagues. There was certainly no shortage of reading pleasure in any issue of *The Sporting News*. I recall my frustration when I used to go to the barber shop for a haircut as a boy and the main reading material for waiting customers was *True*, *Argosy*, and *Mad*. Where was *The Sporting News*, I wondered?

That newspaper alone would have been enough to satisfy the appetite of most baseball fans, but *The Sporting News*, under the baseball fanaticism of Mr. Spink, whose name was synonymous with that company, had a whole line of baseball publications that went into baseball minutiae that would have challenged even the most rabid fan. I faithfully read *The Sporting News Baseball Guide* each year, which was filled with a staggering amount of statistical data from the previous year. Then there were the offshoots, such as the *Baseball Register* and *One for the Book*, which went into even greater detail on players' careers and records of all kinds.

The best of all the *Sporting News* publications, at least to a youthful baseball historical buff such as myself, was a book called *Daguerreotypes of Great Baseball Stars*. There is no doubt that it was a physically intimidating book, not packaged to appeal to the casual reader. On the cover was a faded, serious-looking countenance of Babe Ruth, and inside were the statistical records of the careers of hundreds of retired—and in many cases dead—baseball stars.

That was the book in its entirety: page after page of small print numbers, enough runs, hits, doubles, home runs, and batting averages to drive a normal mind to madness or deep slumber. But for me, it had the tremendous advantage of pointing me directly to the *best* players from the past and explaining, statistically-speaking, why they were the best. Countless hours were spent poring over the stats of Bill Terry, Heinie Manush, Zack Wheat, Chief Bender, Rabbit Maranville, and brothers Paul (Big Poison) and Lloyd (Little Poison) Waner, among so many others. When I think now of the vast amount of time I spent, head buried in some dog-eared *Sporting News* publication like *Daguerreotypes*, I am only glad that I survived the experience and did not pass on these particular genes to my children.

One of my favorite old-timers and a definite Hall of Famer was Cornelius McGillicuddy, or Connie Mack, a Massachusetts native (East Brookfield). The more I read about him, the more fascinating he seemed, almost like a man from outside time. As a manager, he wore a suit and a hat (usually a derby or a straw pork pie hat, from the photographic evidence), rather than a baseball uniform, which always intrigued me. To look at it another way, is it possible to imagine Bill Belichick coaching while wearing a helmet and shoulder pads, or Brad Stevens wearing shorts and sneakers, or Bruce Cassidy wearing hockey gloves and waving a stick at his players? Sartorially, Mack had it right. He also believed in sobriety, back in the day when some players considered a hangover to be part of their game day preparation. (In 1903, the *Cincinnati Enquirer* printed some advice for hitters following a rough night: "Whenever a ball looks like this:

O

O

O

Take a chance on the middle one.")

Mack certainly had enough statistics to satisfy any baseball junkie. He played ten undistinguished seasons as a catcher, but his name was made as a manager. He spent *fifty* consecutive seasons, from 1901 to 1950, managing the Philadelphia Athletics. He won more than 3700 games in his career, but lost more than *3900*, having hung on about fifteen years too long with some terrible teams. He had teams that went 102–48, 104–46, and 107–45, but others that went 49–105 (twice!), 36–104, and 36–117, the last, the 1916 Athletics, featuring a staff that included Jack Nabors (1–20), Tom Sheehan (1–16), Elmer Myers (14–23), and the ace, Bullet Joe Bush (15–24). Mack certainly had seen the thrill of victory and the agony of defeat many times over.

And to show again how much of baseball does come back to the Red Sox, Mack, desperately needing cash, sent both Lefty Grove and Jimmie Foxx, two future Hall of Famers, to the Red Sox in the 1930s. With the Athletics, Grove and Foxx had won three consecutive pennants and two straight World Series. With the Red Sox, Grove won over 100 games, including a 20-win season, while Foxx smashed more than 200 home runs, highlighted by 50 in his 1938 MVP season, when he set the Red Sox RBI record with 175. But, predictably, there were no World Series victories or even a pennant for those Red Sox teams of Grove and Foxx. Grove, however, did bring with him his Belichickian attitude toward the press. Once asked by a newspaperman to recount some of his funniest moments in the big leagues, Grove, who was known to tear down lockers when his fiery temper was unleashed, responded tersely, "I never saw anything funny about baseball."

One possible benefit of all of this reading might have been one of my rare moments of academic success, later, in high school. I apparently produced a work of some merit, at least according to my English teacher, a very enthusiastic and likable man, Mr. W. He gave us an assignment to write a research paper on a "serious" topic. Not too many serious topics were passing through my mind in those days, so coming up with a subject was a bit of a challenge. Mr. W was an open-minded guy, but when I asked him if I could write about sports, he looked less than thrilled. After much discussion, in which he must have realized that no intellectual miracles were about to occur, he agreed to let me write on discrimination in sports.

This was most fortunate for me, as it was a topic that I actually knew something about. I think that most of the "research" for the report was already in my head, some of it having come from an excellent series of articles that *Sports Illustrated* ran in 1968 on the exploitation of "The Black Athlete," but I did read more and pleasantly surprised, if not shocked, him with a detailed examination of racism in sports. He gave me a good grade, along with the gruff but encouraging advice, "just keep writing."

14. Back to Reality

Major League Baseball in 1967 had been blessed by a sensational American League pennant race and a seven-game World Series featuring two tradition-laden teams and both league MVPs. But each year in baseball writes its own story, and the major league season of 1968 would be the calm before the storm, while for the Red Sox it was, unfortunately, merely the calm without the storm, at least on the field. It was the year that the pitchers dominated and the hitters disappeared.

The Red Sox themselves got the message early on when the Orioles' Tom Phoebus no-hit them in April, which set the tone for the entire major league season. If you just consider that the Cleveland Indians' Luis Tiant, later to be a Red Sox immortal, was the American League ERA leader at 1.60, nearly a half run *higher* than Bob Gibson's 1.12 in the National League, you know that the pitchers in both leagues were toying with hitters. There was no thunder coming from any bats in 1968. Regardless, as a twelve-year-old baseball purist, I thought of 1968 as a terrifically exciting year (and still do), but many others saw the lack of runs or even hits as the death knell for the sport.

The statistics of 1968 hadn't been seen in decades, and haven't been seen since. Denny McLain (31–6, 1.96, 28 complete games), Marichal (26–9, 30 complete games), Tiant (21–9, 9 shutouts), and Gibson (22–9, 13 shutouts) led a suffocating barrage of pitching that left hitters in their own statistical infamy. Yaz picked up another batting title, his third, but with an anemic .301 average, the lowest in major league history. Even that took some doing, as he was batting just .270 with six weeks to go and had to hit over .400 the rest of the way to save the American League further embarrassment. "If I can't hit .300, I don't want the title!" was Yaz's own proud take on it, and he just barely made it over the finish line. In fact, there was only one other American League hitter, Danny Cater (soon to be another Red Sox immortal, in the wrong direction), who even hit as high as .290. And no one in the American League came remotely close to getting 200 hits, with Bert Campaneris leading the way at 177.

The National League was barely an improvement, with only five hitters reaching .300, just three outside of the Alou family. Bowie Kuhn must have been grateful to Felipe and Matty for saving Major League Baseball even more shame. The fact that the combined batting average for both leagues in 1968 was .237, a record in hitting futility that still stands, was shame enough.

The All-Star Game, played at night for the first time in more than twenty years and indoors—at the Astrodome—for the first time ever, was otherwise perfectly representative of the season. In the first inning, Willie Mays singled off of Tiant, got to second base on an error, went to third base on a wild pitch, and scored an unearned run when he crossed the plate as Willie McCovey was hitting into a double play. That was it for scoring—nothing but goose eggs for both sides the rest of the way. The game saw a grand total of 8 hits, with the National League's Drysdale, Marichal, Steve Carlton, Tom Seaver, Ron Reed, and Jerry Koosman holding the junior leaguers to a mere 3. Yaz went 0–4 with 2 strikeouts, the second one ending the game. No fan could have expected better in that season of hitless wonders.

Batters did get back on track the following year, with seven reaching 40 home runs, including Yaz and Rico. But pitchers continued to thrive as well. Interestingly, McLain won 55 games those two years, while Marichal won 47. Since, in the National League, only Carlton has matched Marichal's total, while in the American League, no one has approached McLain's. In Red Sox history, you have to go back a full century, to 1916 and 1917, to find the last Red Sox pitcher who won 47 games over two consecutive seasons, and it was none other than Babe Ruth.

Oddly enough, while the 1960s was a boom-to-bust decade for many hitters, it was a veritable golden age for pitchers as hitters, particularly in the power department. In the sports pages of the day, I remember reading that this pitcher or that pitcher had not only hit a home run, but had done so with the bases loaded, and when I recently checked the details on this, it was true: pitchers hit more grand slams in the 1960s than in any other decade, and it's not close. Ten grand slams were hit by American League pitchers, including two by Camilo Pascual and an inside the park job by Mel Stottlemyre (off Bill Monbouquette at The Stadium), and eight in the National League, with the highlight being Tony Cloninger's two in the same game.

Up to the adoption of the designated hitter rule in 1973, the Red Sox themselves had several pitchers who knew quite well what they were doing at the plate. Among players that I saw, Earl Wilson, Gary Peters, Sonny Siebert, and Ken Brett hit a total of 76 home runs in their careers, 32 of them coming in a Red Sox uniform. On the topic of grand slams, no Red Sox pitcher has hit a grand slam in nearly seventy years, Ellis Kinder, in 1950, being the last, but Jim Lonborg, Rick Wise (twice), Wilson, and Peters all hit homers with the bases full—and all while wearing another uniform.

In the hitless year of 1968, the Red Sox had more than their share of statistical nightmares, both at the plate and on the mound, but before addressing the negatives of that year, a positive and memorable performance was turned in by The Hawk, Ken Harrelson. *Flamboyant* hardly begins to describe Harrelson, one of those people you can say has not been cheated by life. His mod, colorful clothing—Nehru jackets were a favorite—flowing locks, ever-quotable mouth, and general love of attention made The Hawk a sensation in staid Boston. After Harrelson came to the Red Sox, I used to get a laugh out of looking back at his 1964 and 1965 baseball cards, with the Kansas City Athletics, when he was as clean-cut as Dobie Gillis.

With a huge new contract from the Red Sox, endorsements streaming in, and the media ever eager to hear more from him, Harrelson was the talk of the town and, in the process, conveniently helped deflect reporters from Yaz, who had never been particularly comfortable in the spotlight. Harrelson managed to give the Red Sox something of a new image, temporary as it was.

And, for a brief, shining moment, he actually did perform. After giving the Red Sox a small boost in the pennant drive of 1967, but not as much as they had hoped, Harrelson flourished in 1968, leading the league in RBI's with 109 and probably in media attention as well. On top of it all, he was at least as well known for being the best golfer in baseball. When he was dealt with Dick Ellsworth and Juan Pizarro to Cleveland the following season for Jose Azcue, Vicente Romo, and Sonny Siebert (partly to let Tony C back into the lineup), fans howled and The Hawk himself "retired" rather than leave Boston before finally agreeing to move on to the Indians, where he went on to hit 30 home runs for the Tribe that year. To any Red Sox fan of the time, The Hawk was gone, but hardly forgotten, even to this day. His lifetime batting average of .239 best sums up his talent on the diamond, but with Harrelson, it was never about the numbers. As mentioned, I enjoyed him more in his later days as an exceptionally candid announcer, but The Hawk was a true presence on or off the field.

Despite Harrelson's heroics, the most painful statistic of 1968 was 6–10, Jim Lonborg's record following a very consequential skiing accident at Lake Tahoe in December. Expected to be the horse of the staff, Lonborg languished in mediocrity, where he sadly stayed for the next few seasons before the Red Sox finally gave up and packed him off to Milwaukee. Remarkably, and typically for the Red Sox, Lonborg then went on to have some outstanding seasons with the Brewers and Phillies. Another telling number for the Red

Sox was .132, the number of points The Boomer's batting average fell (.303 to .171) in a season-long slump in which he did not hit a single homer at Fenway.

But the only statistic that mattered to the Red Sox and to every other American League team was the mounting total in Denny McLain's win column, and with it the Tigers' lead in the American League. I remember the oddness of each passing week that summer. While, as always, I was living and dying with the Red Sox on a daily basis and sensing, with deepening disappointment, that another pennant race was not to be, I was also rooting for Denny McLain to win each of his starts. From my father, I had heard so much about Dizzy Dean and Lefty Grove and the sanctity of 30 wins that to see it happen again, for the first time in three decades, was too historical an achievement to cheer against. And it all unfolded as a very public event, as the Tigers, it seemed, were on the Game of the Week many Saturdays that summer (as were the equally likable Cubs the following year in their fascinating but futile quest to reach the postseason for the first time in twenty-four years), and they honestly were a great team to watch if you were a genuine baseball fan.

It probably goes without saying that my father was not hoping to see McLain reach 30 wins, just as I was not rooting for Mark McGwire or Sammy Sosa to catch Roger Maris. With age comes sentiment, particularly in the sport of baseball, where many old-timers will never cease to argue that the players back in the days of their youth were the true giants of the game. Against my better judgment, I now find myself feeling that way more than occasionally. After all, is it possible that anyone playing today could *really* be a better all-around player than Mickey Mantle or Willie Mays or Roberto Clemente? Maybe, but I don't ponder such questions too deeply anymore—I'm grateful that I saw what I saw.

The Sox themselves were ten games out by mid-June, and padding personal stats was all that remained for Red Sox players to strive for, which is another way of saying that it was a normal year for the Red Sox. The Tigers replaced the Sox in the World Series and vanquished the Cardinals, doing what the Yankees and Red Sox could not—defeating Bob Gibson in a seventh game. Still, the Red Sox had finished in the first division, showing that 1967 was not a mere tease. I was disappointed but not discouraged. But respectability, I would learn, did not necessarily equate to success.

More importantly, for the first time in memory I did not go to any games that year. My Fenway youth was finished. There was no announcement or discussion of this unsettling truth. It just evolved and became a fact. My father did not like fighting the crowds, and he was not getting any younger or richer or more enthusiastic about family affairs. And I was getting closer to the age when it is not desirable to be seen in public with members of the older generation, particularly your parents. I had nothing to complain about, having already been to two dozen games over the past five years. I don't know how many boys had been to more games at Fenway than I had during that time, but it could not have been a very high number. At the dinner table, I did occasionally wonder aloud if we might get to another game. My father fell back on the time-honored crutch of all parents by answering, "We'll see." What I was to see was that I wouldn't be seeing any more games with my father. I was twelve years old. The Nation had been born, but for the foreseeable future I would be relegated to the bullpen of Red Sox life—a couch in front of a television or, more likely, a radio.

As I followed the Red Sox from more of a distance, I was encouraged to see that, after their remarkable success in 1967, the experts did start to mention the Red Sox in the same breath with the Tigers and the Orioles and the White Sox. However, it was also true that it had now been fifty years since their last championship, and the Red Sox had their own "history" that made it difficult for fans to take them entirely seriously. And they continued to build on that history with more of their soap opera saga in the succeeding years, only now on a wider stage.

Inevitably, the old accusations returned in force. The team was a bunch of selfish individuals, not a unified group. All they cared about were their numbers. Dick Williams was a tyrant, particularly toward stars including Scott and Tony C. (Even lesser players suffered under Williams' wrath. Jose Azcue, riding the bench and unhappy a year after being an All-Star for the Indians in 1968, quit the team three hours before a game and flew home to Kansas City. Three days later, he was shipped off to the California Angels.) Most of the players had simply tuned Williams out. They were all wildly overpaid, especially Yaz, and pampered by Yawkey. The team wasn't big enough for Yaz and Tony C. Yaz was seen as being nearly a son to Yawkey, while Tony C was a wounded warrior, a hero to many fans. But when his brother Billy, also an outfielder, made the team, the Conigliaro family was often featured in heated discussions over what was right/wrong with the team, and it looked like the Conigliaros themselves may have been calling the shots. I remember hearing stories about the Conigliaro father, Sal, having various levels of influence within the organization, and Billy C's constant pouting and complaining only added to the drama. The off-the-field Red Sox were my introduction to conspiracy theories in sports.

Dick O'Connell had provided talent on the field, but in some way, the Red Sox, despite the magic of 1967, could not seem to shake their cavalier style that made them the butt end of jokes throughout baseball. Although they continued to have plenty of offense, the old nemeses of not quite enough pitching (painfully illustrated on a Saturday afternoon in June 1969, when Reggie Jackson alone knocked in ten runs in a 21–7 Oakland victory at Fenway) and non-existent speed, at least until the arrival of Tommy Harper in the early '70s, kept them from joining the elite teams.

As the tension surrounding the team increased, it became clear that a change would have to be made, and in baseball, the change in such cases is almost always the same. Undoubtedly knowing that his job was in peril, Williams continued to blast the team, including Yaz, in what he must have understood was a futile effort. Late in the 1969 season, a year in which the Red Sox finished third but a staggering 22 games behind the Orioles, the plug was pulled: Williams was fired reluctantly by Dick O'Connell and not reluctantly by Tom Yawkey. The Red Sox as a team, talented or otherwise, had long been derided as something between a country club and a fraternity house, and Williams's aggressive attempts to change that culture, while initially successful, were doomed to fail in the end, and did. I had grown to like Williams, a man of little sentiment who had brought us the increasingly sentimental Impossible Dream, and his departure stung, for he, unlike the Red Sox, was a winner.

Williams's replacement was the affable Eddie Popowski, a Red Sox lifer who would spend 65 years as a manager, coach, and scout in the organization, once managing a Triple-A Minneapolis Millers squad that included Yaz, Radatz, Schilling, Tillman, and Earl Wilson. Pop never played a day in the major leagues but was a fan favorite as the team's third base coach. His 1969 promotion was the first of Pop's two terms as interim manager, covering a grand total of ten games. As he was 6–4 in those games, Popowski, all kidding aside, may not have done worse than those unfortunate souls who replaced him had he been given the reins long-term.

Nevertheless, the Red Sox were clearly a team with assets in those post-Impossible Dream years, and they did have their individual highlights. Yaz and Rico, as mentioned, each cranked out 40 home runs in 1969, and Yaz repeated the feat the following year. Tony C, continuing his miraculous comeback, added 56 homers over the two years. Ray Culp, a steady and underrated starter who featured a mysterious pitch known as a palmball, won 50 games over three seasons after coming to the Sox in 1968, and the audacious Sparky Lyle was a workhorse closer.

But they also found out that to whom much is given, much is expected. The newly awakened fans, anticipating first place finishes or at least a serious contender each year, were not too happy to find out that the Red Sox were no longer horrible but not much above pretty good, either. For all of us, it was a new kind of frustration that only seemed to increase our impatience. Over the next few years, we watched as the Orioles, with their stellar pitching—Dave McNally went 15–0 to *start* the 1969 season—and a lineup featuring the Robinsons, Frank and Brooks, dominated both the division and the league by going to three consecutive World Series. The Orioles' run was followed by the even more talented Athletics, who not only won three straight World Series, but did so with Dick Williams at the helm for the first two. Why couldn't the Red Sox get a successful manager like that, a cynic may have wondered. Perhaps the strangest managerial sight in those days, at least from a Red Sox fan's point of view, was seeing Ted Williams managing the Washington Senators—and, for that first astonishing season in 1969, *winning*. On second thought, seeing Bob Cousy at forty-one coaching *and playing* for the Cincinnati Royals probably topped the list for most Boston fans.

Following the departure of Dick Williams, the much more placid Eddie Kasko, was given the reins in 1970. Four years earlier, in what can definitely called lateral movement, Kasko had been traded by the Astros to the Red Sox for Felix Mantilla in a swap of has-beens, hitting a lackluster .213 in his only season in Boston. I had Kasko on a 1962 Post card with the Reds, and even though his numbers were decent and he had been an All-Star once, his oversized, rather thick eyeglasses made him look more like your kindly, next-door neighbor than a figure of authority. Roger Angell referred to him as a man with "a perpetually mournful visage."

Kasko was not going to be confused with Williams, and predictably, the clubhouse meltdown continued as the club careened toward another third-place finish, this time coming in 21 games behind the dominant Orioles. Team morale was in free-fall once again, and another shoe was about to drop.

Following the 1970 season, in which he had hit 36 home runs with 116 RBI's in the most remarkable season yet in his improbable comeback, Tony C, in what can be fairly described as a shock, was sent all the way across the country in a trade to the Angels. Apparently, the clubhouse was not big enough for Yaz and Tony C together, so Tony C was out.

While the move stunned both the right fielder and the fans, including me, perhaps it shouldn't have. The Red Sox were still Yawkey's team, and Tony C, who clearly had trade value, had worn out his welcome. The following year, Billy C, after publicly blaming Yaz for, in no particular order, the firing of Pesky, the trading of The Hawk, the trading of his brother, and the platooning of Billy C himself with the not quite immortal Joe Lahoud, met a similar fate, being sent to Milwaukee, along with Lonborg and The Boomer in a housecleaning trade. The Conigliaros had provided great box office theater on and off the field, but Yawkey had seen enough of their act. As a Red Sox fan, I hated both trades. Tony C was Tony C, and Ken Tatum was not Hoyt Wilhelm. And two of my other heroes, Lonborg and Scott, were now gone as well.

Connected to the Tony C story, in my mind, was the earlier and ill-fated career of Tony Horton, a strapping slugger from southern California whose career flamed out in such a bizarre and frightening fashion, almost costing him his life, that his playing days can only be remembered with sorrow. Brought up by the Red Sox midway through the 1964 season to fill in for the injured Tony C, Horton and Tony C were expected to provide years of right-handed power to the Sox lineup once they got their feet wet. Ted Williams himself loved Horton's swing. But Tony Horton was no Tony C. With the Red Sox, he had occasional power, with the emphasis on occasional, and not much else. In Red Sox-speak, he was a right-handed version of Bob Guindon/Sam Horn/Lars Anderson. I didn't go to Fenway hoping that Horton would be in the lineup.

With the first base position open in 1965 after the trade of Dick Stuart, and again the next year with Lee Thomas being shipped out, Horton could not grab what was his to be grabbed, being benched at one point by Billy Herman for "lack of concentration" during a game, specifically, not knowing how many outs there were or what the count was on the batter. In turn, George Scott did not miss his own chance, and Horton was banished to Cleveland in 1967, having hit a total of 8 home runs for the Red Sox and missing out on the Impossible Dream. Liking The Boomer from the start, I did not miss Horton. He did go on to hit some homers for the Indians, 68 in all, but the stress he felt to be the star that he never quite became took such an emotional toll on him that he was done by the age of twenty-five, taking himself out of the lineup and nearly killing himself, literally, as a result. It was a tale of sadness and strangeness, though not at all out of character, most unfortunately, for someone who had worn a Red Sox uniform.

Several other memories come back when trying to capture the essence of the Red Sox in those post-Dick Williams, country club days of big stats, huge contracts, and no pennants. One involved Yaz's role in the heated American League batting race of 1970, a season in which Yaz had already been the MVP of the All-Star game, going 4 for 6 in the summer classic. On September 1, the batting leaders were Yaz (.317), the talented yet exasperating Alex Johnson (.317) of the Angels (he greeted new *Los Angeles Times* beat reporter Ross Newhan that year by noting, "You're no different than those other motherfuckers"), and Twins' hitting machine Tony Oliva (.315). All three hitters, like thoroughbreds streaking to the finish line, then went on a tear over the final month, and when the dust settled on the games of September 30, Yaz's average stood at .329, Johnson's, .327, and Oliva's, .323.

The catch was that while the season for Yaz was over, Johnson and Oliva still had a game to play the next day. Oliva went on to have only an excellent day at the plate, rather than the blockbuster game he needed, going 2 for 3—a double and a triple—and finishing up at .325. Johnson, though, found himself in a much more enviable position. After grounding out in his first at-bat, he singled his next two times up, boosting his average to .3289, a shade above Yaz's .3286. When Johnson left the game for pinch runner Jay Johnstone in the fifth inning after his second single, the batting race had been decided. Alex Johnson, enjoying the game's final eight innings from the bench (the Angels won the game in the thirteenth inning), was the new American League batting champion, the first—and still only—Angel to capture the crown. Of course, the manner in which he did so seemed to spit in the face of a sport that took its sanctity as the National Pastime, a game adored by purists, quite seriously, and left fans in Boston stewing.

But Johnson, in this instance, was not trying to cheat anyone—he had been pulled from the game by manager Lefty Phillips. After spending much of the season fuming at Johnson for his disruptive antics that seemed to occur on a daily basis, Phillips, on that final day of the season, chose to protect his player's batting title in what was a meaningless game in the standings. Still, to those of us who rooted for Yaz, it seemed an unfair and unacceptable blow, possibly costing him his third batting title in four years and fourth overall. He never won another. Of course, to the Yaz-bashers, seeing Yaz lose out to Alex Johnson, of all players, may have been a joy to behold. I was glad not to be in that camp.

For the record, that 1970 batting race was the closest in the American League since the 1949 season, when Ted Williams, at .3427, was barely edged out for the title by the Tigers' (and future Red Sox teammate) George Kell, who finished at .3429. In fact, three other Red Sox hitters—Bobby Doerr, Dom DiMaggio, and Johnny Pesky—finished in the top eight. Far too often in those years, Red Sox fans found their team—and its star players—on the wrong side of history.

And regarding batting champions Kell and Johnson, they were two players who could not have had more different approaches to their livelihoods. Upon retiring as a player, Kell remained in the game and went on to become a popular broadcaster for the Tigers for 37 years. Johnson, on the other hand, eventually took over his father's trucking company in Michigan and never attended another baseball game after his retirement. "The game has no meaning for me anymore," he said. "I loved it. But I found out that the game is a fantasy." For most of Johnson's managers, however, the experience was probably more of a nightmare than a fantasy.

A bona fide baseball "event" took place at Fenway in late May, 1971, one that I eagerly listened to on the radio after getting home from my own Babe Ruth practice. The Sox had gotten off to a hot start and were in first place when the Oakland A's, in first place in the West, came to town. The pitching matchup was a dream: Sonny Siebert, undefeated at 8–0, against young Vida Blue, the talk of baseball with his 10–1 record and an ERA barely over 1.00. In front of a packed house, Siebert outdueled Blue to win his ninth straight, with help from a couple of homers from Rico, sending Red Sox fans home with dreams of October baseball dancing in their heads. But in true Red Sox style, the team almost immediately hit a cold streak, the Orioles—they of the four twenty-game winners—heated up as expected, and while the Red Sox hung around for a while, they finished a too familiar 18 games out when all was said and done. To be fair to Siebert, he did his part with his arm and his bat by winning 16 games and hitting 6 home runs, leading the staff in both categories.

At the same time that the Sox had been teasing the fans with their strong early showing in 1971, Luis Aparicio, the team's newly-acquired and highly distinguished shortstop, was heading in the opposite direction. Eight times an All-Star, including just the previous year with the White Sox when he had batted .313, his highest average ever, and a certain Hall of Famer, Aparicio was a player I was initially very happy to see arrive, even though the Sox had traded the popular Mike Andrews in the exchange. I had Aparicio on so many cards, coins, stickers, tattoos, and other paraphernalia that he felt like a member of the family. Now, however, Aparicio was playing like he thought he was on the 1965 Red Sox.

After getting off to a decent start, he quickly went into a slump that stretched from 0-10 to 0-20 to 0-30 and seemingly on to infinity. As Aparicio hit an endless number of routine ground balls, day after day, across the infield, Ned Martin invoked whatever inspirational rhetoric he could muster in an effort to will some hits from Aparicio's suddenly feeble bat. Despite Martin's heartfelt entreaties, the slump sailed past 0-40 on its way to 0-44 before the law of averages kicked in and Aparicio managed a single off Mike Hedlund of the Kansas City Royals.

But, in keeping with the bizarre nature of what it meant to play for the Red Sox in those days, the skid then proceeded (regressed?) to a nadir of 1-55 before a personal letter of encouragement from President Nixon—"In my own career I have experienced long periods when I couldn't seem to get a hit, regardless of how hard I tried, but in the end I was able to hit a home run"—helped Aparicio to break out of it. And in a vote that may say more about democracy than about baseball, Aparicio, he of a .206 batting average, was elected by the fans to be the starting American League shortstop in the All-Star game. Aparicio himself, displaying a somewhat stronger grasp of reality, voted for Mark Belanger and his own atypical .282 batting average. For Aparicio, refreshingly (and unlike Nixon), it was not all about him.

Curiously, the Nixon-Red Sox connection that year was not confined to the episode with Aparicio. One of Nixon's admirers was Yaz, who had met him at the White House in April and presented his 1970 All-Star MVP trophy as a gift to the president. Undoubtedly of much more significance to Nixon, though, was that he would not find himself with anything resembling a Hall of Fame legacy at the close of his own very checkered career.

15. More Heartbreak

The 1972 Red Sox season would be punctuated by bookends that typified all that was becoming increasingly frustrating about the Red Sox. In a spring training trade that almost made Curt Blefary for Mike Cuellar look good for the Astros, the Red Sox decided to send one of the league's premier closers, a southpaw just entering his prime, Sparky Lyle, to the Yankees for Danny Cater. A fine major league hitter for a number of years, Cater might have been worth acquiring for a fourth outfielder or a draft pick and some money. But to equate Danny Cater with Sparky Lyle was inexcusable, even by traditional Red Sox standards, and they deservedly paid the price.

The intimidating Lyle—it was never clear to me if his wicked slider or his bushy moustache, sideburns and mane of hair scared batters more—went on to save 35 games in 1972 and later won a Cy Young award for the Yankees, while Cater, on the back end of his career, played sparingly for three seasons and was eventually shipped off to the Cardinals for one Danny Godby, who would never play a game for the Red Sox. Dick O'Connell deserved high praise for the majority of his deals with the Red Sox, but he swung and totally missed on this one.

That was how the 1972 season started for the Red Sox. It would end on an even more bizarre note. The Sox reversed the trend of 1971, playing dreadfully for the first half of the season, not even reaching .500 until mid-July. Then they turned it around and actually caught up to and *passed* the first place Tigers. Heading into the final series of the season, a three-game set in Detroit, the Red Sox found themselves a half-game up on the Tigers.

And therein lay the nub of the problem for the star-crossed Red Sox. The Red Sox had played one less game than the Tigers, so under normal circumstances they could have gone into Detroit, settled for taking one out of three games just to stay alive, and then played the make-up game to at least—potentially—force a playoff with the Tigers for first place.

But, unfortunately for the Red Sox, circumstances were not normal in the baseball world of 1972. A players' strike at the start of the season, the first strike in baseball history, had wiped out two weeks of games, giving the teams uneven schedules. And the games would *not* be made up. The decision regarding the standings was that at the end of the regular season, whatever is, is. So, the "whatever is" facing the Red Sox in that last series in Detroit was that they had to take at least two of the games from the Tigers or be eliminated.

Naturally, the Red Sox promptly lost the first game, which featured a classic Red Sox base running blunder when Aparicio rounded third, stumbled, and retreated to the presumed safety of the bag only to find himself sharing it with Yaz, killing a possible rally. Prior to the next day's game, when Kasko was asked by reporters about the Red Sox' lack of artistry on the base paths, he apparently tried to channel his inner poet, with very mixed results, by responding, "If *ifs* and *buts* were candied nuts, we'd all have a hell of a Christmas."

But there would no celebrating for those Red Sox, as they went on to lose the second game before winning the meaningless final game, ensuring that they would finish *one-half* game out of the playoffs. I couldn't believe it, particularly since the Red Sox, unlike a decade earlier, now had the talent to do better. I was not yet at the point of exasperation, but my patience was being severely tested. As a baseball fan, I should add that in the two games of that series that mattered, Kaline went 4 for 7, with a home run, finishing up a Yaz-like run of 22 for 44 in getting his team into the playoffs. Had Kaline helped the Tigers to thump the Yankees in such fashion, I would have been his biggest fan. As it was, I could only privately admire him, as I had been doing for most of my life.

On a more positive note, my favorite memory of that season came on the 4th of July, when a tall, rookie right-hander named Lynn McGlothen got his first major league win by tossing a magnificent, three-hit shutout against the Twins. Imagining that he could be the second coming of Bob Gibson, I immediately became a huge supporter of McGlothen, who went on to have a number of strong starts and finished his half-season with 8 wins and a very respectable ERA of 3.41. Almost unbelievably, another Red Sox rookie, southpaw John Curtis, won 11 games that year. For the Red Sox to produce a solid, homegrown starting pitcher was a pretty rare occurrence in those days, but to have *two* in the same year seemed an embarrassment of riches by Red Sox standards. Hoping I had seen the future, I was eager to watch the development of both, particularly McGlothen.

Unfortunately, my hope turned into wishful thinking, as McGlothen was injured the following year, winning just a single game, and became a throw-in as part of the John Curtis—Reggie Cleveland deal with the Cardinals. The trade, though, would provide another example of buyer's remorse for the Red Sox. McGlothen, having been discarded by the Red Sox, naturally realized his potential in St. Louis. In his very first year, he won 16 games and got votes in both the Cy Young and MVP balloting. He went on to win 44 games (including nine shutouts) and pitch nearly 700 innings over the next three seasons, while Cleveland, an experienced starter and considered the best player in the deal, pitched creditably in Boston over that time with 35 wins, but a total that was barely half of the 68 victories that McGlothen and Curtis secured for the Cardinals. Even Mike Garman, a little-used right-hander also cast off by the Red Sox in the trade, rejuvenated his career by appearing in 130 games and posting a 2.52 ERA over the next two seasons for the Cardinals.

As I faithfully followed McGlothen in the box scores and saw him develop into a workhorse for the Cardinals (no other Cardinal starter won more than 30 games in that stretch), I remembered the flashes he had shown for Boston in that promising first season and thought about what might have been. The story would go on to have a truly tragic ending when McGlothen died in a house fire at the age of thirty-four, just two years removed from the end of his injury-plagued, but at one time so hopeful, career.

Despite the disappointing end to the season, there were additional reasons to believe that 1972 was a harbinger of good things to come for the team. The previous year they had acquired an apparently washed-up Luis Tiant, who had managed to lose 20 games in 1969 and went a somewhat less than encouraging 1–7 in his first season with the Sox. But in 1972, working as a starter and out of the bullpen, Tiant had an amazing rejuvenation, going 15–6 and leading the American League with a 1.91 ERA. Whether Tiant, in his early thirties, could keep it going was the question that would find a happy answer for Red Sox fans over the next six seasons.

Tiant's batterymate that year was equally impressive, and a lot younger. Carlton Fisk, in his first full season, came through in a big way, and his 22 home runs and .293 batting average helped him earn Rookie of the Year honors. Already an All-Star, he looked like he would be the backbone of the team for years to come, and probably would have been had the Red Sox not been the Red Sox. But for now, he was one of the best young catchers in the game. And the fact that he had grown up in New Hampshire and attended the University of New Hampshire only heightened his popularity among Red Sox fans. Two other young players with potential on that team, but just benchwarmers at the time, were Dwight Evans and Cecil Cooper. Twenty years and 4600 hits later, no one would remember much about them sitting on a bench.

A final word on the 1972 season will be devoted to Red Sox right-hander Mike Nagy, who pitched a grand total of two innings that year and soon found himself in the unfailingly embarrassing position of having been traded for a "player to be named later." (In Nagy's case, the player turned out to be southpaw Lance Clemons, who, in between stints at Pawtucket, gave the Red Sox a predictable contribution of 6 innings and a 9.95 ERA.) But before Nagy became a baseball nobody, he had been a somebody for Boston, going 12–2 just three years earlier while being named the American League's Rookie Pitcher of the Year.

It all went south in a hurry, though, for Nagy, as injuries (partly) and not quite enough talent to stay ahead of major league hitters (mainly) limited him to only seven more wins in a Red Sox uniform. As with so many Red Sox players and entire teams before him, Nagy had been a great tease—he whetted our appetites, but the meal was never served. Now past a half-century of championship hunger, Red Sox fans wondered if the famine would ever end.

The Red Sox in 1973 and 1974 continued to be a combination of the good, the bad, and the ugly. They had respectable records and took the pennant races into September each year, but were not able to overcome the Orioles in the East. Tiant, his roller coaster career on the ascent again, did become an ace, winning 42 games (each one no doubt celebrated with his trademark cigar) and gaining great popularity with the fans. Bill Lee, often one toke over the line while in the process of reinventing himself as "The Spaceman" and the king of all Yankee-haters, had developed into a solid starter, with 17 wins each season. He had an uncommon penchant for throwing lots of innings while striking out almost no one. He also had to be one of the easiest pitchers in the majors to hit, I thought, and most players *did* hit him on a regular basis. In 1974, he had what to me seemed to be the outrageous stat line of having given up a league-leading *320* hits in 282 innings but with a very respectable ERA of 3.51. The Spaceman—you had to give him credit—was a survivor. Those hitters got on base and stayed on base. Rail-thin southpaw

Rogelio Moret, who looked like a mild breeze might blow him out past second base, also found ways to win much more than he lost, both as a starter and a reliever.

Fisk, as expected, had erased any lingering trauma from the years when the team would put any warm body behind the plate, too often giving them two automatic outs in the lineup. His problem, unfortunately, was staying healthy, and when he tore up his knee in 1974, there was fear that his career might be over. Yaz could still get around on a fastball and play The Wall better than anyone, carrying with him, always, the pain of the championship-less past, now fourteen years and growing, with his characteristic dignity. Rico, the only starter other than Yaz left from the Impossible Dream team, hit his 200th home run but was beginning to show some signs of age. Eddie Kasko, who had never won fewer than 85 games or more than 89 in his four years as manager and had finished in second or third place each year, was let go at the end of the '73 season for the apparent crime of being quite good but not quite good enough. New manager Darrell Johnson assumed the unenviable task of trying to be good enough with a team that seemed to be moving decidedly sideways.

For me personally, the highlight of 1973 came after the season ended when the Red Sox unexpectedly purchased Marichal from the Giants on December 7. The idea of seeing Marichal and Yaz both playing for the Red Sox seemed almost too good to be true. The pitcher the Red Sox acquired, however, was no longer the pitcher I had admired so deeply. Marichal's tough luck, 1971 playoff loss to the Pirates, on Hebner's home run, was the start of an unanticipated death spiral for his career. The following year he descended to an unsightly 6-16. After a 2-1 loss in mid-May to the Reds (before an intimate gathering of 2,670 fans at Candlestick), the UPI acknowledged the shock in the baseball universe by running a story with the headline, "His name is Marichal, his ERA is 2.84 ...and, yes, his record is 1-7." In 1973, he improved only marginally, to 11-15. As a Marichal fan, I remember watching in chagrin as his career winning percentage sank from spectacular (.670) to merely exceptional (.629).

Still, when your team acquires not only a certain Hall-of-Famer but one of your favorite players, objectivity disappears. I couldn't believe that Marichal would be pitching at Fenway Park, and I fully expected a revival of the Dominican Dandy.

The deal itself was a little complicated simply because of Marichal's stature. His salary was well over $100,000 and the Giants understood that a declining Marichal would not be part of their future, so Horace Stoneham gave the green light to shop him around. But Stoneham, aware that Marichal would not bring much in return, apparently did not want to put his legendary hurler in the undignified position of being traded for a collection of unknown players, so he agreed to sell him to the Red Sox. According to Dick O'Connell, he first had Frank Malzone and Darrell Johnson check with National League sources, including fired San Diego manager Don Zimmer, soon to be a Red Sox coach, on whether Marichal had anything left, and when the reports came back positive, he signed off on the deal. In O'Connell's mind, the chance to purchase Marichal was fortuitous, as the team had been considering giving up Curtis, McGlothen, and/or Garman for a veteran pitcher. O'Connell explained, "What we ended up doing was getting a 35 [actually, 36]-year-old pitcher like Marichal for cash instead of giving the Cleveland Indians some of our young players for 35-year-old Gaylord Perry. We then took our young players and made the deal with St. Louis for Reggie Cleveland and Diego Segui," which also happened on December 7.

So, hopes ran high that the Red Sox would see a rejuvenated Marichal the following season. The *Boston Herald Advertiser*, in fact, was so enthused by the addition of Marichal that the paper ran a full-page article on Marichal—headlined "Marichal Still Can Pitch – Giants"—during spring training, featuring a Bob Coyne drawing of Marichal in his signature windup, with his right leg planted at the bottom of the page and his outstretched left leg touching the top. The article was written by Jim McGee of the *San Francisco Examiner* ("nobody is more qualified to evaluate Marichal's past with the Giants and potential for the Red Sox," the *Herald* noted), and, in 21 adulatory paragraphs, made the case that Marichal was not washed up. The story concluded with Ossie Virgil, a Giants scout, insisting, "I saw him when he started in the Dominican when he was 17. He was throwing strikes then and he hasn't stopped." The Red Sox had already resurrected the career of Luis Tiant. Could the same happen with Marichal?

Not exactly. In fact, it may have been good for Eddie Kasko's blood pressure that he was spared the ordeal of spending the 1974 season in the dugout, as the team outdid itself in leading the fans on another great tease of a pennant ride. This time, the BoSox got off to sluggish start but managed to be leading the division by half a game on June 1. Remarkably, they stubbornly stayed on top, week after week. One memorable June game, a bottom of the 15th, 4–3 loss to the Angels, saw Tiant go the entire 14$^{1/3}$ innings, while Nolan Ryan went 13 demanding innings of his own, finishing with 19 strikeouts (getting Cecil Cooper six times) and 10 walks while facing the staggering total of 58 batters.

Enjoying my first summer out of high school, I watched with growing curiosity as the lead, 2 games on July 1, stood at 2.5 games on August 1 (a month in which they were *never* out of first place), and stretch to 7 games on August 23. Naturally, I was thrilled to see Marichal become a significant factor in the August success, winning three games and allowing only 3 runs over 27 innings while teaming with Tiant to give the staff undoubtedly one of the greatest assortments of deliveries of any team in history.

Apparently feeling the weight of its own history, however, the team reverted to form in memorable fashion. Over the last five weeks of the season, they finished up 14–24, featuring an eight-game losing streak that included back to back 1–0 losses to Baltimore in a doubleheader, to land in third place, 7 games behind the Orioles. The numbers in that stretch, not surprisingly, were ugly. In 12 of the games, all losses, the team scored one run or was shut out. The pitchers, naturally, bore the brunt of such meager support: Moret was 2–4, Tiant 2–5, Lee 3–4, and Dick Drago 1–3. On the final day, barely 5000 fans bothered showing up to Fenway for the game, putting a rather wimpy exclamation point on another season of futility.

Marichal himself finished with an impressive 5-1 record, but also a telltale ERA of 4.87. The Red Sox quietly released him in late October. It was a decision that was hard to accept, but the Red Sox, unlike me, had to look at their roster using their heads and not their hearts. They had made the right choice. And for the record, Gaylord Perry, Marichal's old teammate who the Red Sox apparently could have obtained, went 21-13, with 28 complete games, that year for Cleveland, making the All-Star team and getting both MVP and Cy Young votes. For the Red Sox, the beat went on.

But dreams die hard for Red Sox fans, and 1974 did give us three encouraging reasons for looking beyond the September collapse. That summer, the Pawtucket Red Sox had sent Jim Rice, Fred Lynn, and Rick Burleson up to the big club. Johnson wanted youth, and youth would indeed be served. The stage was set for the high drama of the 1975 Boston Red Sox.

As the 1975 baseball season dawned, Red Sox fans had reason to believe that good things, in the form of the team's young stars, might bring them what only people already in retirement had ever seen: a World Series victory. But the team, in truth, had had talent every year since the Impossible Dream, but always with the same result—eighty-something wins, a reasonably-close-but-no-cigar finish in the standings, and more waiting until next year. And the early returns in 1975 looked barely different. Luis Tiant went the distance on opening day, defeating the Brewers in a game that featured Tony C, at the end of the line, and Hank Aaron, almost at the end. But Carlton Fisk remained out with his knee injury, Bernie Carbo was the

244

team's leading hitter, and the Sox were still mired at .500 in mid-May. The average attendance of 10,000–15,000 each game reflected the level of enthusiasm and optimism of the fans, including me. At nineteen, I was learning to hedge my bets. Devoted as I was to the home team, the Red Sox were still the Red Sox.

What was also true, however, was that the Orioles were not quite the same Orioles anymore, and the Yankees, while much improved from the Jake Gibbs—Ruben Amaro days of disgrace, had not yet made their way back. The Red Sox, for a change, were not facing terribly stiff competition in the East. By June, they had a four-game lead, and that month foreshadowed good things for the Sox that season. Not only did Fisk come back from his injury late in the month, but a few days earlier, Fred Lynn had put on his own demonstration of why the season might be something special, and his own potential even beyond that. On a night when the Red Sox put 15 runs across the plate, Lynn alone drove in 10 of them with 5 hits, including 3 homers. Performances like that could not be ignored.

Like nearly every other fan that summer, my personal favorites were Lynn and Jim Rice, the Gold Dust Twins, as Peter Gammons aptly characterized them. I almost felt bad for Rice. Any other year, he would have been given the star attention he deserved. But being paired with Lynn, side by side both in the outfield and in the batting order, was a cruel twist of fate, for Lynn that year had the magic that every ballplayer dreams of. His theatrical play in center field, making diving catches and dazzling throws seemingly every night, was a joy to watch. And he matched his outfield wizardry at the plate, using his classic, compact swing to hit the ball sharply and often to all fields, for average and power. There appeared to be no weaknesses in his game, and he was honored accordingly, winning both Rookie of the Year and Most Valuable Player awards.

Rice, on the other hand, merely had a great year in the shadow of Lynn. Like Lynn, he could hit to all fields, but with devastating power. When he connected, the ball shot off his bat like it had been launched. His swing, though, was so smooth that the bat looked almost weightless in his hands. With Rice's ability to change the score dramatically on one swing, watching him at the plate was an event, as he struck fear into the heart of any pitcher (with the possible exception of Goose Gossage, who usually made fear work in the other direction for most batters, although probably not including Rice). As a fielder, he was mediocre on his way to getting better, but he was not in the lineup for his glove. When Rice was at the plate, damage control was the first thing on the pitcher's mind—just keep it in the park.

The Red Sox' lead eventually ballooned to nine games. The Orioles hung around until the end, a mild threat mainly due to the ever-present possibility of a Sox collapse, while the Yankees had faded from view by July. The Red Sox, in front of increasingly large crowds of their astonished fans, had cruised to a pennant.

At one of the games, a Red Sox victory, I had been a part of the growing audience at Fenway. But unlike in the good old days when the Red Sox had been bad but you could easily get a decent seat, the park was full, and I was stuck in deep right field, even deeper than where I used to sit with my father. I could see the backs of the right fielders and the first base umpire, but not much else. The pitcher and batter might as well have been playing in Brookline. The key to the game, I quickly learned, was to listen for the crack of the bat. The next key was to join the other 30,000 people in standing up to see—maybe—what had happened. This up and down ritual repeated itself enough times over the course of nine innings that I can safely say I got more exercise in that one game than I had gotten in all of my previous games at Fenway. I left, happy in knowing that the Red Sox were now a legitimate threat in the division but somehow feeling a very misguided longing for the times past when you could buy a ticket, hassle-free, and see the game almost undisturbed.

In the playoffs, the Red Sox' impressive sweep of the defending champion Oakland Athletics was as good as it got for a Red Sox fan. Tiant pitched brilliantly in Game 1, Yaz turned back the clock with some tremendous plays in left field, and the team actually hit the ball in key spots and pitched well enough to embarrass the seasoned and talented A's in three games.

The series win sent the Red Sox to the World Series for the first time since their heartbreaking loss to the Cardinals eight years earlier, but their opponent, the Big Red Machine of Cincinnati, was, if anything, even more imposing than the Bob Gibson-led Cardinals. George Harrison, who had played with a slightly more successful group than the Red Sox, had said that all things must pass. That it might, finally, be true for the championship-starved local nine was the prayer of Red Sox fans. Still, that unspoken but inescapable feeling that the ultimate prize, somehow, would elude us, as it always had, lingered uncomfortably.

And it did elude us, of course, but not without an epic, seven-game struggle featuring likely names (Carlton Fisk) and unlikely ones (Ed Armbrister) that have been deservedly immortalized in baseball history. My own personal memories involve my part-time job in a restaurant, and the weather. The first two games were played during the day, on a Saturday and a Sunday, the Saturday game being Tiant's masterful shutout to begin the Series. But the weekday games were played at night, and my job, unfortunately, was a night shift.

That was not my only challenge, however. After the fifth game had been played on a Thursday, leaving the Reds up 3 games to 2 in what had already been a dramatic Series, the heavens opened up, and it rained all the way through the weekend, washing out the sixth game for days. The game, long to be remembered, was finally played on a Tuesday—at night. At work, I could hear the action, off and on, on the radio, with the lead going back and forth, up to Carbo's momentous, pinch-hit blast off Rawly Eastwick. At that point I finished up work as fast as I could and made a beeline home to get in front of the television. I made it in time to see Fisk's arm-waving, hooking, "if it stays fair, it's gone" home run off the left field foul pole, giving a sport known for iconic moments one of its greatest ever. Reds manager Sparky Anderson remarked later, "I went home, and I was stunned."

Fisk's shot appropriately set the stage for the next chapter of heartbreak for Red Sox fans, which Joe Morgan's blooper to left-center would provide the following night. Some may have thought that the pain could not get much worse for Sox fans after that crushing ninth inning, seventh game defeat. Reality would prove that they had too little imagination.

For me, the difference between 1967 and 1975 was not small. In 1967, I was a kid, deliriously happy that the Red Sox were even *in* a World Series, and thrilled that they had taken a star-filled Cardinals team to seven games. Naturally, I would have been much more thrilled had they won, but considering how things had gone for my entire Red Sox life up to that point, 1967 marked serious progress.

In 1975, however, I was not a kid anymore, and the Red Sox had not been horrible for nearly a decade. Certainly, they were facing a juggernaut in the Reds, and there was no shame in losing to them, but the Red Sox themselves were a team of stars, and anytime you get to the seventh game, the series is truly up for grabs. No one would have been shocked had the Red Sox won. I didn't feel happy for the Red Sox just to be in the conversation anymore—that Series could have been won, and the disappointment was lasting when it wasn't.

The Red Sox had not won consecutive pennants in sixty years, and the streak, it became clear in a hurry, was in no danger of being broken in 1976. Eight games out by May, later falling to as many as twenty games, the Sox never put up much resistance and had to watch the resurrection of the Yankees, back in their accustomed first place. Statistics don't always tell the whole story, but the numbers for 1976 tell you all you need to know about the Sox. Only the old men came through in a big way. Tiant, 35, won 21 games, while Yaz, 36, knocked in 102 runs. That was about it for impressive numbers. Tom Yawkey passed away, Darrell Johnson barely made it past the All-Star Game (in which *he* was the American League manager) before getting axed, and the team finished just above .500.

Probably the most interesting event of the season was something that never happened. At the June 15th trading deadline, the A's owner, Charlie Finley, desperately in need of money even though his team was only one year removed from a run of three consecutive World Series championships, attempted to sell Joe Rudi and Rollie Fingers, both looming free agents, to the Red Sox for a million dollars each.

But Commissioner Bowie Kuhn, citing the deal as "not in the best interests of baseball," shot it down. Typically, Finley then took his own jab at Kuhn, saying he sounded "like the village idiot," and Marvin Miller as well didn't miss his chance to blast Kuhn, calling the decision "sheer insanity." More circumspect but not in disagreement with Finley and Miller, Red Sox GM O'Connell later commented on the transaction in a separate court proceeding, "I thought it was in the best interest of the club. That's all I was worried about." But Kuhn prevailed, and O'Connell continued to have plenty to worry about that season as he watched the Yankees leave his team in the dust.

16. Mission Impossible

In my own personal odyssey through the strange adventure known as teen life, I entered high school in 1971 and graduated in 1974. School itself had always been something of a meandering journey for me, from kindergarten through high school. As mentioned earlier, I started out well in elementary school—my academic decline and fall began in junior high school, although not immediately and not for any single reason. An American truism is that junior high school is a jungle, and my experience would prove no exception. While I always had close friends and can easily remember many humorous and good times during those years, it was also the case that my hair grew, my pimples increased, and my grades slid, all at a steady pace.

The beginning of junior high school, however, was encouraging. At that time, junior high students were leveled by ability, and when I moved on from elementary school, I was put in one of the highest academic levels in seventh grade. Two things that I noticed in my new classes were that most of the students in my level didn't live anywhere near my neighborhood or come from my elementary school, so it was a bit of a culture shock at the start. In fact, about half the kids in my level seemed to come from the *same* elementary school on the other side of town. But I did well that first year, not exactly getting all A's but not getting much below that, either.

The following year, though, I started to slip noticeably, particularly in math and science, and the slide continued unabated in my final year. When the dust settled on my three years of junior high school, I had gone from advanced to average academically. There was no single explanation. I was playing a lot of baseball and basketball. The work was getting harder.

Girls were becoming more interesting to look at. And the subjects, with the exception of English and History, just didn't grab my attention. So, I followed the path of least resistance and focused on leisure over lectures. I struggled with isosceles triangles, but I had a fine time copying Sonny Siebert's windup and Jo Jo White's free throw style during those years, and I was very happy doing so.

Academically, high school for me was the road less traveled. With some generosity from my teachers, I passed most of my classes, but I failed French and Chemistry, and to this day feel a small amount of guilt for the pain and suffering I caused those teachers, who sincerely did try to nudge conjugated verbs and the periodic table of elements into my head before withdrawing in exasperation. If I could apologize to them, I would. Many such apologies are undoubtedly in order, from multitudes of students in countless schools. Such was the unfairness of life for a public high school teacher, a reality that, regrettably, continues apace.

Sports-wise, after five years of Little League, I played three more very enjoyable years of Babe Ruth baseball during my early teens. Two memories that stand out from my Babe Ruth days are a championship-winning triple play and a non-homer homer. In my second year, my team, the Braves (an appropriate fit, from my father's point of view), ended the season in a most unimaginable way. As we clung to a 1–0 lead in the final inning of the championship game, the opposing team (the Pirates) put runners on first and second with no outs. But in electrifying fashion, a line drive to short quickly turned into a 6–3, game-ending, championship-winning triple play. As the first baseman, I caught the last out, and I just remember thinking as our shortstop stepped on second and fired the ball over to me, "Jesus, don't drop this throw!" I don't know how often three outs and a wild infield celebration of a championship have happened in such short order in the history of baseball, but I was certainly thrilled to be a part of it.

The non-homer homer happened in the same season. I had never hit a legitimate home run—over the fence—in an organized game. But in one game, I hit a ball down the left field line that actually did get over the fence. Unfortunately, hooking at the last moment, the ball sailed over the few feet of the fence that stretched into foul territory. As I returned to the batter's box, hugely disappointed, the home plate umpire, a boy a few years older who *had* hit a number of homers in Babe Ruth, said encouragingly, "Don't worry. If you can do it once, you can do it again."

His forecasting skills did not match his batting prowess, though—I never did manage to put one out. Not that I was planning to give it a Cadillac trot, but it would have been nice to go around the bases one time knowing that the deed had been done.

After Babe Ruth baseball, however, the clock ran out on organized baseball playing in my life. In high school I decided to stick with just one sport, and I chose basketball over baseball, not sure that I would even make the baseball team. I felt the oddness of that first spring without baseball—no more game days to look forward to, no more practices after dinner, no more uniforms to wear, no more cleats to bang the dirt from, no more gloves to break in, no more friends to be made while hanging in the outfield and shagging fly balls. There was definitely a sense of loss. However, like everyone else does in many ways all the time, I moved on, or at least tried to.

I spent much of my time in high school playing basketball in the gym and on any outdoor court where I could find a game, and hanging out with friends. The academic range of students in high school was about the same as in elementary school—all levels were represented, only this time I was no longer near the upper echelon.

At one time or another, for nearly every student I knew, high school was stressful, crazy, annoying, intimidating, and confusing. But, often enough, it was fun and carefree as well. I laughed a lot at the time, and I laugh still now when I recall some of the funnier moments. One imaginative and adventurous friend pondered the thrill of parachuting into the high school graduation ceremony, and the only surprise was that he did not make the leap. And I don't doubt that there were many similar schemes and escapades among the various circles of friends in the school. Given the "open campus" nature of the school, we probably had more freedom than we could handle and were sometimes less responsible than we should have been. Had the standardized tests now required of all Massachusetts high school students for graduation been in place in 1974, our graduation rate almost certainly would have taken a hit. That some of us, however, thought more about gap shots and slap shots and make-up and perfume than mitochondria and parabolas should not be a lifetime strike against us. Our immediate futures included higher education, military service, or employment, all honest paths forward. We turned out okay.

My own future to me always seemed fair to partly cloudy at best. As I considered it at length during those years—whether to go to college, what to study if I did, how I would pay for it—one nonstarter was any discussion about it with my father. While we still spoke, sometimes amiably, more often tensely, our relations were clearly on the skids, and it was apparent to me that my father could no more give me advice on higher education or money than he could run the marathon, not that he had any inclination to advise me anyway.

Things were no different concerning sports. While he had gone to just about all of my Little League games, his presence abated considerably at my Babe Ruth games, as did my concern over whether he was there or not. For years, each time I stood in the batter's box, I was aware of my father's presence nearby, with his habitual advice of "don't help the pitcher" and "look for that one good strike" racing through my mind as I dug in. Now, his presence was no longer a big issue, while his words of hitting advice had become part of my normal routine, successfully or otherwise.

And my switch from baseball to basketball held little interest for him. He was no basketball fan, and he never saw me play in a game. Rarely did he ask if we had won or even if I had played. Baseball itself caught less and less of his attention as well, and in fact he never went to another major league game following our last year together at Fenway Park in 1967. Very occasionally we still discussed the sport, but the conversations usually ended with the same conclusions on my father's part: the players were overpaid and not nearly as good as Harry Heilmann and Kiki Cuyler and Paul Derringer and a long list of their contemporaries.

Affecting his growing cynicism were his ongoing mental health issues and the distressing path his working life was taking. In the 1970s, he was approaching his 50s, a challenging transitional period for anyone, but particularly so for someone who has spent the previous decades hoping his ship will come in, only to realize that there are no ships on the horizon. Facing a form of life imprisonment with his factory job stretching out to retirement, still years away, he tried to alter his fate by taking the civil service exam in the hope of landing a job with the post office. His initial optimism—"The post office job would give me damn good benefits"—slowly faded to silence, and I understood that the test must not have gone well, no great shock considering his lack of a formal education. He probably had not taken an exam in more than thirty years. A knowledge of Rudyard Kipling, Admiral Nimitz, Rembrandt, Schumann, and Fred Frankhouse was apparently not the appropriate preparation for a daily life of delivering the mail.

Most likely, though, my father was not surprised. Years earlier, he had submitted a selection of his artwork to the *Boston Globe*. The newspaper's response was the equivalent of "don't quit your day job." And, indeed, my father could not quit his day job, much as he wished to. The result was that his future in the factory, sadly, was assured. While he continued to paint his landscapes and build his warships, those efforts produced little more than occasional spending money. Financially, the future was looking the same as the past: bleak.

In an effort to stem the tide of flowing red ink, I sat down with him one day and tried to explain the basics of his fairly simple budget, my mother having, understandably, withdrawn from the effort long ago. My words fell not on deaf ears—my father did sincerely listen to me—but, worse, on an uncomprehending mind. He just could not grasp how to connect the ebb and flow of money with a healthy balance sheet. The exercise of trying to speculate on what amounts of money might be coming in or going out a few weeks or months down the line was beyond his reasoning powers.

So, here was a man, I remember thinking, who could give me the entire history of World War II (on land *and* sea), explain the finer points of a Beethoven symphony, and recite the starting lineup for the 1945 Boston Braves, but who somehow could not avoid spending twenty dollars when he had only ten. To be totally honest about it, I also realized that if my father *had* understood the essentials of a budget, then we would not have been enjoying ourselves all those nights at Fenway Park, so that was an admittedly illogical but, for me personally, very beneficial side effect of my father's disinterest in family finances. The sole result of our conversation was that the hemorrhaging of money continued.

Predictably, my father's mounting frustration spilled over into family affairs, increasing the sense of frayed nerves and private resentments all around. For me personally, the good news was that I had had a father who was actively involved in my life during my formative years, even if most of that involvement concerned baseball. The bad news, and getting worse, was that my father had largely ceased being a father, as he steadily withdrew from family affairs into his own delusional world of imagined success with his paintings and ships, and was cursed always by his mental illness. The notion of approaching him for advice on anything was senseless. In fact, my father himself could have used a mentor, or some kind of guide

255

through the morass of middle-age and parenthood, but he had none. Relatives and friends helped him financially and with encouragement, but the road ahead for him was always a mystery. In those years of increasing uncertainty, a kind of resentment seeped into my father's behavior. As he felt his future slipping away, he focused almost exclusively on his own issues. Taking care of a family clearly exceeded his grasp. On most days, taking care of himself did as well. The family burdens largely fell on my mother, who made the best of a very challenging situation.

And it was the weight of family caretaking that evidently most troubled my father. For at times he could be jovial and even entertaining with friends and other relatives in situations, away from home, where there was not the pressure to be a provider for a family and he could momentarily indulge the life that he had been better suited for all along—one of far less personal responsibility and more of friendly banter with others.

But at home, when the pressure of being a husband and a father grew overwhelming, usually because of a new bill that could not be paid or, perhaps more often, the unshakable and unnerving sense that he had no future other than what was staring him in the face each day, his reaction was increasingly disturbing and reflected his fragile mental health. His body convulsing as he worked himself into a frenzy of distress, he would storm out of the house in an obscenity-laden exit, going out to the car to go wherever the car would take him, most likely someplace quiet, I imagine, where he could sit and ponder where his youth and dashed dreams of a life as an artist had gone, replaced not only by duties he did not want but by people he could not help, and, more importantly, who could not help him.

At one point, shortly after I finished high school, he packed up most of his belongings in boxes in the very misguided belief that he would move out and, at fifty, "find" himself and capture the life of satisfaction that had eluded him thus far. Of course, since none of the boxes were filled with money, he wasn't going anywhere, and didn't. A decade later, he did move out, taking what would be a temporary and equally unrealistic sojourn as a renter elsewhere until the age-old nemesis, lack of money, drove him back to where he clearly did not want to be, the family home.

A less significant but very annoying situation was the political divide between my father and me that seemed to be growing by the day. In my own primitive yet evolving political mind, I understood that both Democrats and Republicans had plenty of warts but took for granted that anyone with a serious interest in pushing civilization forward probably was not a conservative, at least on social issues.

My father, however, was a conservative. In fact, he was a right-wing conservative. And the growing bane of both our existences at the time, not surprisingly, was Richard Milhous Nixon. I thought Nixon *was* a crook and should be booted out of office. My father, on the other hand, probably thought Nixon was too *liberal* but in any case should not be removed from the White House, especially by Democrats. It was already irritating enough to my father that when Nixon captured the electoral vote in 49 states in 1972, the only state to oppose him was Massachusetts.

Between us, Nixon was a problem without a solution. Tip O'Neill and Bebe Rebozo probably had closer views on Nixon than we did. And when it occurred to me that my father must have voted for Eisenhower (twice), Nixon, Goldwater, and Nixon again (!) without giving it a second thought, I wondered how we could have diverged so sharply in our political beliefs. Somewhat unfairly to my father, I was not shy about expressing my disagreement with his views, which usually took on a combative tone very unlike our good-natured debates of 1930s vs. 1960s baseball. His preference for the National League over the American League was sometimes a little annoying but understandable. Even as a child, I could see both sides of that discussion. But Nixon proved the unbridgeable gap.

The Watergate crisis brought the political conflict between us into the open with, in hindsight, some hilarity. I found the drama to be captivating and watched some of the Senate hearings on TV, which sent my father's blood pressure up to dangerous levels. I sat on the couch, bracing for his onslaught of invective, and he did not disappoint. Standing in the living room doorway, intimating that the proceedings on TV were not worth sitting down for, he offered a colorful and patriotically partisan commentary. When North Carolina's Sam Ervin spoke up with his distinctive southern drawl, my father would wave his hand in disgust at the TV. "For Christ's sake, why don't you learn how to speak English?" he barked at Ervin. As Howard Baker pressed ahead with probing questions of John Dean, my father said of Baker, "For Christ's sake, why doesn't someone remind the god damn fool he's a Republican?" When Dean continued with his damaging testimony against Nixon, my father blasted Dean with, "You're a hell of a lawyer. Who taught you—Benedict Arnold?" Bespectacled Sam Dash brought on pure scorn. "Christ, where'd he get those glasses? You can't trust a man who'd wear those damn things!" And on and on he went. The political theater in my home reached even greater heights during the Iran-Contra hearings when Oliver North said he would stand on his head in support of his commander-in-chief (President Reagan), but that is a story for another time.

The final nail in our political coffin, so to speak, came on a day years later, the main culprits being a portable radio and, at least for me, a most undesirable voice. I walked into the house and saw my father, sitting at the kitchen table, not eating much, just leaning on his elbows and listening to the radio placed right in front of him, lest he miss a word. The speaker, his voice droning on and on, was Rush Limbaugh, and his targets, no different from any other day, were Bill and Hillary Clinton. As Limbaugh's spewed forth his loathing of both Clintons and their conspiratorial, socialist takeover of the country, highlighted by their diabolical plan to provide health care for every citizen, my father, unusually animated, commented repeatedly, "God damn right! That's god damn right!" I stood there momentarily, digesting the unfortunately distasteful scene, before turning away without saying anything. My father, enveloped in his own reality, noticed nothing amiss.

Although we both had strong interests in politics—I occasionally listened to Limbaugh, too, but just to keep the enemy within earshot—I understood that the Rubicon had been crossed. There was nothing we could say about it to one another anymore, nothing at all. And this widening political gulf was like pouring salt in an already open wound, a trend that would continue nearly until my father's life had passed.

In looking back now on the relationship during those early divisive years, it is clear that baseball had been the tie that binds, and when that tie unraveled, so did much of what had kept us together. The increasing crowds and hassles of 1967 had started the process of disengagement, and life's own growing—and impenetrable, in my father's case—challenges hastened it along. As my teen years passed and my father's interest in baseball receded, so did his relationship with me. It was not intentional or mean-spirited on his part. He had his personal demons to deal with, and I had a future to figure out that almost certainly, I assumed, *would* include baseball in some way, along with many other matters that were beyond my father's reach.

With baseball no longer a mutual topic of interest (indeed, it had been a mutual topic of *passion*), there was little else for us to discuss. Silence became the norm. Essentially, life had thrown us a change-up that was unhittable. We just watched it float by, on the black, beyond our reach. Neither one of us got the bat off our shoulder.

17. To Everything There Is A Season

Baseball had been very good to me throughout my life. But while my enthusiasm for both baseball and basketball continued unabated through junior high school and high school, my interest in schoolwork, unfortunately, did not.

This reality became increasingly apparent when I chose to enter college, with decidedly lukewarm support from my parents. With memories of the Depression planted firmly in their minds, and no familiarity with college, they hoped I would find a job—and an income. As a point of fact, I wasn't much more familiar with college than they were. But many of my friends were going, and my part-time job in a restaurant offered no path to the future, so college became the next step.

My actual way forward was more noble than practical. On the savings from my job and some financial aid, I attended Northeastern University, in 1974, commuting from my home with other friends by car or on the T. On the playgrounds of my youth and even up through adolescence, it had been a point of pride to be able to speak knowledgeably on baseball and basketball, particularly regarding the endless statistics that often dominate such discussions. When I sat in my college classes, however, I noticed a couple of things that were not in my favor: none of my professors looked like they knew or cared about the difference between a stolen base and a hit and run, and what they were trying to teach me was not what I was prepared to learn. My baseball education had been excellent, but it had come at the expense of the academic education that I was supposed to have been getting during those formative years in school.

That first year of college was a mix of the foreign and the familiar. I generally enjoyed my classes and professors but was overwhelmed by what seemed like a weekly mountain of homework. In high school, I hadn't paid too much of a price for ignoring much of my schoolwork, as graduation was all but guaranteed if you showed up each day and made a minimal effort, but college was far less forgiving, and I labored mightily to keep up with the coursework.

Part of the reason for my struggles was that, as before, I couldn't resist the pleasure of playing sports. I played basketball in the school gym nearly every day during the lunch break, in games where the other players often included professors and other NU staff, the most noteworthy by far being basketball coach Jim Calhoun, later of UConn fame. Of course, in those games, I was just a body on the court, but the fun of playing remained. Several years later, writing for the short-lived but adventurous college newspaper *The Edge*, I interviewed Calhoun on the NU basketball program, when he was trying to put NU on the college basketball map and viewed any publicity as good publicity. I saw only the grace and none of the temper of the Hall of Fame coach.

More baseball came after basketball in the spring of that freshman year. I was helping to coach a Little League team of eight-year old boys—girls were still relegated to the stands of Little League life in most places, including Norwood—with a friend, Jim, who probably could have recited more Yaz stats than anyone I knew, so we were a good fit.

The team played very well, and I think everyone associated with the team remembers that as a happy season of baseball. For one of those boys of summer (mostly spring, truth be told), however, the happiness would not be forever. John was one of those players who might be termed a "project," but a boy who Little League coaches often find great satisfaction in working with. He was not a natural, needing help in many aspects of the game. He was a little timid at the plate and rather awkward in the field. Like many boys, he was understandably afraid of being hit by the ball, and did not have great instincts in the field. He normally played outfield but was rarely in motion with the crack of the bat.

Still, John took instruction easily, had a great attitude, and steadily improved. At the plate he stopped bailing out on pitches and started getting his share of decently-hit balls, and one day made a legitimately outstanding catch of a high fly ball in the outfield. I still remember the hoopla of the players when he came back to the bench at the end of the inning, beaming from cheek to cheek.

Helping John a great deal was a brother named Tony, who must have been around fifteen years older than John. Tony faithfully appeared at many practices and games, always offering encouragement. John clearly was close to his brother and no doubt benefitted greatly from his support. Occasionally I spoke with Tony and was always impressed by his gratitude for our help and his dedication to his brother. I remember several years later, however, the sadness of learning that Tony had died, I think in a car accident. I immediately thought of John, probably not yet even a teenager, and how the grievous loss must have struck him.

Of course, exceptional people like Tony die every day. We mourn, we remember, never to be quite the same again. But, in our own ways, we do move on. Now, nearly forty years have passed since that tragedy. How John coped with it, I have no idea. Maybe only John knows. But hopefully that one season of baseball, with John coming of age as a player and Tony often there as an admiring and supportive witness, gave both of them a cherished memory that Tony took to the grave and that John used as a small source of courage in facing the unbearable. At least, I'd like to believe that baseball is capable of enabling such small miracles to happen.

Around the same time that I was coaching, I started playing on a supermarket softball team, again managed by Jim, which balanced its consistent mediocrity with a spirited and eclectic group of players. Our left fielder, Phil, generally patrolled his turf while wearing a pair of work boots, but did so with remarkable agility, while our right fielder, Ron, lovingly yet quite aptly gave us our nickname of "The Nonpareils." (Being a recently transplanted ringer from Florida and a fundamentally sound player himself, he may have been accustomed to seeing slightly more polished players in the Sunshine State.) On many occasions, we earned our nickname, such as the time a runner was rounding third base and our catcher yelled out "Got it!" but the cutoff man heard "Cut it!" and thus did yet another run easily cross the plate for the opposing team. The games were always played on Sunday mornings, so comparisons of hangovers were a weekly topic of conversation, if not consternation, in some cases. But as it was a condition that undoubtedly affected both teams equally, neither side worried about being at a disadvantage.

My position was third base, but I was not really a third baseman in that I was all catch, no throw. Butch Hobson, with the bone chips in his nearly useless elbow, looked like Aurelio Rodriguez compared to me. At the plate, my hitting approach was simple: don't swing unless it's a meatball or there are two strikes. Manny Sanguillen, whose theme song could have been the old '60s television ad, "Meet the swinger, Polaroid swinger..." (starring Ali MacGraw), was not my hitting model. So, I took the free pass down to first base many times, and with Jim, our best hitter, batting behind me, I came around to score pretty often.

It was all fun if not always successful. The camaraderie of the teammates and the chance to be on a baseball field, even if just for two hours a week, were enough reasons to continue to pull myself out of bed and spend Sunday mornings on a diamond.

As my first year of college came to a close in 1975, however, my mediocre grades matched my mediocre academic effort, and hanging it up seemed a deserving if not welcome fate. So, facing up to reality, I dropped out of college. Following some looking in the mirror (and at my bank account), I worked at the restaurant full-time for a semester and then enrolled in a much more affordable school that was about a ten-minute walk from Northeastern down Huntington Avenue. In 1976, Boston State College became my new academic home, and I attended classes armed with a new personal approach: seriousness. Educationally, I had years of catching up to do, which meant reading what I was supposed to read and learning what I was supposed to learn.

And I did read—books, magazines, newspapers, anything that would help me to make up for the years of education that I had lost. To this day, more than four decades later, I still feel like I'm trying to recover from those lost academic years, when I knew plenty about Henry Aaron but rather less about Henry Thoreau.

But I owe a lot to the faculty at Boston State, Professors Gainor, Kenney, Petronella, and Bernard in particular, who may have attended much more elite institutions themselves but were always willing to devote hours to my relatively pedestrian needs (such as learning how to write a decent paragraph) and were never less than encouraging and supportive. Writing about the passing of one of his old UMass-Amherst professors, columnist Kevin Cullen of the *Globe* noted that Howard Ziff "was a Renaissance man without airs" who loved "watching some kid from Norwood or Worcester or Ludlow actually start reading books, not because it was required but because it was a joy and a revelation." As one of those kids from Norwood, I certainly benefited from learning under my own Howard Ziffs at Boston State, and it is perhaps appropriate that when Boston State was no longer able to survive on its own, it merged with the UMass system, to become an entrenched, but not forgotten, part of UMass-Boston.

In 1977, new Red Sox manager, baseball lifer Don Zimmer, probably didn't need much education on baseball, but he was about to get plenty of unsolicited and blunt advice on the topic from Red Sox Nation. I had had Zimmer on many baseball cards, when he looked somewhat less hefty, with the emphasis on *somewhat*, than he did in a Red Sox uniform.

Curiously, there was a 1962 Post cereal card sporting a relatively slim Zimmer with the Chicago Cubs, as well as a Topps card from *the same year* displaying a rather heavier Zimmer wearing a Mets uniform with a Cincinnati Reds ID under his name. Zimmer probably never unpacked his suitcase too quickly during his nomadic yet noteworthy career. Later, in his managing days, he looked increasingly like baseball's version of Don Nottingham, a cross between a fire hydrant and a bowling ball.

What he knew—maybe *all* he knew—was baseball. Peter Gammons noted that Zimmer "was a man who slept, ate, lived, and breathed baseball, the first man to the park at 1:30 for a night game and, usually, the last to leave. It wasn't that he didn't care about Iran or the Pine Street Inn; he didn't pretend to have any frame of reference to them. His frame of reference was baseball." Johnny Pesky agreed. "He's no Phi Beta Kappa," Pesky observed, "but he's a darn good baseball man."

While fans and talk radio hosts ("as depraved a group of radio talk-show hosts as ever fouled the air," Shirley Povich wrote in defense of Zimmer) would reach visceral proportions in their mocking of Zimmer for his portly appearance, his gruff demeanor, his hypersensitivity to criticism, and his questionable managerial skills, no one could doubt his physical toughness. He had been beaned in a serious way as a minor leaguer, leaving him unconscious for two weeks, but he came back to play twelve years in the big leagues. You had to admire that part of him, reluctantly or otherwise—he got by on grit. The numbers on the backs of the cards confirmed that it wasn't excessive skill at the plate, although I noticed that he once hit *seven* triples in a season. Imagining Zimmer running nonstop from home plate to third base required some mental gymnastics. I probably did see Zimmer play when he was in the American League, but if so, he has escaped my memory.

Certainly, it was his grit, more than the sizable amount of talent he was managing, that marked his rise and tumultuous fall with the Red Sox. With Fisk, Lynn, Rice, Yaz, Evans, and the return of The Boomer, George Scott, the team was going to score runs. And they did score enough to win 97 games in 1977, finishing just behind the Yankees who, with 100 wins, brought back memories—or nightmares, depending on your team loyalties—of the old Bronx Bombers. On the mound, Soup Campbell performed like the second coming of Dick Radatz by saving 31 games while pitching a gaudy 140 innings out of the bullpen, more innings than a good number of starters go nowadays. In fact, Campbell led the entire staff with 13 wins, a striking commentary in itself on the performance of the starting rotation, led by Tiant's meager 12 wins. That 1977 team became the first—and remains the only—modern major league team to win at least 97 games and have no starters with more than 12 victories.

But when the Sox added Dennis Eckersley and Mike Torrez to the rotation in 1978, it looked like another trip to the playoffs was not so wild a dream. And I had to admit they had a captivating quality to them. With impressive levels of pitching, power, and paranoia, those Zimmer-led teams were never boring.

Unfortunately for Zimmer, the Red Sox and grit were words not often found together, and several of the players, notably Bill Lee ("you can only be young once, but you can be immature forever!"), Ferguson Jenkins, Rick Wise, Bernie Carbo, Dick Pole, and Jim Willoughby, had taken exception to the rigid, old-style ways of their manager. They formed a group known as the Buffalo Heads, and their carousing and frivolity had more in common with Fort Courage than Cooperstown. Had the effervescent Sparky Lyle remained on the team, his affinity for sitting naked on birthday cakes in the clubhouse might have made Zimmer yearn for his playing days with the 1962 Mets or even the 1963 Senators (226 losses between the two teams—Zimmer undoubtedly learned patience the hard way).

Predictably, Zimmer was not amused. He wanted those Buffalo Heads to roll, and most did. Jenkins was shipped off to

Texas (where he won 18 games, probably fondly remembering Zimmer in each one), Wise to Cleveland (where he lost 19 games), and Carbo and Willoughby were gone, too. Lee remained in the rotation but in Zimmer's doghouse as well, before being banished to the bullpen. Staying true to his soul, Lee did manage to get in a one-day protest strike to appropriately note the trade of his friend Carbo, who it would turn out needed all the support he could get in fighting drug demons for decades before finally finding Jesus and, blessedly, going clean.

But all of them could have been helpful to the Red Sox in that defining season of 1978, when a tale of two cities became ecstasy for one and a train wreck for the other. To Red Sox fans, it was no mystery which role the Sox would play, but as in so many other seasons, it was not possible to look away. We were addicted to watching the unwatchable.

The Red Sox star burned very brightly through mid-July of 1978, as the Sox had a sizable cushion on the Yankees and were coasting along. With their powerful lineup and a pitching staff that featured Dennis Eckersley, Luis Tiant, Mike Torrez, and a decent bullpen, they looked like they were in very good shape.

The possibility that all of this was an obvious tease—that the Red Sox would whet our appetite with each passing week, drawing in more and more fans thrilled to jump on the bandwagon, and then find a way to lose, probably in dramatic fashion, possibly in the World Series itself—did occur to many fans, I'm sure. It wasn't as if we hadn't seen it before, and I was not eager to be sucked in again.

And maybe I wouldn't have been, but a funny thing happened to the Red Sox on their way to glory: the despised yet dreaded Yankees, who had been dead since April and had fallen fourteen games off the pace in July and were still 8½ games out on August 20, suddenly were not so dead anymore. The Boston natives were getting restless as the margin narrowed, and by

September, full-scale panic set in when the Yankees seemed unable to lose while the Red Sox seemed *only* to lose.

The bottom of the pit, I hesitate to bring up, was the Boston Massacre at Fenway, a four-game sweep by the Yankees in which the Bombers outscored the Red Sox, 42–9 and pulled even to share first place. In a soap opera that outdid Peyton Place, the Red Sox then actually fell *behind* the Yankees. In a torrid final stretch mirroring a horse race in a photo finish, the Red Sox had to wake up and win their final eight games just to erase a one game deficit and force a playoff game at Fenway against the Yankees, now more reviled than ever.

Such madness could not be ignored. Against all my better judgment, I was again emotionally invested, once more hopeful for the hopeless.

The playoff game was to be played on a Monday afternoon. In hindsight, what I was thinking is a total mystery. How I imagined that the Red Sox, the *Red Sox*, had even a remote chance of beating the Yankees in such circumstances, I have no idea. Not only did the Yankees have Mr. October, Reggie Jackson, batting cleanup and Louisiana Lightning, Ron Guidry, on the mound, but the players in their starting lineup had a total of 12 World Series rings, while the Red Sox featured but one—that of starting pitcher Mike Torrez, earned while hurling for the Yankees. Truly, faith in the Red Sox was an addiction, a brainwashing that had been masterfully executed by the Red Sox for decades, which trapped fans into believing. How else to explain how rational thinking eluded Red Sox fans, including me, on such a regular basis?

The fact that it was an afternoon game was an immediate problem for me and many other people, I imagine, as it was a working day. As early as I could get away from my job in South Boston, I raced off in search of any bar near South Station that had a TV, which was not a tough assignment. When I arrived, true to the script that had been played out so many times over decades, the Red Sox had taken the early lead, encouraging their desperate-for-delirium fans eager to drink the Kool-Aid yet again. The die was cast, the scene was set, the actors were in place. It was a classic opportunity for a Red Sox collapse. But I, and many others, emptied the glass, literally, and asked for more. We got what we deserved.

It seems pointless to recount in detail Bucky Bleepin Dent's shot over The Wall (this, from a player with FOUR home runs all year), or, when we needed some 1967 magic, Yaz's agonizingly ordinary, foul popup to Graig Nettles with the winning run on base. "As Nettles grabbed the ball amid the stunned silence of Fenway Park," Ray Fitzgerald wrote, "you thought, this isn't the way it should end. Not like this. Not with Yaz making the final out." Even now, decades later, it is painful to remember. In his defense, it has to be said that Yaz, thirty-nine years old, had already had a homer and a single and knocked in two runs, half the runs the Sox scored in the game.

One poignant moment from that afternoon that captured both the futility and the humanity that defined the Red Sox of my lifetime warrants mention here. It was the postgame encounter between Yaz and Ned Martin. The pair had come up to the Red Sox together in 1961, seventeen long years previous, and been through the team's epic struggles together. Now, in what may have been (and was, in fact) Yaz's last legitimate chance at a World Series, the pair faced each other in the locker room. With a cracking voice, Yaz said, "I tried, Ned." Martin replied, nearly in a whisper, "I wanted you up there, captain." And, truthfully, we all did. Yaz deserved that shot at history. The following spring, while acknowledging that "it wasn't a good swing, but the guy [Gossage] made a hell of a pitch," Yaz admitted, "I'll always think about that swing." In Red Sox Nation, Yaz is certainly not the only one still thinking about it.

Even the most jaded fan, though, could not have dreamed up that 1978 collapse. If the Red Sox had simply contended but came in a close second in the division, or if they had collapsed earlier in the summer and fallen by the wayside, or even if they had reached the playoffs but lost to any team

OTHER than the Yankees, that might have been acceptable, given some of the calamities that had preceded that particular season. But to lose to the Yankees, of all teams, and on a home run by a barely better than average shortstop, and in our *own* ballpark—there was a limit to the cruel and unusual punishment that the Red Sox could inflict on a soul.

The October debacle came as I was finishing up my final semester at Boston State, having come full circle academically by bringing my grades back to the level where they had been in elementary school. I spent most of the year working at a full-time, public affairs job in a Department of Defense facility in South Boston and took night courses that fall to complete my degree requirements, learning a few more valuable lessons along the way.

One was that members of the military deserved respect, which they certainly weren't getting in those post-Vietnam days, and another was that working for a living was a lot harder than figuring out batting averages. And reading the newspaper on a daily basis and, several years later, doing some volunteer work with refugees and immigrants left an indelible impression. I met a Vietnamese woman who had become one of the "boat people" after seeing family members killed by the Viet Cong for the crime of not being poor enough. Another, a Chinese woman, had gone through Mao's Great Leap Forward, a leap that millions did not survive. A few years later, as a teacher, I read a paper from a Cambodian student who wrote of eating tree bark while hiding in the woods from the Khmer Rouge. I was reminded that not everyone had grown up playing wiffle ball in the backyard. Baseball was rightfully a game, a leisure activity.

The real world had been unceremoniously thrust upon me. I hoped to do some writing, on literature and history, but had no clear idea what lay ahead. To put it mildly, the urgency of checking the box scores had diminished considerably by then, probably with a helping hand from Bucky Dent. Baseball and basketball would remain very enjoyable pursuits but no longer essential. My heart had moved on.

18. Go West, Young Man

The following season the Red Sox again had a solid lineup and put up their usual impressive statistics, with Lynn (.333, 39, 122) and Rice (.325, 39, 130), the Gold Dust Twins once more, leading the way. And for the third year in a row under Zimmer, the team won more than 90 games. But it was all for naught. The Orioles, with yet another ridiculously deep pitching rotation—Jim Palmer was *fifth* on the staff in wins— ran away with the division after the All-Star break, and the Red Sox, not being the Yankees, were not about to catch them. So, 1979 was a comfortably unsuccessful season for Red Sox fans, with no drama at the finish, and was the last time the team would draw 2,000,000 fans until the inglorious year of 1986.

The Red Sox were moderately successful over the next few seasons, generally winning more than they lost, but not enough more to matter much or to save Zimmer his job. The oft-maligned manager was given the axe in the final week of the 1980 season, replaced by Johnny Pesky, who had not managed a major league team since the Red Sox had fired Pesky himself 16 years earlier.

As was often the case with the Red Sox, more off-the-field entertainment followed the season when general manager Haywood Sullivan neglected to send contracts on time to Fred Lynn and Carlton Fisk. The self-inflicted damage saw Lynn, who hit .301 in that final season, shipped off with pitcher Steve Renko to the Angels for a washed-up Joe Rudi, an ineffective Frank Tanana, and an unknown Jim Dorsey. Rudi (.180) and Tanana (4–10) spent a solitary season with the Red Sox, while Dorsey (16.88) appeared in four games over two years, all of the players demonstrating too well why the Angels had sent them packing. Lynn, meanwhile, went on to play ten more years, make three All-Star teams, and hit another 182 home runs. Worse, Fisk was able to walk away entirely, signing with the White Sox. Fisk merely played another 13 years, making four All-Star teams and hitting 214 home runs for Chicago on his way to the Hall of Fame.

Now living with roommates as a graduate student/teaching assistant at Northeastern in the early 1980s, I spent much of my time doing homework and grading papers and managing a tight personal budget that did not include trips to Fenway Park. Still, I followed the team from a respectable distance, and of course liked some players more than others. One player on those Red Sox teams that I did come to appreciate—nothing like the Juan Marichal crush, but then again, I was in my twenties—was Carney Lansford. He had come over from the Angels with Mark (what a curveball!) Clear in exchange for Rick Burleson and Butch Hobson. The Red Sox trading The Rooster was a little like the Celtics trading Kendrick Perkins. It wasn't a total shock, but it was very discomforting, in some way. Burleson played only one way—hard—and was an easy player to admire. I didn't know much about Lansford except that he was going to be the new third baseman.

But Lansford grew on me, if not on American League pitchers. There are more than 700 players in the major leagues, and there are more than 700 different batting stances. Lansford's, however, was particularly intriguing. As he stood facing the pitcher, he used to hold his bat relatively low, not far from his body, and wiggle the bat continuously, to the point that the wiggle became part of the swing as he snapped at the ball. His swing wasn't as wiggly as that of, say, Gary Sheffield in later years, but that bat was moving a lot, never still. But the wiggling bat did not prevent Lansford himself from hitting the ball, and hitting it very well. In his first year with the Red Sox, he led the league in batting with a .336 average, and followed that up with a .301 season. He was also a very good third baseman. But when Wade Boggs was ready to join the Red Sox as a regular, Lansford became expendable and was traded to Oakland. While he had a very productive career, with more than 2000 hits and a .290 average, he seems to be one of those underappreciated names in baseball. At least, I always thought so.

The city of Oakland would soon have a place in my own life. After finishing up graduate school in 1982 and, with my master's degree in English in hand, facing immediate unemployment and another move back home, I got the urge for going. Deciding, with no practical basis, that I would become a global citizen, I considered moving to China or France, to teach, although how I was going to pay for such travel remained a rather sizable unanswered question. A little more in line with reality, but not much more, was a journey to San Francisco, just to be there and live the scene of Ginsberg and Ferlinghetti and so many other writers, and pay a visit of homage to City Lights bookstore. I also understood that I needed at least a temporary break from my father, whose daily struggles were taking a toll on both of us.

In what was really a one-horse race, California won, so with my life savings of about $400 in my pocket I headed west as a young man, a trip that initially had little to do with baseball, but one that eventually would, in moving ways, bring me back to Juan Marichal and Yaz and memories of the 1960s. Regarding the last, how appropriate for a journey to San Francisco, where that decade of protests and flower power will never die and where there may yet be middle-aged, or older, stoners who continue to worship the hallucinogenic corner of Haight/Ashbury (Hashbury, as Hunter Thompson aptly phrased it, most likely based on personal experience), the Human Be-In, and Moby Grape.

So, settling in the Bay Area, I took what would be a very enjoyable and eventful two-year hiatus from the professional working world. Before leaving for San Francisco, I had booked a room in the cheapest place I could find, prepared to live the bohemian life in America's most bohemian city. My new abode turned out to be a flophouse in the pre-gentrified Mission district. The "hotel" took some getting used to—suffice is it to say that while I never did get accustomed to stepping over the sad and wretched men who slept on the sidewalk outside the front door each morning, and then doing the same each night, I otherwise managed the situation tolerably. Those poor sidewalk sleepers, I soon learned, were not at the bottom of the homeless pecking order in San Francisco, as the underside of the Tenderloin district was inhabited by even more destitute souls. (I was well acquainted with the Tenderloin, as I frequently went there to browse through one of my favorite used bookstores in the city, a big barn of a place, with ladders readily available to climb if you wanted to get to the books up near the stratospheric ceiling.)

Mainly I was excited to be in the city by the bay, where undoubtedly like many before me and many since, I felt unfettered and alive. There was nobody calling me up for favors, and no one's future to decide, as Joni Mitchell so accurately put it. I was slightly puzzled, however, over the inferior status given to Oakland, also a city by the same beautiful bay. I once saw a sign over a bar in San Francisco that pretty well summed up the sentiments of the natives: "Eat, Drink, and Be Merry, For Tomorrow Ye May Have To Go To Oakland." It seemed almost a miracle that San Francisco ever allowed the Bay Bridge to be built. For the record, and in defense of Oakland, the East Bay had a lot more sunshine.

The main, and often *only*, issue on the minds of San Franciscans at the time I arrived in 1982 was the still mysterious illness called AIDS. It was one of the lead stories in the papers nearly every day, with coverage ranging from what it actually was, what treatment might stop/cure it (nothing for the moment), and why the Reagan White House wasn't paying more attention to the crisis. The spread of AIDS did present a clear and present danger to the city and was being harshly debated not just between the left and the right but between gays and Mayor Dianne Feinstein, generally a strong supporter of gay positions, and even between gays themselves (the Milk and Toklas groups were at odds on how to move forward). Coming on the heels of the assassination of Mayor George Moscone and Supervisor Harvey Milk by former policeman Dan White, the city had been in turmoil for several years, although some may say that San Francisco was born in turmoil.

My own impression was that while the growing scourge of AIDS appropriately dominated the collective attention of the city, even the AIDS epidemic, horrific as it was, could not extinguish the natural joie de vivre that had been the signature appeal of San Francisco for decades. Having spent my whole life in New England, I never took for granted the warmth of the sun (at least after lunch, when the fog lifted) and the warmth in the hearts of nearly everyone I met in the Bay Area. And, to be fair to my fellow New Englanders, when I returned to Boston two years later and went through another winter of unrelieved snow and ice, I better understood the sometimes-crusty nature of the populace. It wasn't all the fault of the Puritans.

While I remained television-less—and car-less—in keeping with my bohemian pose, one of my personal treats while passing time in my hotel room at night was that on my radio, I could listen to both Giants and A's games. This, of course, was on the occasions that neither team was on the East Coast, in which case a night game might already be over before dark. After so many years of living on the East Coast, when West Coast games often had not even started when I went to bed, it fascinated me that I could get the final scores of *all* the games before falling asleep. In a baseball sense, I felt like I was passing Go and collecting $200 on a nightly basis. At the same time, I never shook the feeling that whatever important was happening in America was taking place somewhere between Boston and D.C. An East Coast prejudice, to be sure, but one that was well-engrained in me, for better or worse.

For the Giants, David Glass and Hank Greenwald were pleasant to listen to, particularly the witty Greenwald, but as a pairing, they did not threaten Martin and Woods. More competitive was the irrepressible Bill King, who did radio play-by-play for the Athletics in what at times was a crowded booth of at least three broadcasters. But King stood out, even next to the revered Lon Simmons. With his flowing gray locks and striking beard and handlebar moustache, he also looked like he would have been perfectly comfortable teaching a course at Cal on revolution or skippering a sailboat, solo, around the world.

In my mind, King was Ned Martin on steroids, or whatever the equivalent of steroids was in the early 1980s. He knew baseball thoroughly, along with many other topics, and he regaled his audience with entertaining reportage ranging from amazement to humor to shock, all spoken with such sincerity and authenticity that listening to him became a kind of addictive experience, sort of like, for many locals, opening the *Chronicle* and reading Herb Caen's column. What I liked most about him was his ability, like Martin, to keep it real—when a player screwed up for either team, King did not try to dance around the fact. In the same vein, if there was a blown call on the field, King, Johnny Most-like, reserved special scorn for umpires, presented with never-hidden sarcasm and with truly genuine outrage. With those mediocre A's teams, it was almost possible to say that listening to Bill King on the radio was more satisfying than being at the game itself.

My days of living in the Mission area were necessarily numbered, and after a couple of months I moved across the bay to Berkeley, where I rented a room in a home with a very nice family—a literary and, of course, liberal father and his two young children—and got a job in a bookstore that had plenty of footnote-filled texts from Cal professors but not too much in the way of baseball literature. And at that time, to keep up with all things Boston, I ordered a daily subscription to the *Globe*, which I continued until I had to admit that regularly reading the Boston news two or three days after the fact was not very practical.

There was plenty happening in the Bay Area itself, however, and that included the baseball scene. I went to see the

Giants several times at gusty Candlestick, where even on a sunny day, the wind-chill factor was likely to remind me of Mark Twain's quip about spending the coldest winter of his life in summertime San Francisco. And the lengthy commute from Berkeley to Candlestick on public transportation was one in which I could easily get through several chapters of whatever book I was reading at the time. Weather and commuting aside, I enjoyed watching current Red Sox hitting coach Chili Davis, who could not replace Willie Mays or Bobby Bonds in the minds of Giants' fans but was an outstanding player in his own right, and Jack Clark, in his slugging prime and a decade before he would find his own way to Fenway, where he had one final, productive season of twenty-eight home runs in 1991 before entering the inevitable terrain of "washed-up" players and retiring a year later.

My favorite Giants' pitcher of the time was a half-Japanese, half-German southpaw with the memorable and dignified name of Atlee Hammaker, which sounded more Nobel Prize-ish than one suited for someone standing astride a pitching rubber. But Hammaker in those days seemed to be a star in the making. A key member of the Giants' rotation, he led the National League in ERA and made the All-Star team in 1983, and the sky was the limit for him. Unfortunately, as happens so often in baseball (and in life!), the sky fell quickly for young Atlee, and he began a long, injury-plagued odyssey through both leagues before finishing up a lackluster career with a record of 59–67. Perhaps that All-Star game itself was a harbinger for him, as he gave up a grand slam to Fred Lynn, three years removed from his glory days at Fenway, and a total of seven runs in a very forgettable performance. Still, when Hammaker was on the mound in the early 1980s for the Giants, they always had a chance.

Across the water, at the Coliseum in Oakland, I saw a good number of games, usually on sun-splashed Sunday afternoons when the wind-chill factor was, thankfully, not an issue. I was destined to watch the A's teams between the dynasties, missing Catfish Hunter and Dave Stewart, but nevertheless enjoyed the games—and the sunshine.

The stadium itself, being so different from Fenway, was of interest. The foul territory alone would have taken up a good chunk of Fenway and must have been a curse to the hitters and a joy to the pitchers. And you could sit in left field, which of course was an impossibility at Fenway, and watch the inimitable Rickey Henderson run down, or occasionally nearly overrun, fly balls. Next to Henderson was a fielding wizard, Dwayne Murphy. Unlike Henderson, who had the unusual combination of being a right-handed hitter and left-handed fielder, Murphy threw as a righty and was a left-handed batter with good power, but he more than earned his salary with his glove and speed alone, covering centerfield like a blanket. Whenever an opposing batter hit a shot to center field, it was worth the price of admission to see Murphy get after it and usually haul it in, often in spectacular fashion.

One other player of note from the Coliseum days was Hall-of-Famer Joe Morgan, near the end of the line but still starting and playing productively. I saw the classy Morgan play for both the Giants (1982) and the A's (1984) in those years, as his career came to a meandering close. Still, the chance to see one of the all-time greats was a thrill, just as seeing Willie Mays at Shea Stadium had been.

None of this, however, touches on my most memorable baseball moments in the Bay Area. One of my goals was to have my first San Francisco beer at "Lefty" O'Doul's restaurant near Union Square, which I achieved a day after my arrival. Walls lined with baseball photos of native son O'Doul, of local San Francisco Seals renown as a player and manager along with his greater fame as a hitting machine with the Phillies and the Brooklyn Robins/Dodgers, brought me back to the days when I pored through *Daguerreotypes* and my baseball encyclopedia in search of the baseball world now displayed before my eyes.

O'Doul, I should note, had his own Red Sox footnote, as he was the "player to be named later" in the 1922 swap that sent Joe Dugan to the Yankees. In his one-year stint with the Red Sox, O'Doul was a mediocre relief pitcher—1–1, 5.43—and didn't return to the majors for another five years. In the restaurant, I recall that I spent far more time looking at the pictures than drinking my beer, a strong commentary on how much I enjoyed the baseball aspect of my visit to "Lefty" O'Doul's.

Next was a kind of baseball "event" in San Francisco, or what at least struck me as an event, being from Boston. In Berkeley, I had met a transplanted New Yorker and diehard Mets fan, Barry, who became a good friend. One weekend he brought me to a stickball tournament that was organized and populated almost entirely by New York natives, apparently in honor of Willie Mays's famous youthful days in the streets of Harlem and as a nostalgic chance to relive their own New York memories of stickball. Whatever the reason, the games were played by men, and some women, of all ages in a large, fenced-in courtyard area, and the day became a very pleasurable cultural experience for me, even though I was a bit of an outsider.

But the fact that I was from "Boorstin," as they put it, did give me a certain distinction, and more than once I was asked to say "Park Street" and "Harvard Square" just to add to the linguistic enjoyment of the occasion. The stickball itself was also very entertaining once I actually learned to hit the rather small ball. We played for several hours that day, and while I can't say that anyone in that courtyard reminded me of a young Willie Mays, I did come away with many good stickball memories and, three thousand safe miles from Boston, a newfound respect for New York baseball fans. They didn't shove the Mets and Yankees down my throat, and with the Red Sox nearly seven decades into their championship-less misery, cut me some much-appreciated slack as a Red Sox fan. Of course, had all of this happened in New York City, the situation might have been quite different. But in San Francisco, everyone gave peace a chance, and the result was one of my happier baseball memories on the West Coast.

The Hall of Fame celebration of Juan Marichal took place at Candlestick on July 10, 1983, a game that I had certainly marked on my calendar. I heard no talk of John Roseboro or second place finishes or lack of Cy Young awards that day. Marichal had been elected to the Hall the previous January, and the ceremony was a remembrance of high kicks, pinpoint control, and true artistry on the mound. The Giants swept a doubleheader with the Cubs (with Hammaker winning the nightcap), and my only regret was in not having seen Marichal at Candlestick during his playing days.

This thought was reinforced by the photo on the cover of the Marichal program, which featured what looked like an older Marichal striding into his leg kick, and behind him a view of the third base seats, a good number of which were painfully empty. What I would have given, I thought, to have been in one of those seats. The Giants of Marichal's heyday were stacked with stars, but the team generally averaged around 19,000 fans, meaning the park was more than half empty most nights. Even on the Marichal day itself, only a modest crowd of 26,000 showed up. Then again, Boston had had Yaz and Tony C and The Monster, and far fewer people went to see them play. But I was one of them, and I absolutely would also have been one of them at Candlestick.

And regarding the Marichal game program from that day, the photos provided a splendid trip down memory lane (and still do now, with its sponsor being Eastern Airlines: "Only our name is Eastern"). One picture features Marichal along with the Meal Ticket himself, Carl Hubbell, and the decidedly less accomplished Ed Halicki, three no-hit Giants pitchers. Another shows Marichal in the Giants clubhouse with fellow Hall-of-Famer Gaylord Perry, before the Giants foolishly sent Perry packing off to Cleveland, where he proceeded to win 64 games over the next three seasons. Interestingly, the program also has a photo featuring, according to the caption, Marichal and the Mets' Tom Seaver. Unfortunately for the program editor, the photo actually features Marichal and Jerry

Koosman, with Koosman wearing his lefty's glove right in front of the camera. Clearly the editor was not hired for his baseball acumen.

The final, and best, memory involved Yaz. I tried to plan my trips to the Coliseum around visits by the Red Sox. In the summer of 1983, I went to what was the final game of the year between the two teams. The Red Sox were in the midst of a mediocre season, destined to finish twenty games behind the last of the great Orioles teams. As was typical at the time, and undoubtedly remains true today, there were at least as many Red Sox fans in the stands as A's fans, the crowd being an altogether modest turnout in Oakland.

For me personally, the reason for going to that particular game was Yaz. He had announced his retirement earlier that year, so I knew that this was my last chance to see him in action. Many other Red Sox fans, at least some of whom probably could have said of Yaz what Neil Young once famously said of Stephen Stills—"We've had our ups and downs, but we're still playing together"—were there as well. That season must have been a nostalgic but rather bittersweet experience for Yaz. With his team going nowhere in the standings, he knew there would be no more trips to the World Series and no championship ring in his storied 23-year career.

The story of Yaz was so familiar to me, going back as far as anything I could remember in my life. In fact, I had never seen a Red Sox team without Yaz. He was already a star on the first Red Sox team I ever saw in person, in 1963. In his prime, at twenty-eight, during the Impossible Dream season, he could not have imagined the crushing disappointments that lay ahead of him. He was thirty-six before he reached his next World Series, in 1975, when he turned back the clock and hit over .300 in a fine Series performance. And he was nearly forty when the 1978 playoff disaster occurred. Now, five years later, in the winter of his career at forty-four, he was on his last tour of the league, and I wanted to get a final look.

Appropriately and not surprisingly, in his last at bat late in the game, Yaz turned on a misplaced pitch and drove it deep to right. Like so many before it, the ball was long gone. I stood and clapped, as did nearly everyone else, to give Yaz his final due as he rounded the bases. Over nearly a quarter of a century, he had earned it.

Following my return to Boston after the two years in California, I experienced the most important and meaningful events in my life. I met my future wife, Cristina, who was a scientist at the UMass Medical Center at the time, and we were married in the spring of 1987 in her hometown of Trieste, Italy. Our children, Julia and Timothy, were born in 1989 and 1992, and raising a family became the new challenge and joy in my life. From my wife, my daughter, and my son, I learned early and often of the subjects that filled their minds, the compelling worlds of art, nature, language, and, yes, soccer, a sport that had barely existed in my own youthful world when Dick Radatz was firing fastballs past a frustrated Mickey Mantle. It was, and continues to be, an adventure that has enriched my life far more than I could have imagined and, given my years of struggles with my own father, one that I have deeply appreciated.

19. Darkness, Darkness

While I was away, I hadn't missed too much concerning the Red Sox, who continued to play pretty well but not well enough to get to the postseason. The 1982 season, when the team won 89 games, was a prime example. The team's staff featured two relievers, Bob Stanley and Mark Clear, who won 26 games, matching the win total of the top two starters, Dennis Eckersley and John Tudor. In fact, Stanley was called upon to carry so much of the pitching burden that he tossed a total of 168 innings, an American League record for relief pitchers that still stands. By comparison, Dick Radatz himself topped out at 157 innings, in 1964. Stanley, who once pitched ten innings in relief in *one game*, and Radatz may have enjoyed pitching back in the days at the turn of the century when most hurlers were used as both starters and relievers. Indeed, in the Boston Braves' championship 1914 season, the team of miracles had twelve pitchers, and each of them started at least one game.

The summer of 1984, when I returned, presented another familiar sight. The Red Sox had sluggers galore in that lineup—Rice, Armas, and Evans all topped 100 RBI's—but no pitchers who could do much with it. Roger Clemens and Bruce Hurst were not yet stars. Dennis Eckersley, 20-8, 2.99 in 1978, slumped to 9-13, 5.61 in 1983 and with the blessing of much of Red Sox Nation had been traded to the Cubs for the ill-fated Bill Buckner on a day in late May when, oddly enough, I was attending a Cubs game at Wrigley Field with an old college friend, Tom, during our meandering journey east from California by car. (Eckersley's reinvention of himself as a Hall of Fame closer with Oakland would become one of baseball's great stories, and he chose to finish up his legendary, 24-year career with a final season—50 games, 4-1—in Boston in 1998.) Bobby Ojeda was good but only good, and Oil Can Boyd was himself: a moody, bizarre, outspoken, very talented, but often unreliable pitcher who probably made each of his managers feel more like a psychiatrist than a skipper. Altogether, it was a recipe for 86 wins and a fourth place finish, making it a very typical, post-Impossible Dream season—modestly successful, largely disappointing.

It was also Ralph Houk's 20th and final season as a big league manager. He had come in with the Yankees of Mantle, Maris, and Ford and won two World Series in his first two seasons. Those days must have seemed long ago and far away in his autumn of 1984.

Around the same time, baseball played a prominent role in a sports-related event that will live in infamy, at least in the financial story of my life. After returning from California to Norwood, I had some free time while looking for gainful employment, and this lack of work inspired me to unwittingly put into practice the saying, "idle hands are the devil's workshop."

Much of my childhood was stored in boxes in my parents' attic in the form of baseball cards, baseball magazines, baseball newspapers, baseball pennants, baseball yearbooks, and other baseball memorabilia, and football cards, and basketball cards (including a Wilt Chamberlain card that seemed almost as tall as Wilt the Stilt himself), and hockey cards, and stacks and stacks of comic books. I had plenty of available time, and my various collections were all gathering dust, just taking up space, hadn't been touched in years, were no longer of any obvious use, so naturally they needed to be.... How many times has this story been told in America? When I was a child, I spoke as a child, but when I was an adult, I put away childish things. My own father had told me of all of the Hall of Famers he had on cards, now all a distant memory, having been discarded— such a painful but appropriate word—without a hint of the monetary damage being done.

On my own fateful day in the attic, I did have second thoughts. Something did not feel right about this at all. But there I was, surrounded by oversized boxes stuffed with—stuff. I had to do it, I told myself. Childhood was over, adulthood was well upon me. Besides, wasn't such cleansing supposed to be good for your soul in some way, turning the page, starting fresh? All of that wasn't really in my character as a sports hoarder, but I tried to make myself believe it was. And those boxes were, in fact, taking up a lot of room that could be used for other—stuff.

So, I reluctantly dug into the piles, bringing bags and boxes of things down to the car, thrown into the trunk, destined for the mother of all collections, the town dump. Even now, my mind resists focusing on the carnage of that day, and all of it self-inflicted. There was no one to blame—just my conscience telling me to grow up. April may be the cruelest of months, but conscience has to be the cruelest of emotions. The only lesson I learned from the experience was that if you have no conscience, your chances of gaining fabulous wealth probably increase greatly, which some historians and ethicists might say has considerable basis in fact.

First to go were the comic books, the easiest items to part with. But even those boxes and boxes of comic books carried with them untold—and unknown, unfortunately, to me—hundreds, possibly *thousands*, of dollars in value. Everything was there, and still in excellent condition. *Top Cat, Dennis the Menace, Richie Rich, Archie, The Green Hornet, Zorro, Gomer Pyle, Get Smart, Flipper, Daniel Boone* (has anyone ever worn more coonskin hats than Fess Parker?), *Beetle Bailey, Voyage to the Bottom of the Sea, The Man from U.N.C.L.E.* and many others lost to memory—much of my reading education as a child, about to go up in smoke. (The dumps still burned trash in those days, with flames leaping up from the piles of debris every smoke-filled Saturday morning.)

But all of that was just the prelude to the true Armegeddon. Throwing out the sports stuff was hard, and of course throwing out the baseball trove was the biggest challenge of all. In my best attempt to delay the inevitable, I considered how best to pack the items, which in fact had already been pretty much packed long ago, but for *keeping*, not for tossing, and how to arrange the boxes in the car, and how to do just about anything except actually move the possessions. The far greater matter, though, was the emotional toll it would take. I knew the effort I had made to find and collect all of the material in the first place, spending much of my hard-earned savings from lugging around newspapers largely in order to assemble much of what I was now about to usher into oblivion. I had stored it so that it would not get ruined with age, at least as much as could reasonably be done. The irony of it all...

The story has good news and bad news, most likely indicating that part of me had grown up and part of me, clearly, had not. My baseball cards—at least the singles—from Topps or Post cereal boxes or jello boxes or wherever else cards could be found, were, most mercifully, saved. Also avoiding the town bonfire were dozens of metal and plastic coins, with player photos and info, which had come in packs with the cards, as well as years' worth of copies of the *Sporting News* and *Sports Illustrated*. And singles of my football, basketball, and hockey cards, not quite as coveted but nevertheless too difficult to toss, were safe, as were the boxes of newspaper and magazine clippings.

Everything else went. Stacks of *Sport*, *Baseball Digest*, and many other magazines, numerous pennants, yearbooks, scorecards, various things that came with cards such as decals, paper rings, stickers, stand-up figures, rub-ons and iron-ons, player photos, posters, and countless doubles and triples and quadruples of any card in any sport, a total that certainly exceeded all of my singles—all were cast out. Much of it had economic value, some of it quite a bit, but all of it had sentimental value to me, and I took no pleasure from the task. The deed, however, was done. The stuff, like turning gold into lead, was tossed. The baseball cards that I kept, including some "near mint" cards of Yaz, would bring in some helpful cash later, but, to use a worn refrain, it was never entirely about the money. I took it, not wishing to be a fool twice, but to me the cards and other things had really been about my childhood fascination with baseball.

The Red Sox, under new skipper John McNamara in 1985, showed little more sense in their own endeavors than I had in mine. Making no moves with a World Series in mind, the team had less hitting and about the same pitching, allowing them to reach the pinnacle of major league mediocrity at 81–81. But it was a noteworthy year in a couple of respects: it was the last time the Red Sox would draw fewer than two million fans, excepting the strike-shortened 1994 season, and it gave Red Sox fans absolutely no warning of the cataclysmic year to follow. McNamara would be pilloried for the next generation, until Grady Little placed that albatross upon himself. But Little, unlike the much-maligned McNamara, would be bailed out within a year by the miracle worker, the unflappable Terry Francona.

The 1986 season was quite similar to the 1975 season in that the Red Sox again sat atop the division by June 1, and were rarely positioned otherwise for the rest of the year, even losing nine of their final fourteen games while still finishing well ahead of the pack. The similarity, along with the previous sixty-seven years of Red Sox history, probably should have given pause to all fans. But the addiction remained, the burden had to be borne, the fight had to be fought.

For me, the regular season itself had some memorable distinctions. Finishing in a Red Sox uniform, Tom Seaver won his 311th—and final—game in the big leagues. His was a career that I could never quite grasp, and I had seen it, from a distance, from beginning to end. With the Mets, Seaver had done everything that a pitcher could do. With three Cy Youngs and the immortal 1969 championship, he joined Palmer, Hunter, Jenkins, and Carlton as the best starting pitchers of his time. His delivery looked like something from a pitching textbook.

Smooth, no wasted motion, able to throw hard and accurately—Seaver was a pleasure to watch and obviously a challenge to hit.

Then, after a decade of brilliant success in New York, Tom Terrific became Tom Terrible in the eyes of the soon-to-be-vilified Mets owner M. Donald Grant. A contract dispute between Grant and Seaver that featured rumors of Seaver's wife, Nancy, becoming upset over Nolan Ryan's higher salary with the California Angels, resulted in Seaver being shipped off to Cincinnati for four nobodies, a trade that sent Mets fans into a tirade. Seaver, oddly enough, would be traded three times in his career, and the best anyone got in return for him was Steve "Psycho" Lyons. Now, here he was with the Red Sox, finishing out what was a certain Hall of Fame career, against the Mets. But, due to an injury, the drama of Seaver facing his old team was not to be. I had always enjoyed watching Seaver, and had been fortunate to see him pitch at Shea Stadium, in his prime, on my 1973 visit there. So, as with Marichal, I was pleased to see Seaver make a late tour through Boston on his way to Cooperstown.

On the youthful side of greatness that year was Roger Clemens, a pitcher not at all unlike Tom Seaver himself in his prime. The Rocket had the whole package—power, control, and pride. And he put it all together brilliantly that season, his 24 wins earning him both the Cy Young and the MVP. Watching Clemens dominate hitters while leading the Sox into the playoffs must have reminded Seaver of his own magical summer of 1969, when he was the young Turk carrying the amazin' Mets into baseball history. Whether the ending would be as happy for Clemens remained to be seen. I remembered the Red Sox riding the strong right arm of a young Jim Lonborg into a World Series, hopeful, as always with the Red Sox, that the past was not prologue.

Another intriguing story of that year for me was the performance of Jim Rice, who had a renaissance of sorts at the plate. He batted .324, his highest average since 1979, collected

200 hits, also for the first time since 1979, and drove in 110 runs. He was a strong third in the MVP voting, finishing behind only Clemens and Don Mattingly, who both had off-the-charts seasons. And at thirty-three, there was every reason to expect that Rice would crank out at least one or two more similar seasons before starting the inevitable decline.

But for Rice, 1986 was truly his last hurrah. Within inches of being a lock for the Hall of Fame—just a few more decent seasons would have done it—his fearsome skills suddenly vanished. He didn't have a Steve Blass (19–8, 2.49; 3–9, 9.85) collapse, but his drop was precipitous and stunning to Red Sox fans, and undoubtedly to Rice himself. He had three more mediocre/poor seasons (31 home runs, total) before hanging it up for good. What had happened? Some said it was nagging injuries, others said his eyesight had deteriorated, still others said he was just washed up. Whatever the reason, Rice never recovered. I thought back to his rookie season, when it had been easy to imagine that both Gold Dust Twins, Rice and Lynn, were on their way to the Hall of Fame. Those hopes seemed dashed. But in 1986, Rice still had a dangerous bat, and unlike in 1975, he would be able to use it in the playoffs.

The fate of the Red Sox in the playoffs and World Series should have been unknown only to fans with amnesia. I won't get fooled again, I told myself. I was at the September game at Fenway with my brother when Oil Can Boyd won the clincher, but even as the fans screamed and got swept up in the thrill of the moment, I tried to steady myself and take the long view. Calmly and rationally, I thought, this is the Red Sox. In Texas, they remember the Alamo. In Boston, I remembered 1978. And 1975. And 1974. And 1972. And 1967. It was not in the Red Sox genetic make-up to win a decisive game. And once again, they didn't, of course. I didn't want to witness the futility, yet struggled to look away. With the Red Sox, you truly were damned if you did and damned if you didn't. There was no exit.

Several years earlier, Leigh Montville had spoken for all of us when he put the Red Sox fan on the couch and gave his analysis: "The Red Sox never give you a break," he wrote. "They will be bad enough to hate. They will be good enough to love.... You're pretty sure you're going to be hurt again, that you're going to be screaming again, that you're going to be picking this team apart as if it were last Thursday's chicken, but you're not sure enough. Not 100 percent sure. Ninety percent? Ninety-five? Not sure enough. You'll follow the familiar lure. You'll hope the familiar hope. You're a Red Sox fan. Nothing is easy for a Red Sox fan." His words were right on the mark.

The entertainment factor was always undeniably high when the Red Sox and the postseason collided, and that proved to be the case once again. The team managed to come back from a 3–1 deficit in the ALCS, and then blew a 3–2 lead in the World Series. The larger point was that the Red Sox had now endured nearly seventy years of championship-free seasons and had lost not only their last four seventh games in the World Series (to this day, they remain 0–4 in their last four seventh games of World Series), but had done so in a manner that, inconceivable as it may have seemed, was *more* painful than the 1978 fiasco. In the competitive field of baseball teams coming up short, the Red Sox were all too competitive. Few teams had lost so many times, in so many ways, over so many years, in so many big games, as the Red Sox. I remembered the Brooklyn Dodgers, and their aggrieved fans, but found little solace. Perhaps most distressing of all, the misery of the team would continue for nearly two more decades before Red Sox Nation suffered the ultimate pain and humiliation, the 2003 playoffs against the Yankees.

The pitch by pitch details of the disaster in 1986 don't need to be presented. In Red Sox Nation, probably such an effort should be declared illegal. But, again, there are storylines in the experience that bear mention. In my own mind, for humanitarian reasons, Donnie Moore must come first. Why he killed himself, and nearly his wife, is unknown, but considering the state of his marriage, his finances, and his health, he obviously had mounting personal issues to contend with. Still, if his performance in Game 5 and its aftereffects did have something to do with his violence against himself and his own family, as some, including Brian Downing, have claimed, how can anyone begin to understand such events? Of the many bad memories of the 1986 postseason, Donnie Moore's story is easily the saddest.

The story of Calvin Schiraldi, on the field, is worse than Moore's, as his collapse happened in two clinching games and on a much bigger stage. What does it say about the Red Sox when a pitcher who had a 32–39 career record with five different teams—the epitome of a journeyman—remains almost a household name in Red Sox Nation? There are times when moves in a game just feel wrong, and Red Sox manager John McNamara produced that feeling too often, however unfair that may be toward him, considering that he got them to the final game of the World Series.

Using Schiraldi in key situations in both games 6 and 7 may have given many Red Sox fans that sinking feeling. He had had an excellent regular season out of the bullpen, and a very good playoff series against the Angels as well. There were reasons to justify putting him in there, and the necessary acknowledgment of that fact still rankles. There is also the legitimate question of, if not Schiraldi, who? Dick Radatz of 1964 was not walking through that bullpen door.

At the same time, Schiraldi was only twenty-four and had pitched in a total of 40 games in his entire career up to that postseason. When you're in a position to be the hero or the goat, the whole season riding on your arm, the pressure must be tremendous on someone so young. Naturally, Red Sox fans were exasperated when Schiraldi became the goat—twice—but maybe we should not have been surprised by the turn of events. Didn't we remember Bucky Dent? Jim Burton? Julian Javier? How far back did you want to go? The stage was set for the thrill of victory or the agony of defeat, and one of the teams on the field was the Red Sox. We had forgotten our history.

In closing on that season, of course, there is Bill Buckner. He shouldn't need any defense, no pun intended, but I'll try to provide one anyway. When the Sox traded Eckersley for Buckner, I didn't like the trade, just figuring you should almost never trade pitching for hitting, especially if you are the Red Sox. But I had always thought of Buckner as a very solid, at times underappreciated player. And, until Game 6, he played as advertised. He was out there almost every day, always hustled, and hit the ball with men on base, driving in 212 runs in 1985 and 1986. I don't recall anyone having a problem with Buckner ... until Game 6.

There have been many Bill Buckners in baseball. Fred Snodgrass, Mickey Owen, Johnny Pesky, Ralph Terry, Willie Davis, among others—players, some of them very accomplished, who are renowned for one pitch, or one play, or one inning, in a key spot, when it all unraveled. King of the hill, so to speak, in this regard was Brooklyn's Ralph Branca, who lived in notoriety for more than six decades for a single pitch that was heard 'round the world when Bobby Thomson nearly cost Russ Hodges his voice with one immortal swing. ("That was one time when the pennant winners didn't pour the champagne all over each other. No sir—we drank it. We needed it," declared the Giants' Monte Irvin.) Bob Stanley himself probably should qualify, for if he had done his job in the first place, Bill Buckner would not be "Bill Buckner." Maybe ditto for Rich Gedman. But Bill Buckner is who he is. He took his adversity like a professional, even coming back to Boston in 1990 to finish his career. And fans have forgiven him as well, so the story has a happy ending, undoubtedly helped along by the comfort of three world championships in the meantime.

Through the late 1980s, I kept one eye—but not often both eyes—on the Red Sox, as I had accepted the fact that I could not ignore them entirely. I continued to go to games, but more to enjoy a few hours of baseball than to scoreboard watch. The team, as usual, had talent, which had often been part of the dilemma for a Red Sox fan. When you knew they would contend, there was the remote possibility that they might actually reach the promised land that year. So, you could not simply look away as you could in, say, Kansas City when they had the Athletics, or in Houston when they had Colt .45s. With the Red Sox, something great *might* happen. It just hadn't *actually* happened in seventy years.

On the mound in those years, Clemens and Hurst gave the team an outstanding top of the rotation. And they had the usual potent offense, led by Mike Greenwell, Ellis Burks, Dwight Evans, and, most impressive of all, Wade Boggs, who had been a hitting machine since his .349 rookie season in 1982. In fact, after his first ten seasons with the Red Sox, five of which produced batting titles, Boggs's lifetime average sat at a gaudy .345.

When I attended games in the 1980s and 1990s, I usually sat along third base, which was a perfect location from which to observe the left-handed hitting Boggs. His repetitive plate mannerisms prior to each pitch, his careful cocking of the bat, always with a bit of a twitch, his steely fixation on the pitcher's delivery, and then the liners he so effortlessly sprayed around the field, most often to center or left, were all clearly visible from where I sat. Each of his plate appearances was worth staying in your seat for, as Boggs was probably as close to Ted Williams as anyone my age was likely to see in a Red Sox uniform.

As remarkable a batter as Boggs was in the 1980s, however, his accomplishments served as a striking reminder of how truly dominant his 1970s predecessor as a hitting genius, Rod Carew, had been. In 1977, for example, when Carew won the sixth of his seven batting titles, his .388 average put him 52 points ahead of his runner-up, and teammate, the wonderfully talented but ill-fated Lyman Bostock, a differential not seen before or since in the majors other than in the very first year of the American League, in 1901, when Nap Lajoie won the title by a whopping 86 points. The Red Sox themselves played an unwelcome role in Carew's overpowering success in 1977, as he torched them for a .422 average, including a blistering .500—13 for 26—at Fenway. Boggs's own best differential was 33 points, winning the batting title over George Brett in 1985, a number surpassed by Carew on three occasions.

The 1988 season was a fine example of the Red Sox tease at the time. Despite the presence of Boggs and the other reputable names in their lineup, the Red Sox, still led by John McNamara, floundered around .500 for half the year, barely an improvement over the previous season when they had finished twenty games out. Not surprisingly, and not to the regret of any fans that I knew of, the hammer came down on McNamara in mid-season, paving the way for the magic of Joe Morgan.

Under Morgan, the Sox proceeded to win 19 of their next 20 games, almost all of them at home before packed houses, to reach first place. In the middle of the streak, Morgan, who drove a snow plow in the winter and was not afraid to speak truth to power, showed who was in charge when he pulled a slumping Jim Rice and sent up light-hitting infielder Spike Owen as a pinch hitter. Rice, unwisely, got in Morgan's face about the unexpected and unwelcome decision. As much as I admired Rice, I was embarrassed for him now, as his pride, in full public view, had come before the fall. Deservedly, Morgan got the better of him, and fans thought this might be the dawn of a new era at the Jersey Street country club.

But Morgan Magic, while fun to watch, wasn't the solution, either. The Sox went on to finish the season with a 27–30 mark over the final two months, hanging on to win the division by a single game before being swept by the Athletics in the playoffs. The Sox repeated as division champions two years later, only to be swept again by the A's, with the added insult being that Dennis Eckersley, sent away six years ago for Bill Buckner and now a lights-out closer, got saves in six of the eight games. And not to belabor the point, but after the Red Sox survived three seasons in the non-playoff baseball wilderness with Butch Hobson at the helm, they again made it to the postseason in 1995 where, this time, it was the Indians who swept them. For those keeping track, the Sox were now 0–13 in postseason action since that fateful, innocent ground ball to first base in 1986.

The pattern remained essentially the same through the close of the century, now more than eighty years since the Red Sox had captured a World Series. Great players were coming (Pedro Martinez, Nomar Garciaparra) and going (Roger Clemens), but the Sox always hung around respectably, not that the Yankees ever made it easy. In 1998, the Sox won 92 games, more than enough to get into the playoffs but still *22* games behind the dominant Yankees. The Sox managed to win a game against Cleveland in the ALCS before being eliminated. The following year, in the playoffs again, the Sox this time got past Cleveland to face the Yankees, which resulted in a 4–1 drubbing. The postseason for the post-Buckner-ground-ball Sox now stood at an ugly 5–22. Perhaps mercifully, they played well but not quite well enough to make it to the playoffs over the next three seasons.

From a comfortable emotional distance, I watched the goings-on, always interested in seeing a good baseball game but not believing anymore that the Red Sox were capable of doing more than what they had been doing my whole life. Two quotes from Red Sox general managers themselves helped to illustrate, with humiliating clarity, a large piece of the problem. "We spent more days in first place than the Yankees," and "Where would we play Willie McGee?" were not quotes from Solomon. It may be unfair to attach these words to the legacies of Dan Duquette and Lou Gorman, who did put competitive teams on the field. Duquette himself brought in many of the key players who would produce the elusive championship. But the quotes do reflect at least some of the muddle-headed thinking that sustained the drought for 86 years.

The new millennium for the Red Sox brought even jaded fans to new levels of heartache and, finally, joy. It got off to a rather tumultuous start with Jurassic Carl Everett, aptly named by Dan Shaughnessy after Everett questioned whether dinosaurs ever roamed the earth, plummeting from stardom to ridicule in securing his own well-deserved place in Red Sox infamy. Sadly, three men who were much more serious in their baseball pursuits in Boston—Ned Martin, Ted Williams, and Dick O'Connell—passed away within two months of one another in the summer of 2002. Their collective time spent with the Red Sox had covered a period of well over one hundred years, with none of them destined to see the team win a single championship. Even Martin might have struggled to find the words to describe such misfortune.

What happened in 2003 and 2004 was so like/unlike the Red Sox that *any* baseball fan would have been hard-pressed to ignore the drama that unfolded in the greatest rivalry in baseball history. Had any baseball team ever gone from similar depths of postseason disappointment (embarrassment?) to the heights of a championship in such fashion, and in consecutive seasons? No candidates come readily to mind.

The collapses of the Red Sox have certainly claimed their share of victims over many decades, and one of the more sympathetic of the group is Grady Little, who managed the team in 2002 and 2003. Had Little managed the Pittsburgh Pirates or the Baltimore Orioles and won 85 games a year during those two seasons, either team might have offered him a long-term deal, happy to be at least in the middle of the pack.

Instead, his fate was to lead the Red Sox to 188 wins over his two years in Boston and be released in disgrace. The Red Sox championship the following year, with Little out of the picture, is the only thing that prevented Little's name from becoming Bucknerized for years in the exasperated minds of Red Sox Nation. How curious, and unkind, are the changing winds of baseball. Little had won more games over two seasons than any other Red Sox manager since Don Zimmer. And while Zimmer would be forever cursed by the name of Bucky Dent, Little in 2003 would have his own albatross in the names of Aaron Boone, Pedro Martinez, and the hard-charging, slightly crazed ... Don Zimmer.

How managers are judged in general seems to be an all too human pursuit, based on factors that may have scant connection to the manager himself. If the owner and the general manager don't get along, if the owner won't spend money, if the owner spends money on the wrong players, if the owner is a racist, if the general manager can't identify talent, if the farm system is no good, if the players are too young, or too old, or simply injured—any or all of these issues could sink a team, and a manager, but they have little to do with the manager himself.

Examples abound as to whether it's the players or the managers or other factors that produce success. Going way back, Miller Huggins had a 1925 Yankees lineup featuring five Hall of Famers (Ruth, Gehrig, Earle Combs, Waite Hoyt, and Herb Pennock) that went 69-85, finishing in seventh place (but still 21 games ahead of the last-place Red Sox). Just two years later, with the same five Hall of Famers plus Tony Lazzeri, Huggins rode the most famous Bronx Bombers team of all to a World Series title. Johnny Pesky may have been a great manager had he been with the Yankees of 1961 (109-53), but with the Red Sox of 1964, he had no chance. Johnny Keane was the World Series winner in 1964 with the Cardinals (over the Yankees!—"I never dreamed a human being could be this happy," was Keane's own understandable reaction), and then, in a headspinning turnaround, was hired by Yankees general manager Ralph Houk (who *was* the manager of the 1961 Yankees) to manage the team. But after a sixth place finish in 1965, Keane survived only twenty games (4–16) into his second season of misery before being replaced by ... Ralph Houk, who himself then led the aging and injured Bombers to a last place finish. And it bears repeating that Houk completed his managerial career with four years in Boston, all of them out of the playoffs. More recently, John Farrell may or may not be a good in-game manager, but if Rick Porcello and David Price, two pitchers with stratospheric salaries, pitch clunkers to start a playoff series, managerial wisdom goes out the window.

Common sense does tell us a couple of things, however, about managing in the big leagues: a manager has to get at least some credit when a team wins as often as Little's teams did, but managers also can lose games, and Little's decision-making in the eighth inning of the 7th game against the Yankees, by any measure, was spectacularly flawed. In that sense, Grady Little was most appropriate as a Red Sox manager. No matter how many games his teams won, in the end, they didn't win enough, and he could look in the mirror to see one of the reasons why. But his failures certainly set the stage for the sensational turnaround of 2004, and the blessed end of "wait till next year."

Very little on baseball, however, came up in my conversations with my father in those years, when he struggled mightily to keep his life intact as he passed through his sixties and seventies. Baseball was barely an afterthought, as there were other, far more pressing issues for him. The biggest remained money, always in short supply, resulting in episodes demonstrating a mysterious form of capitalism that I've yet to understand. Banks routinely issued him credit cards that he easily maxed out with no hint of how the money would ever be repaid. Once when he was sitting in the kitchen filling out a credit card application form, I watched in exasperation until finally asking him why he was applying for yet another credit card, and how he thought he would get it. Displaying his unique view of reality, he replied, "Oh, they'll give it to me. They always do. Why the hell shouldn't they?"

Eventually, he was flat on his back financially. A compassionate local attorney took on his case and, fortunately, managed to keep the moneylenders at bay. Through all those years, going back to the days of my money jar in the pantry, my father and I had the same economic relationship: he was the debtor, I was the lender. However, there was no repayment schedule, as there would be no repayments forthcoming. The money was always meant to "tide him over," but we both understood that the loans were gifts, and that no reasonable amount of money would be sufficient to "tide him over" for

299

more than a week or so. When the losses mounted from the hundreds of dollars to the thousands and seemingly to infinity and beyond, I learned to dread the sound of a ringing phone if my father hadn't called in a few days. And when the conversation started with, "How are you doing for cash these days?", I knew the outflow would resume momentarily. How do you ask your father to stop calling?

Steadily, his life faltered in other ways as well. One of the worst blows, yet one that was legitimately overdue, was the loss of his driver's license in his early seventies. His mind was rarely focused on the road ahead when he drove, as he was not relaxed enough to concentrate anymore, and after being stopped a couple of times by police for erratic driving, the deed was done, and my father was carless.

His reaction was swift and typical—"How the hell can they take away your car? What am I supposed to do now, for Christ's sake?"—but, as usual, irrelevant. As much as possible, family members and relatives helped out with rides. He tried walking and using buses, and to his credit, he did put what proved to be his last burst of physical strength into that effort. One day when I came home to visit, he proudly showed me a new pair of shoes he had recently bought. His misplaced optimism sadly on display, he told me enthusiastically, "These shoes really work, god damn it! They're comfortable as hell—I can walk uptown in fifteen minutes!"

I don't doubt that he may have covered that modest distance in fifteen minutes, but it was not a situation destined to last, and it didn't. He continued to wear the shoes, but his walks outside diminished, and over time his legs grew weaker while his frustration grew stronger. He became more restless as his body was giving every indication that it was close to taking a permanent rest. Homebound, he was not going to go down without a fight, but that he was going down was increasingly obvious. By then, thoughts of Yaz and Rico and Spahn and Sain in our lives seemed almost a part of antiquity.

20. Francona Delivers

As unsuccessful as the Red Sox had been in the eighty-six years leading up to 2004, they certainly had stiff competition among the ranks of historically underachieving teams in baseball history. The often-abysmal Phillies, for instance, were a deserving rival, as they passed the first *ninety* years of their own existence before winning a World Series, in 1980. Their futility included a particularly brutal stretch of twenty-five years, from 1921 to 1945, in which they lost 100 games twelve times. The 1930 edition was a classic. The team featured eight players with batting averages of .313 or higher—Lefty O'Doul hit .383 and finished three points below *his own teammate*, Chuck Klein—and yet the team managed to lose 102 games in coming in dead last, 40 games behind the pennant-winning Cardinals.

But baseball fans most often tended to compare the Red Sox with the Chicago Cubs in debates over which club had suffered the most. If you define "suffering" as unrelieved pain, then surely Cubs fans could claim victory, unwanted as it was. The Cubs had not only not won the World Series in nearly a century, the last time being 1908, but they lost the Series in their next *seven* appearances, only once managing to reach the seventh game. Perhaps more amazing, the Cubs had not even been *in* a World Series for almost seventy years. Only the Cubs' neighbors, the White Sox, could come close to matching the futility of the Cubs in actually getting to the Series, but even the White Sox had at least made it there in 1959, their only appearance in a period covering eighty-five years before they won it all, for the third time, in 2005. The relentless lack of hope for Cubs' fans certainly qualified as a deep form of suffering, and no one could begrudge them their sweet taste of champagne, at long last, in 2016.

The heartache of the Red Sox, on the other hand, lay in the fact that they had been tantalizingly close to winning it all on several occasions, yet always managed not to win, often in jaw-dropping fashion. The Cubs were pathetic, the Red Sox were failures—the distinction was all too clear to Red Sox fans, particularly those of us who could remember Bob Gibson and Julian Javier and all the false hopes that followed.

When the Red Sox finally did get their championship in 2004, it was unlikely that it could happen in any normal manner, and it didn't. (For that matter, their previous World Series victory, in 1918 over the Cubs, could hardly be called normal, either, with both teams taking the field an hour late in Game 5 after threatening to go on strike over wages—this, as numerous ballplayers were serving overseas in World War I and a number of wounded vets were in the stands.) Sweeping the Yankees after almost getting swept themselves, and then legitimately sweeping the Cardinals in the World Series, was a perfectly appropriate way for the Red Sox to erase memories of all the calamities since the trade of Babe Ruth.

The next championship, in 2007, was more of an old-fashioned romp through the playoffs. Even when they were down three games to one to Cleveland in the ALCS, the Red Sox showed that their pre-2004 collapses were truly in the trash heap of history, as they went on to outscore the Indians 30–5 over the next three games, and then overwhelmed the Rockies as well, 29–10, in a mercifully short, four-game series. For stat freaks, that's a 59–15 slaughter over seven games against supposedly the best of the best baseball teams from both leagues. These were no longer your grandfather's Red Sox.

And while seeing the Red Sox win a World Series was astounding, my age was somewhat against me. I was excited that they had finally done it, but I would have been much more excited had it happened in 1967, or 1972, or 1975, or 1978. Still, there was no denying that it was a historic occasion not only in Boston, but in the hearts and minds of the countless Red Sox fans spread throughout the country. As with a decent number of Red Sox fans, I could remember so clearly the years when I thought the day simply would never come. I just wished that it had actually come during those same years, when it very well could have.

The "cowboy-up" players who broke the drought, and then repeated as champs three years later, are certainly memorable, but I was more intrigued by their boss, Terry Francona. The story of Terry Francona is compelling on a number of levels, from his family to his playing/managing career to his ultimate success—and failure—in one of the most competitive markets in baseball. His relatively unassuming ways did not conjure up memories of Dick Williams, Leo Durocher, Earl Weaver, Billy Martin, or Lou Piniella, kicking dirt on umpires or blasting players in public. Still, his obsessive chewing of tobacco or whatever it was in his mouth that he was constantly grinding away on was a pretty clear indication that even Francona could feel stress. Relaxation was not in the job description of a major league manager in Boston.

To baseball card collectors, the name *Francona* was well-known decades ago, as Terry's father, Tito, had a long, if not illustrious, major league career. I had Tito on several cards, seemingly always for different teams and, for whatever reason, often on doubles. I remember that fact because a card of Tito Francona, not being a particularly desirable commodity, was hard to trade, so getting him on doubles was not a real advantage in any way. But while his name was quite familiar to me, I once gave it a Kafkaesque spelling of "Frankona" in my baseball memo book of lineups.

What I did like about him was that he had played many years during my pre-baseball life, so studying his cards, like those of Bill Bruton, Dick Donovan, and Del Crandall (all of whom had been signed by the *Boston* Braves) and many others, was a kind of educational experience. One lucky point in Tito's favor is that he played long before the steroid era, as he once had a career year that would make Brady Anderson blush. In the span of two years in the late 1950s, his average went from .254 to .363, and his slugging percentage from .330 to .566, including an increase in home runs from one to twenty. Those are numbers that a baseball fan could hardly take with a straight face nowadays, but maybe Tito started lifting weights, or whatever players did in the 1950s to stay in shape. Undoubtedly it was above board and was just one of those years that make baseball statistics (pre-1998) so fascinating to ponder. For the statistical record, Francona followed up his Ruthian year with 17 homers and a .292 average—nothing to be ashamed of.

Alas for Tito, the first year was more indicative of his talent than the next two, and after a few solid seasons he wandered from team to team and league to league, ending his career by playing for the Cleveland Indians, St. Louis Cardinals, Philadelphia Phillies, Atlanta Braves, Oakland Athletics, and Milwaukee Brewers in the span of just seven seasons, and wearing the uniforms of nine teams in total. He appeared annually on baseball cards with, not surprisingly, steadily dwindling numbers each year. But Tito Francona was a baseball standard, a name known to anyone who kept half an eye on the game through the 1950s and 1960s.

So, the father Francona was no mystery to me. The son, on the other hand, was nearly a total stranger. When Terry Francona became manager of the Red Sox, I had only the vaguest recollection that he had ever played in his own right, and no memory of seeing him at all. His statistics again reminded me of what baseball numbers reveal, and do not reveal. In ten seasons as a utility player, he hit over .300 on three occasions, batting as high as .346, but never with more than 223 at-bats in a season. One year he produced 19 doubles in just 214 at-bats. Two major injuries, though, robbed him of a better career.

But while Terry Francona may have deserved better as a player, his record as a manager begs questions in the other direction. When the Red Sox hired him, I thought, "Based on what?" His managing record with the Phillies was unimpressive, to be polite, and terrible, to be honest. In four seasons, he never finished over .500 and twice lost over 90 games. His teams never made the playoffs. And the year after he left the team, the Phillies improved their record by 21 wins under Larry Bowa. There was nothing on the surface to recommend Terry Francona as a manager for *any* team, let alone for one of the most storied franchises in baseball history, with a player payroll to match. I thought for sure he would be in over his head in Boston.

Yet Francona, for much of his tenure with the Red Sox, was a resounding success. Anyone (including Red Sox upper management) who says they saw this coming is almost certainly misremembering. He had been a mediocre-to-poor manager, arriving with a solidly losing record, who went on to end an 86-year-old drought in his first season and then win another World Series three years later. It's true that Francona took over a veteran club with skilled players at most positions and a starting rotation that included Curt Schilling and Pedro Martinez. Still, as I could painfully attest, the Red Sox had had serious talent nearly every year since 1967, and with a small amount of luck could have won at least one championship. But the fact remains that no matter how much talent they had, and no matter who managed them, the Red Sox did not break through until Francona arrived, and he did it in his first try. It is just what it appears to be: an astonishing achievement.

What most interested me in Francona was his demeanor and his treatment of players, on and off the field. In this sense, he reminded me of Walter Alston and Joe Torre, two managers who also had the players each year to win and whose patient, supportive approach to players actually did get them to win on a regular basis. With these managers, there were no scenes reminiscent of Billy Martin fighting with Reggie Jackson in the dugout, or even Joe Morgan jawing with Jim Rice over a pinch hitter. They were the steady, quieter types, humble after victories and unflappable after defeats, not afraid to give credit to others for success and shoulder the blame for failure.

As Red Sox Nation knows well, Francona for years brilliantly handled a cast of characters that would have tried many managers' souls. From superstars/divas like Pedro Martinez and Manny Ramirez to regulars like J.D. Drew to virtual footnotes like Jay Payton, Francona was remarkably able to deal with their issues while keeping the rest of the team, and often the recalcitrant player himself, performing at a high level. In cases that might have created significant clubhouse dissension, if not outright rebellion (how many normal people can show up for work each day and see a co-worker—e.g. Manny—just take days off whenever he feels like it and still try their hardest with such an outrage right in their faces?), Francona managed to deflate the issue. Whatever he said, always behind closed doors, kept relations with the player under control and seemingly satisfied the rest of the team.

One aspect of his managing style that must have gained Francona serious respect among players was his relationship with the media. Although this annoyed some fans, no question from a reporter, even about Manny, caused Francona to lose his cool. He never threw a player under the bus, and frequently expressed confidence in players who had given him precious little reason for such confidence.

And if a player was playing well, Francona repeatedly offered praise bordering on adulation. Any fair-minded player for the Red Sox under Terry Francona had to know that if he showed up, gave his best effort, and produced even marginally well, the manager would give him every possible opportunity to play. I once heard an interview with Francona in which he was discussing the play of outfielder Darnell McDonald, who was hitting around .200 at the time. Francona never mentioned the batting average, preferring instead to point out that McDonald had hit the ball well the previous night and had had other "good swings" lately, leading Francona to conclude that McDonald was on the verge of breaking out and therefore would be in the lineup that night. "He's a good kid, and he's come up big for us before," Francona observed in all sincerity. Leo Durocher never spoke that way about .200 hitters, or probably even some .300 hitters.

Whatever his magic was, it ended quickly and disgracefully in a matter of weeks during the month that cannot be named. The fact that had the Red Sox managed to win even *one* of the numerous games that they coughed up that month, they would have been in the playoffs, is disgrace enough. But the manner in which his players betrayed him, particularly Josh Beckett and John Lackey, the supposed "leaders" of the staff, was really an unpardonable sin.

The shameful, unprofessional, juvenile, and selfish behavior of those players, who had no reason whatsoever for jeopardizing Francona's job—or their own—was the kind of outrage that made me prefer to think back to Billy Williams playing in more than 1100 straight games, or Mickey Lolich tossing 376 innings in a season, or Randy Hundley catching 160 games in one year. Those were not players who fretted about how many days off they had, or how their hammies were feeling when they got out of bed, or whether they felt a tweak during batting practice, or whether the media hadn't said anything good about them for a couple of days. I imagine they also carried their own luggage. Had the Red Sox immediately banished Beckett and Lackey in trades, that would have been fine with me. Obviously, Lackey was later a huge part of their 2013 championship run, so this is my heart speaking over my head. Still, it's hard to respect Lackey, even now—paranoia strikes deep, especially if you are a Red Sox fan.

But Francona's legacy speaks for itself. As a Red Sox manager, Francona won more playoff games (28) than the next three most successful team managers—Farrell (11), Bill Carrigan (8), and McNamara (7)—combined. Even if John Farrell matches Francona by winning a second championship himself, he will not catch Francona in respect. Only Francona ended the drought of nearly a century. Bottom line on

Francona: he will be remembered as the best of all Red Sox managers, with a place in Cooperstown a serious possibility.

In my own working life, an unexpected connection between baseball and Japan came about. Teaching for more than two decades at Showa Institute in Boston, a study-abroad campus for English majors from Showa Women's University in Tokyo, gave me an additional link to the Red Sox, particularly the 2007 and 2013 championship teams, which I certainly could not have imagined during my earliest days of following the team.

Baseball, it was true, had been popular in Japan for generations and had attracted some American players from as far back as I could remember. In my baseball history readings, I learned about Negro League and Major League barnstorming tours in Japan between the wars, with one team featuring Ruth, Gehrig, and Foxx, and with Don Newcombe and Larry Doby also going over there as a final stop in their careers. Lefty O'Doul was a veritable hero in Japan, having gone there many times as a player and coach, and in 2002 became the first American named to the Japanese Baseball Hall of Fame. Of course I had never seen any of these players. The first players that I remember going to Japan in the 1960s were Don Blasingame, George Altman, Dick Stuart, Willie Kirkland, and Jim Gentile, all of whom I had on cards nearly every year that I collected them.

But while American players established a well-worn path to Japan, players coming in the other direction were almost non-existent. After Masanori Murakami's two-year stay with the Giants in 1964 and 1965, there was a drought of nearly three decades before Hideo Nomo had his auspicious debut season with the Dodgers in 1995. The Red Sox started bringing in Japanese players several years later and can thank Japan in large part for their last two championships. And as a teacher, I was thankful that the Red Sox-Japan connection gave me an easy topic for discussion when getting to know my students.

The Red Sox started with Tomo Ohka in 1999, not that I recall that Ohka left a marked impression on the students (or on major league batters) during his three years with the team. The arrival of Nomo in 2001, however, was a different story, as the students already knew Nomo as a star in Japan, and he didn't disappoint in Boston, throwing a no-hitter in his very first start and going on to lead the league in strikeouts. The name "Nomo" was a quick conversation starter that summer. But the 2001 season for the Red Sox overall was forgettable, and the nightmare of September 11 deservedly became the only memory that mattered from that dark year.

What was truly a Japanese event not just at Showa but in the city of Boston was the 2007 arrival of Daisuke Matsuzaka, who evidently had been the equivalent of Cy Young in Japan. Japanese tourists flocked to Boston, "Daisuke" souvenirs flew off the shelves, and sales of sushi soared in Beantown. Many Showa students became huge Fenway fans, and several met Daisuke and teammate Hideki Okajima at Fenway and presented them with a traditional origami gift on behalf of the school. That first year in Boston, when Daisuke won the clinching ALCS game and had a World Series victory, as well as the second year (18–3, 2.90), I used his name early and often to help form bonds with my students. Some were more excited than others about Daisuke, but all were very proud of the Japanese connection. One student unfailingly reminded me each time Daisuke was scheduled to pitch.

In subsequent years, Daisuke would unfortunately drive an increasing number of Red Sox fans, including me, to distraction with his agonizingly slow pitching regimen on the mound. Even when he won, he usually won ugly. But in those first two seasons, the name Dice-K, as locals pronounced it, was golden in Boston and at Showa.

By 2009, the team roster included four Japanese pitchers—Matsuzaka, Okajima, Takashi Saito, and Junichi Tazawa. And when Koji Uehara played a huge role in the 2013 championship, the Red Sox continued to profit magnificently from their Japanese investment. Being in the same city as the Red Sox, and its trove of accomplished Japanese players, gave Showa an unexpected but very welcome benefit as a Japanese college with many young baseball fans, a reminder of truth sometimes being stranger than fiction.

Certainly the news of my teaching position at Showa must have seemed like something beyond truth *or* fiction to my father, who undoubtedly harbored sharp opinions, if not incredulity, regarding my choice of employment. At the top of his list, I'm sure, was the thought that his son would be teaching, possibly, the grandchildren of men who may have been involved in the bombing of Pearl Harbor. I'm certain of that because, in his mind, Japan and World War II were connected in the way that Nixon and Watergate were connected—one didn't exist without the other.

Concerning baseball, Japan and the war, my father was not alone in his sensibilities. Soon after the Pearl Harbor attack, the *Sporting News* itself editorialized that while baseball may be popular in Japan, the essence of the sport could not be truly appreciated by such a militaristic nation: "Through our great game runs an inherent decency, fair dealing, love of the game, and respect for one's opponents.... It is the very soul of baseball. We may cut a few corners on the playing area, but we do not stab an 'honorable opponent' in the back.... No nation which has had as intimate contact with baseball as the Japanese could have committed the vicious, infamous deed of the early morning of December 7, 1941, if the spirit of the game had ever penetrated their yellow hides." Again, connecting the horrors of war with the game of baseball seems very ethically questionable.

Regarding the "inherent decency" of the sport, evidently the Black Sox scandal, the rampant drinking by players before, after, and even during games, the strict enforcement of the dictatorial reserve clause, and, most glaringly, the exclusion of black ballplayers for decades did not taint Major League Baseball in the partisan eyes of those publishing baseball's Bible.

The *New York Times* carried the importance of American baseball superiority even farther when its senior sports columnist, the erudite and esteemed John Kieran, declared three days after Pearl Harbor that the U.S. would defeat the Axis powers because American boys had grown up on the competition of baseball, with war apparently qualifying as a higher level of sporting conflict to Kieran. Certainly, the positive attributes given by Americans to the game of baseball had strong roots. Shortly after the turn of the twentieth century, when the U.S. was flush with pride in its imperialistic venture in the Philippines, transplanted American teachers included baseball lessons in their determined attempts to westernize the Filipino natives, inspiring the *Manila Times*, an American newspaper, to commend their efforts in demonstrating that baseball "was more than a game, a regenerating influence and power for good."

Yet, while my father may have largely agreed with the baseball propagandists (and jingoists), he did not lapse into an Archie Bunker soliloquy from the far right, to my surprise and relief. Instead, he sincerely congratulated me on getting the job. Still strong in his mind, no doubt, were memories of the Depression, and the stability of a full-time job was no trivial matter, even so many years later. I'd also like to think that, maybe, my father had realized—and accepted—the irony, both beautiful and tragic, that the country he had so instinctively thought of as "the enemy" now was the employer of his grateful son, and that the issues linking the two countries included education and baseball. I would be immensely pleased if I knew that my decision to teach at Showa had such a beneficial effect. Of course, I can never know, but the change alone in my father's outlook, while an outlier, was reward enough.

21. The Faithful

There is no doubt that the birth of Red Sox Nation can be traced to 1967, but something of a longer historical view is needed to see how that miracle came to be. As with so much else in baseball, the numbers tell the story, and the moral of the story is that it is better to win than to lose.

My interest in the team's attendance stems from the still amazing (to me) fact that I came to know of Fenway Park as a boy sitting in a largely empty stadium year after year even at a time when nearly every boy I knew loved baseball, while the vast majority of Red Sox fans now regularly attending sellouts or near sell-outs cannot imagine such a scene even at a time when apparently far fewer boys play baseball at all.

Before getting started on the more recent—"recent" meaning within sight of my own lifetime—ebb and flow of Red Sox attendance, it is worth noting that there was rabid interest in the team going back more than a century, with the famed 1912 season providing a colorful example. The Sox had their own cheering section, known as the Royal Rooters, who were so obsessed with the team that before one of the World Series games against the Giants, when too many tickets had been sold at Fenway, police on horses had to do battle with the Rooters to move them from the grass in front of the left field wall. (They succeeded, but not before the Rooters had taken part of the center field fence with them.) Smoky Joe Wood called the Rooters "the most fanatical fans you could imagine," and he offered up more of their antics during the World Series that year as proof. The Rooters traveled with the team back and forth to New York, with Wood recalling that "we didn't get much rest on the train rides because they were a noisy bunch; loyal and good-natured as all get-out, but noisy." At the park, they may have been noisiest of all in support of Wood himself, who won 34 games that season and then won another three in the Series.

In more modern times, in 1948, winning came often for both the Red Sox and the Braves in Boston. With Spahn and Sain (and apparently not enough rain, at least in the World Series, when they lost to Cleveland), the Braves won the National League pennant with a record of 91–62, and led the league in attendance at more than 1,400,000, nearly half a million fans more than it had been just two years earlier, when the Braves finished fifteen games out of first place.

The Red Sox, of course, with the return of Ted Williams from the Pacific, had actually been in the World Series themselves in 1946. When Shirley Povich had heard of the Japanese surrender, he remarked, "That settles it. The Red Sox can't miss the 1946 flag." He was right, and their attendance reached a million for the first time, more than doubling that of the previous year, a seventh-place finish.

In 1948, still with a strong team led by Williams, Dom DiMaggio, Vern Stephens, Bobby Doerr, Johnny Pesky, and an outstanding rotation headed by Jack Kramer, Joe Dobson, and Mel Parnell, the Red Sox tied for first before losing their infamous "Denny Galehouse" playoff game to Cleveland and ruining the possibility of a Boston-Boston World Series. (That Galehouse, four years earlier, had shut out the Yankees on the next-to-last day of the season to keep his St. Louis *Browns* tied for first place, only adds to the ignominy of the occasion.) But the Red Sox won 95 games and drew more than 1,500,000 fans, giving the city of Boston a major league attendance total of more than 3,000,000 for the 1948 season.

The following year brought more heartbreak for the Red Sox, as the team took a one-game lead into Yankee Stadium for a two-game series to end the season. And the season, frustratingly, did end for the Red Sox, as they dropped both contests and watched the Bombers pass them for the pennant, the second straight season that the Red Sox had

313

finished one game out of first place. Fans could only dream about how the Red Sox would have fared had the same series been played at Fenway, where the club went 61–16 and drew nearly 1,600,000 fans.

But by 1952, just three years later, the teams' fortunes had shifted. The Braves finished in seventh place, out of eight teams, 32 games off the lead. Their attendance reflected their poor play, as they drew a mere 281,000 fans, the fewest in the league, and the team moved on to Milwaukee the following year, leaving behind some mourning fans, including my father, but not enough of them to make a difference. When the Boston Braves' youngsters of Eddie Mathews and Lew Burdette developed into stars in Milwaukee and, with a bit of help from a new arrival, Hank Aaron (a Boston Braves signee), brought a World Series championship to that city in 1957, the mourning in Boston only grew. No teammates ever hit more homers than Aaron and Mathews, and a panoramic shot featuring the sweet swing of Mathews, in fact, had graced the very first cover of *Sports Illustrated* in 1954, just to pour a little more salt in the Boston wounds. For the record, after leaving Boston, the Braves had *thirteen* consecutive winning seasons in Milwaukee, and added a fourteenth in Atlanta. Clearly, parting was not such sweet sorrow for those Braves teams.

The Red Sox fared somewhat better than the Braves in 1952, ending up in sixth place, with attendance at an almost respectable 1,100,000. Still, it was a decline of about 500,000 fans from 1948, and their string of seasons with a million-plus attendance would be interrupted at eight the following year. The Sox did get back up to a million four more times in the 1950s, but fan support was hardly feverish. Only twice did the team average as much as 20,000 fans a game, and during most of those years of a million-plus, the emphasis was on the million, not the plus, as the team barely squeezed over the seven-figure mark. With a lineup featuring Williams, Billy Goodman, Jackie Jensen, Piersall, Malzone, and some less than memorable but generally reliable starters—Tom Brewer, Frank Sullivan, and

Willard Nixon—along with reliever Ellis Kinder (who once had Derek Lowe-like seasons of 23 wins and 27 saves), the Red Sox had some decent teams throughout the 1950s. Still, they had no hope of challenging the Yankees, Indians, and White Sox, and were never in serious contention. By 1961, following Ted Williams's retirement, the Red Sox had begun their annual run of being near the bottom in the standings.

The Red Sox had never been a huge box office draw, but the summers of the 1960s, pre-1967, were an embarrassment for a city with such a rich baseball history. It was obvious that even some hardcore fans had given up buying Red Sox tickets. Most casual fans, of course, were strangers to Fenway. With such a pathetic team on the field, there was apparently no compelling reason to show up at all at Fenway. I say *apparently* because, at the time, I didn't see the problem of going to Fenway and enjoying the stars on the visiting team, as long as you cheered for the Red Sox. The evidence showed, however, that not many Sox fans shared my approach to the game, unfortunately for the Red Sox front office.

Given the level of interest in baseball that I saw all around me—in school, in playgrounds, and in backyards, not to mention the fathers that sat through countless Little League games watching their sons, and the mothers who routinely had to do extra loads of laundry and sewing because of sons sliding into second base—it is obvious that Red Sox Nation could have been born sooner, and probably *would* have been born sooner, had the Red Sox been owned and run by men with a serious interest in the quality of both the product on the field and Fenway Park itself, particularly the former. Interest in baseball in Massachusetts absolutely had been strong—to repeat, *every* boy I knew played at least some baseball—even in the darkest days of the Red Sox. Boston was not Tampa Bay.

Where were these many baseball fans all summer? Where had they been hiding out when the double play combination was Eddie Bressoud and Dalton Jones? Most likely nowhere farther away than the beaches at Salisbury,

315

Revere, Nantasket, and Hyannis. They might have been at Fenway, had the team put some talent on the field. When talent finally did arrive at Fenway in 1967, The Nation was officially born. Going to a Red Sox game went from being a father-son thing to a family outing, a night with friends, a date, a place where nearly anyone could find some enjoyment. The Impossible Dream season attracted 1,700,000 fans, more than twice that of the previous year. Despite having seen it with my own eyes, I still marvel at the transformation.

But it's not as though the Impossible Dream alone created Red Sox Nation. What it did was give the countless baseball fans who already existed in New England a legitimate reason to get excited about their own major league team for the first time in a generation, and attract the additional, casual fans who, in almost any city, will enthusiastically follow a winner.

The improvement was not fleeting, and the explanation why is clear. It comes down to one word: winning. Since 1967, the Red Sox have had only nine losing seasons. Even the three consecutive losing seasons under Butch Hobson in the 1990s, or the recent last place finishes under John Farrell, did not seriously dampen the enthusiasm for the home team. Clearly, the magic of 1967 lit a spark of excitement among Red Sox fans that has not only endured but intensified. The World Series loss that year was certainly a letdown, but the team had come from nowhere to make the Series in the first place, and everyone, including eleven-year-old boys, understood.

The larger point was that a new generation of Red Sox fans had tasted success, and ever since then it has been the case that Red Sox fans hope to win, expect to win, and *have seen* a lot of winning since 1967, including three final games of the entire baseball season. Attendance has never dropped below 1,000,000 again, a span covering fifty years (and counting), and broke the 2,000,000 barrier for the first time during the tragicomic 1977–1979 years of Don Zimmer.

More impressively, after hitting 2,000,000 again in 1986, another tragicomic year, it has stayed above that threshold for the past *thirty* years, with the exception of the strike year of 1994. The Red Sox even had a five-year stretch of *three million* fans, broken only—and barely—by the improbable year of 2013, when apparently some still shell-shocked fans were not beating a path to Fenway, a departing gift of the hapless Bobby Valentine, as the team made its unlikely way to a championship that no one saw coming.

Red Sox baseball thrives no matter the prices of tickets, lack of parking, occasional frigid April and September nights, obstructed view seats, or last place finishes. Grandparents yet to be born may be the next ones to witness a season, as I did, of under a million fans for the Red Sox. First or worst, the Red Sox are never less than entertaining and always manage to spark adulation or admonition (sometimes both) among their devoted fans. The well-established intrigue of the Red Sox attracts fans not only to Fenway but to stadiums around the major leagues, a very happy outcome for baseball owners and fans alike. Red Sox Nation is no misnomer.

The question of who exactly are these many millions of fans is certainly worth asking. When I went to games as a boy, I saw some families at games, but mostly fathers and sons, or two or three adult guys, of any age, together. I have few memories of women with other women, college students, minorities, or chatterers (people who are physically at the game but are not actually watching the game). I don't have any sociological data on any of this—I can only comment on what I have seen with my own eyes. And with HD television, it is easy enough now to see who is at the games, and what they are doing, even while sitting on your couch.

So, who started flocking to Fenway to add to (or replace?) the die-hards who sat there with my father and me through the many losses of the 1960s, and why? What is clear is that the seats are filled by a wide range of people, and, judging from the fans' behavior, there are many different reasons why they are there. Some are clearly tuned into the game, watching each play and cheering or booing as appropriate. Others are more relaxed, maybe there to enjoy the Fenway experience and hoping to see a victory by the home team. Still others may go for a social day/night out, happy to tell others that they are going to a Sox game, and have varying levels of interest in baseball.

The only category of Red Sox fan that remain a mystery to me are those whose attention to the game appears to be almost totally absent. I imagine that, at any given point in the game, they would not know what the score is, what the inning is, or even which team is at bat. Considering the money that is required to buy a ticket, park your car, get a souvenir or two, and consume hot dogs and beer for three or four hours, the motivation of such fans is puzzling. It is safe to say that I saw few of those people at Fenway in the mid-1960s.

In the end, though, "live and let live" applies—those fans enjoy the Fenway experience in their own way, as is their right, regardless of whether they know a fastball from a foul ball, and they now make up their own piece of Red Sox Nation. The Red Sox owners are wise to cater to fans of all stripes by at least attempting to put talented players on the field (for the baseball fans) and making a trip to Fenway a reasonably comfortable and enjoyable event (for everyone else). In the old days, the game itself was the thing, and luxury boxes, jumbotrons, ubiquitous ads, "foodie" choices, and musical entertainment between innings (other than the notable—and very positive—exception of John Kiley and his memorable organ interludes) were not part of the experience. But it was also true that in the old days, almost no one bothered showing up for games. Tom Yawkey may not have cared so much about that, but no modern owner is going to be unconcerned about empty seats in the ballpark. The Red Sox have certainly been masterful at attracting fans to Fenway, never more so than in the last decade, and members of The Nation show no signs of losing interest.

22. Conclusion

By the time the Red Sox did get to the mountaintop, in 2004, I was nearly fifty. My memories of the role baseball had played in my life were overwhelmingly good, even including the remarkable futility of the Red Sox. I looked back sentimentally on those teams, focusing more on the thrill of the chase rather than the empty-handed finish. And, as Ned Martin had pointed out so eloquently, there was a certain poetic touch to baseball, even as the hapless Red Sox had played the game. There were rhythms and undercurrents not only to each game but to each inning and each pitch. A pitcher going for a shutout, a batter going for the cycle, a suicide squeeze, a 3-2 pitch with the runners taking off, a line drive that hits the chalk, a first baseman's foot coming off the bag and a storm of protest ensuing, and endless other possibilities all contributed to the drama and charm of the game.

But each moment of excitement in a baseball game was just that: a snapshot of action. Then there was a pause, the baseball universe was reset, the pitcher returned to the rubber, and the next pitch set the wheels in motion again. While boring to some, for obvious reasons, the game of baseball, especially to me as a child, was never less than exciting, whether I was looking forward to my next at bat or to the next ball that would come my way in the field.

At fifty, however, certain realities could not be ignored. Not to sound like an old curmudgeon (while sounding exactly like an old curmudgeon), professional ballplayers made obscene amounts of money to play a game three or four hours a day, and owners made even more obscene amounts of money from the same simple game (while often crying that they were not making obscene enough amounts of money). Why couldn't that kind of money go to childrens' hospitals or to veterans' services? Granted, the fans willingly provided the profits, but this was far from the same experience I had had when I had gone to games with my father on barely five dollars for tickets, food, souvenirs, and T fare.

And now that we know more about the personal lives of the players, it was probably easier to enjoy the game when we didn't. If Ken Coleman said that Paul Casanova or Tom Satriano was a fine young man, that was good enough for me. The use of PED's has been a huge stain on the game and—rightfully—has tarnished the legacies of stars who would have been automatic Hall of Famers on their natural ability alone. Who knows—maybe Ernie Banks, skinny as he was, also took something back in the day to add power to those quick wrists of his, but as a boy I didn't know about it and was glad I didn't. Banks said every day was a great day for two games, and I believed him. Certainly, if someone had told me that Yaz or Marichal were doing anything illegal, I don't think I could have believed it. The end of the innocence, I'm assuming, has made being a sports fan a very different experience for youngsters.

The unfortunate bottom line may be, as many have pointed out, that athletes are what they do, period. They should not often be looked upon as heroes or role models. You don't want your child to emulate someone who acts like the world revolves around himself just because he can hit a ball 400 feet once or twice a week, or has the arrogance to insist on a daily basis that he is "clean" until the evidence, inconveniently, proves dramatically otherwise. Barbara Tuchman once wrote of the insufferable Patrick Hurley, U.S. ambassador to China under FDR, that "vanity was Hurley's security." The same sentiment could be applied to some of baseball's biggest stars of the steroid era—they believed that they were too big to fail. And if most of them eventually end up being voted into the Hall of Fame, the ultimate lesson of that time may be that crime pays. The juicers may yet have the last laugh.

Still, for me, the love I had for playing baseball as a young boy remains a treasured memory. The passion of a childhood consumed by baseball is worth examining. I'm not saying that such a preoccupation is desirable, especially from a parent's point of view, but it has merits for that child that are quite meaningful. The biggest of all may be what can be called the "hopefulness" factor. There was always something to look forward to. Another practice or game to go to, another pick-up game with friends to organize, another game to watch at Fenway or listen to on the radio, another pack of cards to be opened, another sports article or book to be read— undoubtedly I had moments of boredom as a child, but they were the exception, not the rule. Even a good chunk of a rainy day could be spent poring over the ever-present statistics that filled the backs of baseball cards and the pages of *The Sporting News*.

Baseball gave a kind of continuity, or flow, to each year, leading with anticipation into the next spring. The fact that you could play, or try to play, every day from late March to early October, provided a comfortable rhythm. For some boys, if nothing else, it kept them out of trouble, which must have made parenting a whole lot easier in many families.

This optimistic view of baseball does not apply only to boys. Adult fans benefited from the sport as well. Following the watershed year of 1968, when major league bats fell silent nearly a half-century ago, sportswriter Ray Robinson observed all of the handwringing over the future of the sport and wrote, "I am getting bored reading that baseball is the great national bore. I am getting battle fatigue reading that baseball is dying, that it is too dull... If it is "decaying," as announcer Howard Cosell keeps telling us ... then something quite decent, pleasant, charming and civilized will have deserted our lives." Robinson did concede, with prescience, that "perhaps some pitchers *do* dawdle unnecessarily, while some batters fidget and fuss too much time away," but concluded, "baseball, with all of its warts and imperfections, is still a tranquil and joyous moment for many."

Time has shown the accuracy of Robinson's words. More than 70 million fans attended major league games in 2016, while millions more watched minor league games, college games, Legion games, high school games, Little League games—clearly, reports of the death of baseball, usually validated by sightings of empty summer baseball fields, have been greatly exaggerated. Even when the sport has tried to kill itself with strikes, steroids, and other forms of stupidity, the game faithfully replenishes the optimism of home fans each spring, and rightfully so.

Not only is baseball not dead, but interest in baseball and other sports seems to be at a feverish pitch. There is now what can be called the sports "obsession" factor that, with big screen televisions and full-scale entertainment rooms standard features in many homes, is becoming part of the everyday landscape for fans, particularly since nearly every professional sporting event can now be seen on television. The arithmetic on this may seem a little hard to believe for anyone who can remember watching infrequent games on a black and white television set with antennae sticking out of it, but, in this case, statistics don't lie. For example, a Boston sports fan who watches *just* the pre-season, regular season, and playoff games of the Red Sox, Patriots, Celtics, and Bruins will spend well over 1000 hours a year, or 20 hours a week, watching games. If such things as games between non-Boston professional teams, college games, and local and national sports talk shows are added to the mix, as they probably should be, those numbers of viewing and listening hours may double. And all of this still does not include the now-ubiquitous fantasy leagues. To put it another way, sports-think for many Boston fans may involve more hours each week than their actual jobs, and this may apply in many other American cities as well.

Of course, such a lifestyle was not possible or even imaginable in the relatively low-tech 1960s, when sports involved children more than adults, especially in the "passion" department, and was much more about *playing* or even reading than watching, as there were not all that many chances to see a game unless you actually went to it. Nowadays, though, many neighborhood ballfields are, in fact, empty much of the time, even on sunny days, while Fenway is packed on a nightly basis.

But weariness does not seem to be an issue among members of Red Sox Nation. It is the ongoing enthusiasm of fans that is a key element in the success of the Red Sox both as a baseball team and as a brand. The fans have been coming to Fenway for decades, and now generations of Red Sox fans cannot remember when it was otherwise. In Boston, the winters are cold, the summers are hot, the State House is corrupt, and Fenway is full—these are facts of life unquestioned by locals. Who knows how many present members of The Nation were the children, like myself, worshippers of baseball, who were sitting in the near-empty confines of Fenway Park in the dark days of the 1960s, unaware that they were viewing the calm of irrelevance (and irreverence) before the storm of near-annual pennant fever? Or how many are the children, or the grandchildren, of those same faithful fans? No matter—all are beneficiaries of the sudden transformation of the Red Sox, from stumblers in 1966 to stars in 1967, which gave birth to Red Sox Nation. And it is a number that has made Red Sox management very happy ever since.

Will Red Sox Nation, at some point, cease to exist? Possibly, if new owners come in, payroll is cut, free agents are ignored, the farm system languishes, and Fenway Park is finally abandoned in favor of a spacious, new park where baseball is just a small piece of the total entertainment package. But none of that seems likely to happen any time soon. What can be said for sure is that the spark of Red Sox fever was lit in 1967, and it has burned brightly for decades. Now, at a half-century, The Nation continues to get a clean bill of health, even in subpar seasons. Nothing lasts forever, but for Red Sox Nation, there is no end in sight for the ageless and lovable baseball soap opera known as the Boston Red Sox.

The enviable success of the Red Sox and the other professional sports teams in Boston has deep roots. While many observers have focused on the remarkable number of titles for the local teams over the course of the 2000s, I take a longer view of the city's sporting grandeur. In my mind, the run of champions in Boston has been noteworthy *since I was born*. Of course, it is true, in that time, our four teams have fielded some spectacularly bad clubs: the 1965 Red Sox (62–100), the 1990 Patriots (1–15), the 1996–97 Celtics (15–67), and the 1961–62 Bruins (15–47–8, 38 points) certainly qualify.

But the numbers also highlight unrivaled success. Starting with my birth year, 1956, Boston has produced a total of 29 championship winners in the four major sports, more than any other city including—dare I say it?—New York, which has 28. Next in line are Los Angeles with 21, Montreal with 17 (amazingly, all from one team!), Chicago and Pittsburgh with 14 each, and Detroit with 10. Moreover, since I was born, Boston has only once gone more than four years without having a team at least *in* the championship game or series, and even that was a relatively brief interim of six years between 1991 and 1996. (Interestingly, Boston teams have also *lost* 20 times in the championship finals, a record somewhat akin to Jack Nicklaus winning 18 majors and finishing second 19 times and a testament to how challenging it is to put away that final opponent.) Relative to other cities, "these are the good old days" is nearly a ceaseless refrain for Boston sports fans.

And the Red Sox' World Series record, comparatively speaking, is quite admirable. The Red Sox have won eight championships—oddly divided and positioned, like two facing cliffs, astride the infamous abyss of nearly a century of heartache—that rank the team as one of the most successful ever in baseball, hard to believe as that may still be for any fan my age or older. In fact, the Red Sox have a very impressive 8–4 record in the October classic. While it doesn't rival that of the

Bombers (27–13) or the Cardinals (11–8), it compares very favorably with the Athletics (9–5). The only other teams remotely relevant are the Giants (8–12) and the Dodgers (6–12), two storied teams that can be justly praised as being among the most outstanding and influential franchises in baseball history. But they've also combined to lose about twenty percent of all of the World Series ever played, including two losses to the Red Sox. So, the Red Sox, often—and deservedly—maligned in baseball lore, must also be seen for what the numbers say they are: one of the most successful baseball franchises in history.

As I look back on my life, I can see that, baseball-wise, I started at the top, with an insatiable appetite for all things Red Sox and baseball when I was a boy, so I had nowhere to go but down. And, as I saw more of life outside of baseball as an adult, I did move on, believing that an endless fixation on Fenway was probably not the most appropriate way to pass my time.

Still, I enjoy my childhood memories of the sport, and over the years random pieces of baseball news occasionally have brought flashbacks of those days of innocence. When the Athletics' Bob Welch, in 1990, won his 27th game, something Marichal had never done (failing in his final start in 1968, 3–2, to the last-place Astros), I noticed. When yet another Alou, Moises, came along in the early 1990s, I noticed. When Cal Ripken (consecutive games played) and Alex Rodriguez (grand slams) passed Lou Gehrig, I noticed. When Barry Bonds won his 4th MVP, leaving behind Foxx, Musial, Campanella, DiMaggio, Berra, Mantle, and Mike Schmidt as 3-time winners, I noticed. When Eddie Mathews died in 2001, I noticed. Ditto, two years later, for Warren Spahn.

Now, with the Red Sox having ended the 86-year drought and won the World Series, Yaz and Rice (with a tireless and deserving boost from Red Sox PR maestro Dick Bresciani) having made the Hall of Fame, and Fenway itself having dodged the wrecking ball, the team's inglorious past, to those who can even remember it, seems increasingly long ago and far away. I

325

learned over time to follow the team from a more relaxing distance, reading box scores with interest but not passion. What remains is the comforting sentiment that the Red Sox, exasperating to exhilarating, have always been well worth the ride.

It is easy for me now to think back to those early days of going to Red Sox games with my father, and how simple it was to wrap my whole life in the innocence of baseball. It wasn't that I was aware of other things in the world but chose to ignore them—I don't recall, from my childhood, anything else that was remotely close to capturing my attention as much as the details of the Red Sox and the entire major league season each year, and my own baseball playing. But the real world was out there, whether I wanted to recognize it or not, and when it made its presence felt in my life, it was not always possible for me to make sense of it, and as time passed it did not have a beneficial effect on my relationship with my father.

Much more significantly, with my father, I witnessed the sad, inexorable damage that poverty inflicts over time. When you are poor and young, you can think that things will change, you'll find a better job, you'll go back to school, you'll win the lottery—something will come along to improve your lot and rescue you from what you had to assume, in youthful optimism, was a temporary condition of rotten living. But when you are poor and not young anymore, the desire to look ahead inexorably fades. The job from hell isn't going anywhere, returning to school is a pipedream, and trying the lottery is throwing good money after bad, and yet the effort to go on must be made regardless, as much in despair as in hope. Weeks turn into months, months into years, years into decades. The cute, little children are no longer cute or little, growing families require growing amounts of money that are not forthcoming, work means the ceaseless monotony of early mornings and deadening 8-hour (and longer) days, and, worst of all, you recognize that you're getting older, weaker, and more beat up every day.

Added to this were the serious mental and physical illnesses that made my father's life—and family life—only more challenging. As he entered middle age, his running commentary on the state of things, often muttered to himself, generally ended with "Who gives a damn anyway?" When he finally left his dreaded factory job at the earliest possible age, sixty-two, it was not important that he did so with no financial plan for his "golden" years, as there was no gold to make the plan with.

Still, the complicated truth of my father's last years—indeed, his whole life—is that despite his bleak situation, he never totally lost his hope for a brighter day even when all the evidence pointed in the other direction. Occasionally when he called me in those years, almost always to ask for money, what he really wanted to talk about were the various schemes he had dreamed up to produce some of his own income, usually involving the marketing of his warship models to a public that unfortunately was not going to bed at night dreaming of buying World War II ship models. I recall the persistent, often even enthusiastic, hope in his voice, when he still didn't have a nickel to his name, as he would tell me about someone who had called him to purchase a particular ship model, or a kindly storeowner who would allow him to display his ships in the front window—each represented a new chance, a possible signal that things were starting to turn. In fact, he had studied the history of the U.S. Navy in the war years—its ships, planes, admirals, battles—diligently, so he knew the subject matter. His idea was not without merit. But such schemes always need a bit of luck, and luck was not something my father ever had any experience with in financial matters.

My father struggled with multiple health issues in his final years. He once spent a night in a psychiatric ward, where there were sights and sounds that no one should ever experience. At that point, it seemed merciful if the end would come soon for my father. I don't write that to be mean. My father himself voiced the same thought to me in those days when he was bedridden. He knew perfectly well that he couldn't build ship models or paint landscapes in his condition. The dream, finally, had died.

I can't say that I ever really understood my father, particularly outside my happy days of childhood baseball. But it is true that, as the expression goes, you have to walk in another man's shoes to know how he feels. I was entering my own middle age as my father's health declined, and I was beginning to see a little more clearly some of what he had faced. I assumed (hoped) that I had a decent grasp on things myself and was making my way in the right direction, but the rest of the world apparently did not always see it that way, presenting me with challenges ranging from the solvable to the absurd, as is the case with most people.

My father, however, never had a decent grasp on things, and every problem that came his way was a potential calamity that affected not only him but a family as well. To live with that kind of pressure, day after day for an entire life, with little understanding of it all or a glimpse of a way forward other than to continuously call relatives and ask for help, must be the kind of stress that makes most people simply give up. And, slowly, my father did give up on quite a bit, including baseball. I mention baseball because I suspect that my father as a child loved baseball as much as I did, and he still loved it when he went out of his way as a parent to find out if I would share his enthusiasm. Losing the satisfying escape of baseball must have been a cruel blow to him, but by that time it was part of such an escalating number of blows that I don't know if he had the mental energy anymore to grieve the loss.

Yet, to a small extent, there was a limited thawing of the ice between us in those last months when I visited him in hospitals and nursing homes. As it became clear that my father would not be long for this world, I saw him, or tried to see him, in another light. When we were together, there certainly was still a gulf, and I had not forgotten that he had not been a good parent for most of my life or that he had given far more thought to his own cares than to mine or anyone else's. To be fair, I had not been the easiest son, either.

But with my father I saw less of a pathetic figure than I did images of Brooks Robinson, Mickey Mantle, Tony Oliva, Al Kaline, and of course Yaz. This is what he had given me long ago. Occasionally in those visits, when I wasn't sure what to talk about with him, I would bring up the names of players from our past, some of whom we had seen perform at Fenway, and the sound of their names seemed to stimulate him, as if those remembered moments were indeed a time that gave a measure of meaning to a difficult life. With baseball in the air, we could communicate, however briefly, in a timeless manner. During one of these visits, when I mentioned something about the Red Sox, he grumbled in a burst of energy, "Christ, what would Spahn be worth today?" That was the spirit of the old time, diminished but not yet dead. When I replied, "And how about Wally Berger?," he growled, "Damn right." Baseball, in the end, remained the tie that binds.

My father died in 2003, as penniless as ever and having lived seventy-seven years without ever seeing the Boston Braves or the Boston Red Sox win a championship. Timing in life had never been his strong suit. Sadly, nor had much else.

One exception, though, had been his love of baseball, leaving me with unanswered questions. Why, so long ago, did he focus so much of his time on me and baseball? Was it because he genuinely wanted me to develop a love for baseball that he must have once had as a boy, back in the days of Ruth and Gehrig? Was it because he himself still enjoyed the game and found it a respite from his daily grind of work in a factory? I recalled reading, as a boy, the moving story about Mickey Mantle's father, Mutt, who worked in the Oklahoma mines and dedicated himself to teaching young Mickey how to hit a baseball (from both sides!), a story with its own tragic ending. Or was it a reason I may never know?

The answer, clear to me now, is that it doesn't matter. More than anyone else, he put baseball in my life, as it was his tireless trekking in and out of Fenway Park, the endless fly balls and grounders he hit to me in the backyard after coming home from a wearying day of work, the packs of baseball cards that he would buy for me on a Sunday morning after church, the baseball practices and games that he drove me to and sat patiently through, that established my childhood addiction to the sport. I have to be honest with myself about that—it would not have happened without him.

There is another point of significance that led to my reconsideration of my father: his books. My main academic interest as a child was reading, so seeing those books in his bookcase every day, as well as the pile of newspapers that I delivered around the neighborhood, got me started early in appreciating words on a page. And most of the words on the pages that I was reading were about baseball.

Years later, as my father grew distant and started shedding interests, one of the casualties was his collection of books. I remember one day finding the bookcase in the living room half-empty. The discarding of books has always seemed to me to be nearly a sacrilegious act, so I quietly rescued some of the books before they met a similar fate. Two of them, purchased by my father when he was about twenty years old, and oddly protected by aging, wrapping-paper-style book covers, are very worthy of mention in this story.

One is entitled *The Basic Teachings of the Great Philosophers*, written by S.E. Frost and published in 1942. On the inside flap of the book cover, my father had written, "Painting, music, poetry, history, science, ships, philosophy—interests are very important to me and to men. They keep you going. Amen." In the table of contents, underlined are the chapters ""The Nature of God" and a subtitle, "Recent and Present-day Conceptions of the Soul and Immortality." In a chapter entitled, "Fate versus Free Will," he underlined the following sentences: "Inevitably death must overtake man.... But ... death is no defeat, but is actually a victory for the will of man.... *I am the master of my fate, I am the captain of my soul.*"

The second book, also published in 1942, is *The Story of Science* by David Dietz. Again on the inside flap, he had written, "Science, the most important study for the health and progress of mankind. This book is the 'best' book on science I ever had or ever read. I 'love' it. L.E.H. 45." He then added, "Chapter XIX [The Structure of the Atom] wonderful chapter."

Those words were written by someone who had grown up in the Depression and was a high school dropout, at the close of World War II. Although I knew my father as a difficult man with many regrets at the end, I also understood that the person who had bought such books, read them, and composed those words was not a bitter person beaten down by reality but a young man full of hope, inquisitive for knowledge, and undoubtedly imagining a future far different from the one he lived. That was a person I wish I had known, and perhaps, in a sense, I had, not only through those two books, but even more so through the game of baseball and the Boston Red Sox.

Acknowledgments

This book initially started out as the story of my love of baseball as a child and how it was shaped by my devotion to the Red Sox. My father was going to be a minimal presence in the book, mainly because of the difficulty I knew I would face by addressing his complex influence on my life. I didn't get too far in my first draft, however, before realizing that not only would I need to acknowledge my father's role in some way, but that his role had been a major reason for my interest in baseball at all. It wasn't possible for me to tell the story without focusing on this important but personally awkward truth. My father taught me how to play the game and gave me much of my early education on the history of baseball, with of course an emphasis on the National League and his beloved Boston Braves. But he knew quite a bit about the Red Sox as well, so I received a thorough telling of baseball's past. And it was my father and my mother (and other relatives) who put up the money, scarce as it was, to buy my first bats and balls and gloves, as well as those prized, early baseball cards, and pay for my trips to Fenway Park—I was the fortunate, and quite innocent, beneficiary of their generosity. Matters became far more complicated as years went by, but it would be unfair of me not to acknowledge the patience that both of my parents, my father being the driving force, showed by indulging and encouraging my childhood passion for baseball. For that, I am extremely grateful. I trust, and hope, that my daily excitement over the sport at the time gave them the gratitude that they certainly deserved for their efforts.

Many have taken the time to improve my work. Special thanks to Kevin Baker for his enthusiasm and encouragement at an early stage of the book. His detailed thoughts on the manuscript and his musings on baseball and his own past provided valuable guidance and inspiration. Both helpful and entertaining was the response of Leigh Montville, who, among his comments, noted that his own father (unlike mine) was no fan of Pinky Higgins. Bob Brady, the esteemed keeper of the flame for the Boston Braves, generously offered his encyclopedic knowledge of not simply baseball but the history of Boston in clarifying numerous points. Larry Lucchino recommended Rick Swanson to me as a Red Sox historian of note, and Rick proved Larry's words were right on target—I appreciate the assistance of each. Rick's careful reading of the manuscript caught factual mistakes that I never would have noticed. Many thanks to Larry Johnson for his kind permission to use his baseball drawings from nearly a half-century ago, when I used to cut them out from the *Globe* and save them in my treasured boxes of sports history. I enjoyed doing the same with the engaging illustrations of Phil Bissell, and I'm very grateful for his enthusiastic support.

Longtime friends and Red Sox fans Jim Duggan and Gary Olshan graciously read the entire manuscript and provided helpful insights and encouragement. Colleagues helped as well. Cathy Sadow, after finishing the manuscript, offered substantive comments and heartfelt support, nostalgically recalling her own Canadian childhood days of attending Royals games with her father at Delorimier Stadium in Montreal, where she saw former Celtic and future Rifleman, Chuck Connors, play first base. Carole Thieme's steadfast belief in my work over many years is also much appreciated.

I am very grateful to Bob Cullum for permission to use photographs from the fascinating archive of his grandfather, Leslie Jones, whose work graced the pages of the *Boston Herald* for many years, and to Danielle Pucci and Monica Shin at the Boston Public Library for their assistance regarding the Leslie Jones Collection. I also appreciate the help of Jeff Thomas at the San Francisco Public Library. And for permission to use their material, I am grateful to Post Consumer Brands, LLC.

A special note of gratitude concerns the late Dick Bresciani, who agreed to read my manuscript even while, unknown to me at the time, he was enduring the final stage of his valiant bout with cancer. He indicated that he wished to speak with me about my work, but the call never happened, as his life ended shortly thereafter. But I was very moved by his interest in my writing and his effort to help despite his exhausting circumstances—I understood why he had earned the praise and respect of so many throughout the baseball world. I also appreciate the consideration shown to me by Debbie Matson in my communication with Dick Bresciani, and I thank Sarah Coffin for all of her help in providing photos from the Boston Red Sox.

I am very indebted to Nell Minow at Miniver Press for her initial belief in my work and her unwavering support throughout the publishing process. Thanks also to Rani Gold for her careful editing of the text and for many helpful suggestions.

My wife, Cristina, not only read the manuscript and discussed it with me at length but skillfully took the photos of my baseball collection that appear in this book, including the cover photo of the glove from my Babe Ruth League playing days of nearly fifty years ago. I deeply appreciate her involvement in my work. The encouragement of my children, Julia and Tim, is always an inspiration. Writing is never easy, but having your family behind you makes the process far more enjoyable.

Index

Praise for *We All Have Fathers:*
A Red Sox Memoir

"A thoroughly enjoyable, poignant, intimate story of the making of the Red Sox—and a Red Sox fan. For those who like baseball, and love family."

 – Kevin Baker, co-author with Reggie Jackson, *Becoming Mr. October*

"Take a ride in the Wayback Machine with Peter Hartshorn, back to when a family of four didn't have to get a second mortgage to buy seats along the first base line at Fenway Park, back to when the athletes weren't multi-millionaires, back to when baseball seemed to be a more simple game. Enjoy the scenery. Very nice."

 – Leigh Montville, author of *Ted Williams: The Biography of an American Hero*

"Baseball in New England draws much of its popularity from a solid core of supporters whose loyalty to the Red Sox can be traced back through generations. After the 2004 Red Sox World Series victory, many visited local cemeteries to decorate in Red Sox regalia the final resting places of loved ones who missed the momentous breaking of the 86-year-old 'Curse.' In his book, Peter Hartshorn warmly recalls how baseball created a strong father and son bond in his family. In the author's case, however, it took a somewhat atypical path as his dad grew up not as a follower of the Crimson Hose, but of the old Boston Braves. Hartshorn's reminiscences preserve invaluable memories of those days when Boston also was once the 'Home of the Braves.'"

 – Bob Brady, president of the Boston Braves Historical Association

Praise for *I Have Seen the Future: A Life of Lincoln Steffens*

"Absorbing ... [Hartshorn] has produced a biography that is prodigiously researched, fantastically interesting and extremely well-written. Steffens would have been pleased by how well Hartshorn has turned him inside out."
— *New York Times*

"Well-researched and well-written"
— *Wall Street Journal*

"This big, lively book is very well-researched and presents a fascinating history of the age when magazine writers steered national opinion—a role Steffens embraced with vigor ... This is an extraordinary book about a complex man."
— *American Journalism Review*

"This well-researched book adds new luster to one of America's notable journalists. Highly recommended."

— *Choice*

Miniver Press publishes lively and informative non-fiction books, specializing in history and popular culture. For more information, see http://www.miniverpress.com or email editor@miniverpress.com.

We All Have Fathers